EJB 3.1 Cookbook

Build real world EJB solutions with a collection of simple
but incredibly effective recipes

Richard M. Reese

D1557946

BIRMINGHAM - MUMBAI

EJB 3.1 Cookbook

First published: June 2011

Production Reference: 1030611

Published by Packt Publishing Ltd.
32 Lincoln Road
Olton
Birmingham, B27 6PA, UK.

ISBN 978-1-849682-38-1

www.packtpub.com

Cover Image by Dan Anderson (Dan@CAndersonAssociates.com)

Credits

Author
Richard M. Reese

Reviewers
Krum Bakalsky

Andrey Gotchalk

Deepak Vohra

Acquisition Editor
Amey Kanse

Development Editor
Chris Rodrigues

Technical Editor
Arun Nadar

Project Coordinator
Vishal Bodwani

Proofreader
Mario Cecere

Indexer
Monica Ajmera Mehta

Graphics
Geetanjali Sawant

Production Coordinator
Shantanu Zagade

Cover Work
Shantanu Zagade

About the Author

Richard Reese is an Associate Professor teaching Computer Science at Tarleton State University in Stephenville, Texas. Previously, he worked in the aerospace and telephony industries for over 16 years. He earned his Ph.D. in Computer Science from Texas A&M University. He also served four years in the Air Force primarily in the field of communication intelligence.

Outside of classroom, he enjoys tending his vegetable garden, maintaining his aquariums, and running with his dog, Zoey. He also enjoys relaxing with an episode of Firefly and is ever hopeful for the return of the epic series.

Dr. Reese has written numerous publications and contributed to *Turbo Pascal: Advanced Applications*.

No book can be written without the help from others. To this end I am thankful for my wife Karla and daughter Jennifer whose patience, support, and reviews have made this effort possible. In addition, I would like to thank the editorial staff of Packt and my reviewers for their input which has resulted in a much better book than it might otherwise have been.

Lastly, I am indebted to my doctorial committee chairman, Dr. Sallie Sheppard, who years ago spent countless hours helping me to learn how to write.

About the Reviewers

Krum Bakalsky has finished his MSc studies in theoretical computer science from Sofia University. Afterwards he joined SAP, where he is currently part of the Java server team. He drives different EJB related topics, and is responsible for JPA tasks as well. He is SCJP6, SCBCD5, and SCWCD5 certified, and is very enthusiastic about the new Java EE 6 platform, hoping that it will gain great adoption and will receive good popularity. His professional interests include popular open source frameworks, like Spring, Hibernate, and Quartz. He has some basic involvement in several tooling projects in the Eclipse family, and is interested in cloud computing topics as well.

Being an amateur mathematician, in his spare time Krum likes to enjoy different math activities, often related to his great math library, that he continues to maintain and expand. Krum is a great koala lover and donator. His dream is to live one day a peaceful idyllic life in his own house, far from civilization and surrounded by several koalas.

Andrey Gotchalk has more than 12 years of experience in software development. He is certified by Sun Microsystems and Microsoft. He has worked for multiple multilingual international software companies in Europe and North America, where has served in different roles as senior software developer, team leader, and project manager. He speaks four languages and he has lived and traveled at many places of the world. Currently he lives and works in Montreal, Canada.

He has strong OOA/OOD and RDBMS skills, extensive experience in various technologies as Java/JEE, PHP5, X++, Object Pascal, PL/SQL, Web development, ERP systems, and so on. But his last preferences are JEE and mostly standard solutions like EJB, JPA, JSP, JSF, and much more. He is also interested in analyzing and using various JEE open source projects. You can reach him at a.gotchalk@gmail.com.

Deepak Vohra is a consultant and a principal member of the NuBean.com software company. Deepak is a Sun Certified Java Programmer and Web Component Developer, and has worked in the fields of XML and Java programming and J2EE for over five years. Deepak is the co-author of the Apress book, *Pro XML Development with Java Technology* and was the technical reviewer for the O'Reilly book, *WebLogic: The Definitive Guide*. Deepak was also the technical reviewer for the Course Technology PTR book, *Ruby Programming for the Absolute Beginner*, and the technical editor for the Manning Publications book, *Prototype and Scriptaculous in Action*. Deepak is also the author of the Packt Publishing books *JDBC 4.0 and Oracle JDeveloper for J2EE Development*, and *Processing XML Documents with Oracle JDeveloper 11g*.

www.PacktPub.com

Support files, eBooks, discount offers and more

You might want to visit www.PacktPub.com for support files and downloads related to your book.

Did you know that Packt offers eBook versions of every book published, with PDF and ePub files available? You can upgrade to the eBook version at www.PacktPub.com and, as a print book customer, you are entitled to a discount on the eBook copy. Get in touch with us at service@packtpub.com for more details.

At www.PacktPub.com, you can also read a collection of free technical articles, sign up for a range of free newsletters, and receive exclusive discounts and offers on Packt books and eBooks.

http://PacktLib.PacktPub.com

Do you need instant solutions to your IT questions? PacktLib is Packt's online digital book library. Here, you can access, read, and search across Packt's entire library of books.

Why subscribe?

- Fully searchable across every book published by Packt
- Copy and paste, print, and bookmark content
- On demand and accessible via web browser

Free access for Packt account holders

If you have an account with Packt at www.PacktPub.com, you can use this to access PacktLib today and view nine entirely free books. Simply use your login credentials for immediate access.

Instant updates on new Packt books

Get notified! Find out when new books are published by following @PacktEnterprise on Twitter, or the *Packt Enterprise* Facebook page.

Table of Contents

Preface

Enterprise Java Beans enable rapid and simplified development of secure and portable applications based on Java technology. Creating and using EJBs can be challenging and rewarding. Among the challenges are learning the EJB technology itself, learning how to use the development environment you have chosen for EJB development, and the testing of the EJBs.

EJB 3.1 Cookbook addresses all these challenges and covers the new 3.1 features, along with an explanation of useful features retained from previous versions. It brings the reader quickly up to speed on how to use EJB 3.1 techniques through the use of step-by-step examples without the need to use multiple incompatible resources. The coverage is concise and to the point, and is organized to allow you to quickly find and master those features of interest to you.

The book starts with coverage of EJB clients. The reader can choose the chapters and recipes which best address his or her specific needs. The newer EJB technologies presented include singleton beans which support application-wide needs and interceptors to permit processing before and after a target method is invoked. Asynchronous invocation of methods and enhancements to the timer service are also covered.

EJB 3.1 Cookbook is a very straightforward and rewarding source of techniques used to support Java EE applications.

What this book covers

Chapter 1, *Getting Started With EJBs* presents the creation of a few simple EJBs followed by recipes explaining how they can be invoked by a client. Client examples include the use of servlets, JSP, JSF, SE applications, and applets. The use of JNDI and dependency injection is also presented.

Chapter 2, *Session Beans* talks about the stateless, stateful, and the new singleton session bean. The use of single and multiple singletons is illustrated along with how concurrency can be managed. In addition, examples of how to use asynchronous methods are presented.

Chapter 3, Message-Driven Beans explains how these EJBs provide a useful asynchronous approach for supporting an application. The numerous types of messages that can be sent are illustrated along with typical application scenarios. Access to the message queue is also discussed.

Chapter 4, EJB Persistence covers the creation and use of entities including the use of a facade class. In addition, numerous validation techniques are presented in support of entities.

Chapter 5, Querying Entities using JPQL and the Criteria API covers how to query an underlying data store with emphasis on the use of JPQL and the Criteria API. The use of annotations in support of these queries is illustrated.

Chapter 6, Transaction Processing, covers transaction processing which is central to many EJB supported applications. In this chapter, we examine how this support is provided using both container-managed transactions using annotations, and bean-managed transactions using code. Also, the use of timeouts and exception handling in support of transactions is illustrated.

Chapter 7, EJB Security covers the process of handling security using annotations and using code. The relationship between the support provided by the server and the roles used by an application is examined.

Chapter 8, Interceptors, explains how the interceptors provide a means of moving code that is not central to a business method outside of the method. Here, we learn how to use interceptors to handle a number of different concerns including security and transactions.

Chapter 9, Timer Services, explains how the timer services provide a means of periodically executing a method. We will examine the use of declarative and programmatic timers along with the use of persistent and non-persistent timers.

Chapter 10, Web Services explores how to create and use EJBs with JAX-RS and JAX-WS web services. Also covered is the use of a message-driven bean with a web service.

Chapter 11, Packaging the EJB details the packaging and deployment of EJBs. It covers the class loading process and the use of deployment descriptors for various interceptors such as timers and callbacks. The use of deployment descriptors with transactions and security is also addressed.

Chapter 12, EJB Techniques, examines techniques that are applicable to a variety of EJB technologies in this chapter. These include the use of logging and exception handling as they apply to EJBs. Also presented is how to create your own interceptor and efficient techniques for using strings, time and currency.

What you need for this book

The software required for this book includes NetBeans 6.9.1 and GlassFish Server Open Source Edition v3.0.1. Mozilla Firefox or Google Chrome can be used to display the output of servlets.

Who this book is for

The book is aimed at Java EE and EJB developers and programmers. Readers should be familiar with the use of servlets in the construction of a web application. A working knowledge of XML is also desirable.

Conventions

In this book, you will find a number of styles of text that distinguish between different kinds of information. Here are some examples of these styles, and an explanation of their meaning.

Code words in text are shown as follows: "The `ApplicationStateBean` uses an enumeration variable called `state` to store the state of the application."

A block of code is set as follows:

```
@Stateful
@DeclareRoles("manager")
@RolesAllowed("manager")
public class VoucherManager {
  ...
}
```

When we wish to draw your attention to a particular part of a code block, the relevant lines or items are set in bold:

```
public class VoucherManager {
  ...
  @EJB
  VoucherVerification voucherVerification;
  ...
  @RolesAllowed("employee")
  public void submit() {
    System.out.println("Voucher submitted");
    voucherVerification.submit();
  }
  ...
}
```

New terms and **important words** are shown in bold. Words that you see on the screen, in menus or dialog boxes for example, appear in the text like this: "Enter a name and press the **Add Name** button".

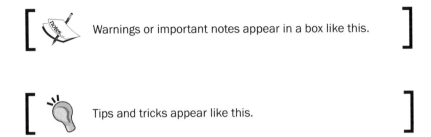

Warnings or important notes appear in a box like this.

Tips and tricks appear like this.

Reader feedback

Feedback from our readers is always welcome. Let us know what you think about this book—what you liked or may have disliked. Reader feedback is important for us to develop titles that you really get the most out of.

To send us general feedback, simply send an e-mail to feedback@packtpub.com, and mention the book title via the subject of your message.

If there is a book that you need and would like to see us publish, please send us a note in the **SUGGEST A TITLE** form on www.packtpub.com or e-mail suggest@packtpub.com.

If there is a topic that you have expertise in and you are interested in either writing or contributing to a book, see our author guide on www.packtpub.com/authors.

Customer support

Now that you are the proud owner of a Packt book, we have a number of things to help you to get the most from your purchase.

Downloading the example code

You can download the example code files for all Packt books you have purchased from your account at http://www.PacktPub.com. If you purchased this book elsewhere, you can visit http://www.PacktPub.com/support and register to have the files e-mailed directly to you.

Errata

Although we have taken every care to ensure the accuracy of our content, mistakes do happen. If you find a mistake in one of our books—maybe a mistake in the text or the code—we would be grateful if you would report this to us. By doing so, you can save other readers from frustration and help us improve subsequent versions of this book. If you find any errata, please report them by visiting http://www.packtpub.com/support, selecting your book, clicking on the **errata submission form** link, and entering the details of your errata. Once your errata are verified, your submission will be accepted and the errata will be uploaded on our website, or added to any list of existing errata, under the Errata section of that title. Any existing errata can be viewed by selecting your title from http://www.packtpub.com/support.

Piracy

Piracy of copyright material on the Internet is an ongoing problem across all media. At Packt, we take the protection of our copyright and licenses very seriously. If you come across any illegal copies of our works, in any form, on the Internet, please provide us with the location address or website name immediately so that we can pursue a remedy.

Please contact us at copyright@packtpub.com with a link to the suspected pirated material.

We appreciate your help in protecting our authors, and our ability to bring you valuable content.

Questions

You can contact us at questions@packtpub.com if you are having a problem with any aspect of the book, and we will do our best to address it.

1
Getting Started With EJBs

In this chapter, we will cover:

- Creating a simple session EJB
- Accessing a session bean using dependency injection
- Accessing the session bean using JNDI
- Creating a simple message-driven bean
- Sending a message to a message-driven bean
- Accessing an EJB from a web service (JAX-WS)
- Accessing an EJB from a web service (JAX-RS)
- Accessing an EJB from an Applet
- Accessing an EJB from JSP
- Calling an EJB from JSF
- Accessing an EJB from a Java Application using JNDI
- Accessing an EJB from a Java Application using an embeddable container
- Accessing the EJB container

Introduction

Creating and using Enterprise Java Beans (EJBs) can be challenging and rewarding. Among the challenges are learning the EJB technology itself, learning how to use the development environment you have chosen for EJB development and the testing of the EJBs. The examples used throughout the book were developed and tested using NetBeans 6.9.1 and GlassFish Server Open Source Edition v3.0.1. NetBeans and GlassFish can be downloaded bundled from `http://netbeans.org/downloads/index.html`. On this page are several bundle combinations. Use the one title Java. The GlassFish Enterprise Server v3 Prelude also supports EJB 3.1.

In addition, Windows 7 Professional 64 bit edition, service pack 1, was used to develop the applications. The Mozilla Firefox v3.6.15 browser was used to display web pages.

EJBs can be used in many different contexts and called from many different types of applications. In presenting EJBs, a fundamental question is this: how do we go about illustrating the use of an EJB before we know what an EJB is? How do we learn about EJBs unless we know how to call them? The approach taken in this chapter is to first demonstrate how to create simple Session Beans and Message-Driven Beans. Knowing how to create these beans will then allow us to use them from different contexts. The details of session and message bean construction and their use are covered in subsequent chapters. We are concerned with identifying some of the more common clients and then seeing how they call and use EJBs. EJBs can be used within a number of different clients including servlets, JSP, JSF, applets, Java SE type applications, and other EJBs.

From the client perspective, it is accessing an EJB as if the EJB existed in the same **Java Virtual Machine** (**JVM**). Depending on the client, this may be true. Regardless, EJBs are managed by an EJB container that provides support not readily available to other objects. This support can be in the form of security, transaction processing or concurrency management.

Using a bean involves declaring a reference to the bean, creating an instance of the bean and then calling the methods of the bean. There are two techniques for gaining access to an EJB: **Dependency Injection** (**DI**) and the **Java Naming and Directory Service** (**JNDI**). DI is the easiest when we can use it, but JNDI can be used in places where DI is not supported. We will look at both of these approaches. However, EJBs should not be created using the Java **new** keyword. If the EJB is created using this keyword, then it will no longer be an EJB but rather a regular object. It will not be able to take advantage of the support provided by the EJB container.

When an application is created using NetBeans, it will normally consist of an `application-ejb` and an `application-war` module. Other development environments may take a different approach. In addition, Java EE applications are normally deployed as an `.ear` file.

An important element of Java EE applications is entities which support the persistence of application data. The **Java Persistence API** (**JPA**) supports the use of entities in an EE application and the traditional Java application. While they are not introduced here, they are typically called indirectly through a session bean. This topic is covered in *Chapter 4, EJB Persistence*.

Some of the recipes are dependent on earlier recipes. For example, the session EJB developed in the first recipe is reused in the second recipe. This approach permits the reuse of code which is always a good development practice.

Creating a simple session EJB

In this recipe, we will create a simple session bean that returns either a formal or an informal salutation based on a string parameter. In the next recipe we will see how to invoke this EJB from a servlet.

Specifically we will create a stateless session bean. A stateless session bean does not remember its previous invocations. A user will call the bean and the bean will return a result. A stateless bean is not good for maintaining the state of an interactive session such as required to maintain a list of purchases. However, it is useful for one-time calculations. Our bean returns one of two simple greetings.

Getting ready

The creation of a session EJB consists of two steps:

1. Create the EJB class annotated with a session bean annotation
2. Add business method to the EJB

These steps have been made easier through the use of annotations.

How to do it...

In this example we will use the **@Stateless** annotation. Create a Java EE application called `SalutationApplication`. The application should have both a `SalutationApplication-ejb` and a `SalutationApplication-war` module. Add the following Stateless session bean to a package called `packt` and name the bean `Salutation`.

In this EJB we will add two simple business methods which return different types of greetings.

```
package packt;
import javax.ejb.Stateless;

@Stateless
public class Salutation {
  public String getFormalSalutation(String name) {
    return "Dear " + name;
  }
  public String getInformalSalutation(String name) {
    return "Hi " + name;
  }
}
```

How it works...

The process of creating a stateless session EJB involved defining a class to support the desired functionality of the bean and using the **@Stateless** annotation to specify the class as a stateless session EJB. In order to use the **@Stateless** annotation we needed to use an import statement.

The two class methods took a string as an argument and returned the string prefixed with either a formal or informal greeting.

There's more...

Annotation is at the heart of the EJB declaration. Annotations are embedded in the application's source code and allow further processing of the source code either:

- Before a source code file is compiled
- During development by a compiler, IDE deployment tool or similar application
- During the execution of the application

An annotation can be applied to many different program elements including but not limited to classes, methods, parameters, fields, and packages. In essence, annotations are used to provide metadata about an element. Metadata is usually defined as data about data. We may have a program element, such as a method, requiring in some circumstances additional information about how it is used.

For example, we might want a particular method to correctly override a base class method. The **@Override** annotation does exactly this. This annotation is useful should we accidentally mistype the method name and fail to actually override the annotation. We may think we are overriding it but we are not. If we use the **@Override** annotation and fail to actually override the method a syntax error is issued by the compiler.

The **@Stateless** annotation provides information to configure the environment and treat the class as an EJB. The annotation is used at runtime and has attributes affecting its visibility. In particular, the `mappedName` attribute is used in the generation of the bean's JNDI name.

```
@Stateless(mappedName="salutationBean")
public class Salutation {
```

The bean can now be referenced in certain contexts using the name: `salutationBean`. An alias can also be defined for an EJB in the project's `ejb-jar.xml` file.

Session beans are not limited to a stateless form. The use of the **@Stateful** annotation declares a bean to be stateful. This means field variables can maintain their values as a user interacts with the application over a period of time called a session. In addition, session beans frequently interact with entities to persist data to a database.

A session bean can also have a local, remote and no-interface client view. The interface used determines the intent and scope of the bean. The no-interface view is new to EJB 3.1. This approach allows the developer to use EJB without having to declare a business interface. In later recipes we will see how these aspects of session beans are used.

See also

The next recipe illustrates how we can use the session bean in other parts of our application.

Accessing a session bean using dependency injection

A session bean has limited value by itself. To be useful it needs to be used by a client such as a servlet or JSF page. In this recipe we will see how to use dependency injection to use a session bean in a servlet.

Getting ready

The essential steps to access a session EJB using dependency injection include:

1. Inject the EJB using the **@EJB** annotation
2. Access its methods as needed

First we need a session bean. To keep things simple, we will use the Salutation session EJB developed in the previous recipe. We will add our servlet to the `SalutationApplication`.

How to do it...

We will be developing a **HyperText Transfer Protocol** (**HTTP**) based servlet named `SalutationServlet`. This servlet will use the `Salutation` EJB's methods and display their return value. Create a package in the WAR module called `servlet`. Add the servlet to this package.

The servlet consists of a class declaration and three methods:

- ▸ doGet—A standard servlet method
- ▸ doPost—A standard servlet method
- ▸ processRequest—Is invoked by both the doGet and doPost methods

The servlet begins with the **@WebServlet** annotation then declares an instance of the Servlet EJB and uses it in the processRequest method.

```
package servlet;
import javax.ejb.EJB;
import packt.Salutation;

@WebServlet(urlPatterns = {"/SalutationServlet"})
public class SalutationServlet extends HttpServlet {
  @EJB
  private Salutation salutation;

  protected void processRequest(HttpServletRequest request,
    HttpServletResponse response)
    throws ServletException, IOException {
      response.setContentType("text/html;charset=UTF-8");
      PrintWriter out = response.getWriter();
      try {
        out.println("<html>");
        out.println("<head>");
        out.println("<title>Servlet SalutationServlet</title>");
        out.println("</head>");
        out.println("<body>");
        out.println("<h1>" +
          salutation.getFormalSalutation("Sherlock Holmes") +
          "</h1>");
        out.println("</body>");
        out.println("</html>");
      } finally {
      out.flush();
      out.close();
    }
}

  @Override
  protected void doGet(HttpServletRequest request,
    HttpServletResponse response)
```

```
        throws ServletException, IOException {
            processRequest(request, response);
    }

    @Override
    protected void doPost(HttpServletRequest request,
        HttpServletResponse response)
        throws ServletException, IOException {
            processRequest(request, response);
        }
}
```

Enter the URL as shown in the following screenshot into a browser. When executed, the salutation **Dear Sherlock Holmes** will be displayed in the browser.

How it works...

To provide a reference to an EJB in a servlet we used the **@EJB** annotation to inject the bean. However, before we could use the annotation two import statements were required. The first one was for the annotation and the second one is for the Salutation EJB.

```
import javax.ejb.EJB;
import packt.Salutation;
```

The declaration of the servlet began with **@WebServlet** annotation. The **@WebServlet** is a class level annotation marking the class as an HTTP servlet. The **urlPatterns** parameter specifies the URL pattern which maps to this servlet. This pattern is important because this is how a user of the servlet is able to locate it on the server.

```
@WebServlet(urlPatterns = {"/SalutationServlet"})
public class SalutationServlet extends HttpServlet {
```

The salutation variable was declared as a field of the servlet. The **@EJB** annotation immediately preceded the variable declaration and effected dependency injection. This allows the EJB container to support the EJB.

```
    @EJB
    private Salutation salutation;
```

HTTP Servlets typically respond to `doGet` and `doPost` HTTP commands. The `doGet` and `doPost` methods are invoked depending on whether a **GET** or **POST** HTTP command is issued. In this example, both of these methods called the `processRequest` method using the common servlet logic in the `processRequest` method.

The `processRequest` method used standard servlet code to generate the HTML response sent back to the browser. Of particular interest to us was the use of the salutation object. The `getFormalSalutation` method was invoked and its return value was sent forward to the browser.

```
...
out.println("<h1>" +
    salutation.getFormalSalutation("Sherlock Holmes") + "</h1>");
...
```

See also

The next recipe illustrates the use of JNDI to access an EJB.

Accessing the session bean using JNDI

JNDI can also be used to access an EJB but using this technique is not as easy as DI. The `Salutation` EJB from the first recipe and the servlet from the second recipe are used to illustrate this technique.

Getting ready

To use JNDI in a client:

1. Obtain an **InitialContext** object
2. Use the context to look up the EJB

Familiarize yourself with the `Salutation` session bean and its two methods as developed in the *Creating a Simple Session EJB* recipe. We will also modify the `SalutationServlet` from the second recipe to use JNDI instead of DI.

How to do it...

A portable JNDI name syntax has been added to EJB 3.1. We will use this syntax as it makes the use of JNDI less dependent on the deployment server.

The modification of the `SalutationServlet` involves removing the **@EJB** annotation and adding code to perform the JNDI look up. This code is placed immediately before the servlet's `try` block.

```
. . .
   Context context = null;
   try {
     context = new InitialContext();
     salutation = (Salutation) context.lookup(
       "java:global/SalutationApplication/
       SalutationApplication-ejb/Salutation");
   } catch (Exception e) {
       e.printStackTrace();
   }
. . .
```

How it works...

In order to initialize and assign an instance of the bean to the `salutation` variable, the bean needed to be looked up using an object implementing the `Context` interface. The `Context` interface provided the information necessary to locate the server and to create a reference to a `Salutation` object. First, we needed to create an `InitialContext` object. This class implemented the `Context` interface. Exceptions resulting from the creation of the `InitialContext` object and the subsequent `lookup` method were caught.

Once the `Context` has been established, the `Context` object's `lookup` method was invoked and a reference to the `Salutation` EJB was provided. The `lookup` method used a portable JNDI name to identify the EJB. In this case, a global name was used.

The syntax starts with one of three different prefixes. In this example the prefix was `java:global` specifying a global name. Following the prefix is a series of names separated by forward slashes. The first name was the name of the application, `SalutationApplication`. The second name was the name of the JAR file where the bean is held, `SalutationApplication-ejb`. The name of the bean was the last name. Names are automatically generated for EJBs.

Prior to EJB 3.1, a JNDI name was server-specific and limited the portability of EJBS. With EJB 3.1 this problem goes away and we can create more portable and maintainable applications.

There's more...

There are two features of JNDI needing further scrutiny.

- Portable JNDI naming syntax
- EJBS supporting multiple interfaces

Portable JNDI naming syntax

JNDI is used to look up resources such as session beans within an application and across the network. A JNDI server allows resources to be registered and then clients can look up and use these resources. Each EJB is automatically assigned a unique name by the server though it is possible to assign a specific name if desired. This name is then combined with one of three JNDI namespace prefixes to form a complete portable JNDI name.

The following table details the string prefixes and implications.

String prefix	Visibility of the resulting name
`"java:global/"`	A globally accessible name
`"java:app/"`	Can only be seen by code in the same application
`"java:module/"`	Can only be seen by code in the same module

A Java EE application is organized around a series of JAR files. An EJB may be packaged in either an `application-ejb.jar` or an `application-war.war` file. The `application-ejb.jar` can also be packaged within the `application.ear` file.

Let's look at the syntax for portable global session beans in more detail.

```
java:global[/<app-name>]/<module-name>/<bean-name>
```

There are three sections that follow the `java:global` prefix:

- ▶ `<app-name>`—This name is optional and is only used if the bean is packaged in an `.ear` file. The `<app-name>` is the name of the `.ear` file minus the file extension. The `<app-name>` can also be specified in the `application.xml` file.

- ▶ `<module-name>`—This is the name of the `ejb-jar` file or the `.war` file containing the bean excluding its extension. An explicit name can be specified for the `<module-name>` using either the `ejb-jar.xml` or `web.xml` files.

- ▶ `<bean-name>`—This is the name of the bean. As mentioned earlier, this name is automatically generated but can be given an alias.

The JNDI name used is dependent on the location of the client in relationship to the EJB module. For example, the module namespace can be used for looking up names within the same module.

```
java:module/<bean-name>
```

The application namespace can be used for looking up names within the same application.

```
java:app[/<module-name>]/<bean-name>
```

Using more than one namespace can make our code more stable and less susceptible to breaking when code changes. For example, we could use a global namespace for a client and a bean within the same module.

```
java:global/app1/module1/bean1
```

If the client and bean are moved into a different module then this lookup will fail. However, if we had used the module namespace, the lookup would not fail.

```
java:module/bean1
```

EJBs supporting multiple interfaces

Each of the JNDI names may be terminated with `[/interface-name]` and are only required if the EJB implements more than one business interface. For example, a session bean may implement a local interface and a remote interface.

```
public class Salutation implements
   SalutationLocalInterface,
   SalutationRemoteInterface {

   }
```

Either of these two names could then be used:

```
java:global[/<app-name>]/<module-name>/Salutation/
SalutationLocalInterface
java:global[/<app-name>]/<module-name>/Salutation/
SalutationRemoteInterface
```

Creating a simple message-driven bean

Message-Driven Beans (**MDB**) are used to support asynchronous communication within an application. Typically, they are used in conjunction with a queue. A client will send a message to a queue and the MDB will then process the message in the queue. The client does not call the MDB directly, but instead communicates through messages. The MDB never returns a value to the client.

Java Message Service (**JMS**) is the basis for communication between a client and the MDB. Fortunately, many of the details needed to use JMS are hidden thus making the job of the EJB developer easier.

In this recipe we show how to create the MDB. In the next recipe, we will modify the `SalutationServlet` developed in the second recipe to send a message to our MDB.

Getting ready

The creation of an MDB involves three tasks:

1. Using the **@MessageDriven** annotation to designate the class as an MDB
2. Implementing the `javax.jms.MessageListener` interface
3. Overriding the `onMessage` method

Our MDB, which is called `SalutationMessageBean`, will simply log each time a salutation message is processed.

How to do it...

Open the `SalutationApplication` and add the `SalutationMessageBean` to the `SalutationApplication-ejb` module and the `packt` package.

```
@MessageDriven(mappedName = "jms/SalutationQueue",
   activationConfig =  {
      @ActivationConfigProperty(propertyName = "acknowledgeMode",
      propertyValue = "Auto-acknowledge"),
      @ActivationConfigProperty(propertyName = "destinationType",
      propertyValue = "javax.jms.Queue")
      })
public class SalutationMessageBean implements MessageListener {

   public SalutationMessageBean() {
   }

   @Override
   public void onMessage(Message message) {
     try {
       String name = message.getStringProperty("name");
       Logger.getLogger("SalutationLog").log(Level.INFO,
         "Salutation processed", "");
     } catch (JMSException e) {
        throw new RuntimeException(e);
        }
   }

}
```

The next recipe will demonstrate the use of this MDB.

How it works...

The **@MessageDriven** annotation is more complex than most annotations but understanding it is by no means insurmountable. The annotation has five possible attributes. For our `SalutationMessageBean` we used only two of them, `mappedName` and `activationConfig`.

The `mappedName` attribute is the simplest one. It is a vendor-specific name and maps the MDB to a JMS queue. When a message appears in the queue, it is sent to the MDB's `onMessage` method. We used the name `jms/SalutationQueue`. This is the name configured by the server and represents the queue we want to use. Most servers provide a way of creating and naming JMS resources, such as a queue.

```
mappedName = "jms/SalutationQueue",
```

The `activationConfig` attribute is concerned with how the MDB works in its environment. This can include issues such as how messages are acknowledged and the type of destination used. We addressed these two issues in our MDB. Nested within the **@MessageDriven** annotation were two **@ActivationConfigProperty** annotations. These were used to specify the acknowledgement mode and the destination type.

The **@ActivationConfigProperty** annotation has a `propertyName` attribute and a `propertyValue` attribute. These are used together to specify the name and value of a property. For our MDB the acknowledgement mode was set to "Auto-acknowledge" and the destination type was the `javax.jms.Queue` interface.

```
@MessageDriven(mappedName = "jms/SalutationQueue",
    activationConfig = {
        @ActivationConfigProperty(propertyName = "acknowledgeMode",
        propertyValue = "Auto-acknowledge"),
        @ActivationConfigProperty(propertyName = "destinationType",
        propertyValue = "javax.jms.Queue")
        })
```

When a message arrives at the message queue it is sent to the `onMessage` method of the MDB. This method has a single parameter, a `javax.jms.Message` object. Depending on the type of message sent, various methods can be applied against this object to return information needed by the bean. In the earlier code sequence, the value of a `name` property was returned and used as part of the logging operation.

There's more...

There is a lot more to MDBs than what we have seen here. But let's not spoil the fun; many useful MDB recipes are found in *Chapter 3, Message-Driven Beans*.

See also

The next recipe shows how to send a message to this MDB.

Sending a message to a message-driven bean

Message-Driven Beans (MDB) are used in an asynchronous fashion. A client will create a message and then send it to a queue for processing. The MDB will effectively remove the message from the queue and act on it.

In this recipe, we will use the `SalutationServlet` to send a message to the queue each time a salutation is processed.

Getting ready

The process consists of two steps:

1. Adding declarations for a queue factory and a message
2. Adding code to actually send the message

Review the `SalutationApplication` project as developed in the *Accessing a session bean using dependency injection* recipe. We will be modifying the `SalutationServlet`.

How to do it...

Start by adding declarations for a queue factory and a message queue as instance variables in the `SalutationServlet`.

```
@Resource(mappedName = "jms/SalutationQueueFactory")
private QueueConnectionFactory queueConnectionFactory;
@Resource(mappedName = "jms/SalutationQueue")
private Queue queue;
```

Next, we need to add code to send the message. This code is placed in front of the servlet's `try` block. This code can be used regardless of whether the salutation object is instantiated using DI or JNDI. In this code we will create a connection to a server-based queue. Once we have a connection we create a session which serves to facilitate communication. The session creates a message producer which sends the message. And of course, we need to handle exceptions.

This might sound kind of involved but don't worry; most of the individual steps are simple.

```
try {
  String message = "Salutation generated";

  Connection connection =
    queueConnectionFactory.createConnection();
```

```
    Session session = connection.createSession(false,
      Session.AUTO_ACKNOWLEDGE);
    MessageProducer messageProducer = (MessageProducer)
      session.createProducer(queue);
    TextMessage textMessage = session.createTextMessage();
    textMessage.setText(message);
    messageProducer.send(textMessage);
    Logger.getLogger("SalutationLog").log(Level.WARNING,
      "Message sent successfully", "Message sent successfully2");
  } catch (JMSException ex) {
      Logger.getLogger("SalutationLog").log(Level.WARNING,
        "JMSException in SalutationServlet",
        "JMSException in SalutationServlet");
  }
```

How it works...

First, we needed to create a connection to the queue. This step used a connection factory. As you are probably aware, the software factory pattern is used to, among other things, hide the details of how an object is created.

In addition to a connection factory, a destination queue was created. Most IDEs will assist in the creation of these resources. However, it may be necessary to use the server's administration console to create these resources. The connection factory was created by the server, GlassFish in this case, with the name `jms/SalutationQueueFactory` which is of type `QueueConnectionFactory`. The **@Resource** annotation was used to inject it into the servlet.

```
    @Resource(mappedName = "jms/SalutationQueueFactory")
    private QueueConnectionFactory queueConnectionFactory;
```

The queue is of type `javax.jms.Queue` and used the name `jms/SalutationQueue` as defined within the server. The **@Resource** annotation was used again to inject this resource.

```
    Resource(mappedName = "jms/SalutationQueue")
    private Queue queue;
```

A `try` block was needed to catch and handle any JMS exception thrown. Within the `try` block a message string was defined. This string was sent to the queue. Next, the `QueueConnectionFactory` object is used to create a `QueueConnection`. The `QueueConnection` represents a connection between two point-to-point JMS elements. Any exceptions were handled in the `catch` block.

```
    try {
      String message = "Salutation generated";
      Connection connection =
        queueConnectionFactory.createConnection();
  ...
```

```
} catch (JMSException ex) {
    Logger.getLogger("SalutationLog").log(Level.WARNING,
        "JMSException in SalutationServlet",
        "JMSException in SalutationServlet");
}
```

The next step created a `Session` object used for sending and receiving messages. The `Connection` object's `createSession` method uses two parameters. The first one indicates that the session is part of a transaction. The second argument specifies the type of acknowledgment to be made. Using `Session.AUTO_ACKNOWLEDGE` meant the session automatically acknowledged the receipt of the message.

```
Session session = connection.createSession(false,
Session.AUTO_ACKNOWLEDGE);
```

The `Session` object was used to create a `MessageProducer`. The `MessageProducer` object was used later in this code sequence to send a message to the destination queue. The queue was used as the argument in the `createProducer` method.

```
MessageProducer messageProducer = (MessageProducer)
    session.createProducer(queue);
```

Next, a `TextMessage` was created using the `createTextMessage` method. A `TextMessage` is one of several interfaces derived from the `Message` interface. These JMS interfaces represent different types of messages used within JMS. The `setText` method assigned a string to be sent.

```
TextMessage textMessage = session.createTextMessage();
textMessage.setText(message);
```

The `messageProducer` then sent the message.

```
messageProducer.send(textMessage);
```

The output was displayed in the log file used by the `SalutationMessageBean`.

INFO: Salutation processed

See also

The previous recipe explains the MDB used in this recipe.

Accessing an EJB from a web service (JAX-WS)

Java EE 6 supports **Java API for XML Web Services** (**JAX-WS**) based web applications. These are frequently referred to as "big" web services because they use **Simple Object Access Protocol** (**SOAP**) XML messages. This protocol provides a standard approach for accessing remote objects. The functionality supported by the service is provided in a **Web Services Description Language** (**WSDL**) file. This file is a standard way of describing an application's services.

In this example, we will create a `TimeOfDay` class with a single method. The method will return a string representing the current date and time. We will use a singleton session bean to support the time service. A singleton is a session bean for which there is one and only one instance ever present in the application.

Getting ready

To create a web service:

1. Create a supporting EJB for the functionality of the service
2. Create a class annotated with the **@WebService** annotation to provide the service

Creating the EJB and web service are both straightforward.

How to do it...

Create a new web application called `TODService`. Within the application we will create a web service and a stateless EJB. Next, create the singleton EJB in a package called `ejb`. Add an EJB called `TimeOfDay` using the **@Singleton** annotation.

```
package ejb;

import java.text.SimpleDateFormat;
import java.util.Calendar;
import javax.ejb.Singleton;

@Singleton
public class TimeOfDay {

  private static final String DATE_TIME =
    "yyyy-MM-dd HH:mm:ss";

  public String timeOfDay() {
```

```
    Calendar calendar = Calendar.getInstance();
    SimpleDateFormat simpleDateFormat =
      new SimpleDateFormat(DATE_TIME);
    return simpleDateFormat.format(calendar.getTime());
  }
}
```

The next step is to create the Web Service. The JAX-WS Web Service is defined using the **@WebService** annotation. We will use the **@EJB** annotation to inject the `TimeOfDay` EJB and then create a single **@WebMethod**, called `timeOfDay`.

```
package service;

import ejb.TimeOfDay;
import javax.ejb.EJB;
import javax.jws.WebMethod;
import javax.jws.WebService;

@WebService
public class Time {
  @EJB
  private TimeOfDay timeOfDay;

  @WebMethod(operationName = "timeOfDay")
  public String timeOfDay() {
    return timeOfDay.timeOfDay();
  }

}
```

The easiest way to demonstrate service is to use the testing service available as part of the server. Enter the following URL into a browser to observe the behavior of the service:

```
http://localhost:8080/TODService/TimeService?Tester
```

The following screenshot shows the `TimeService` Web Service Tester. This page is automatically generated and provides a way of testing web services. Since this type of application uses the SOAP protocol to invoke a service, the service tester provides an easier to use graphical technique to test the service. Without this capability the developer would have to develop a more convoluted SOAP message.

Click on the **timeOfDay** button. The following screenshot displays the string returned. The SOAP request and response used for the service are not shown in the screenshot but can be seen in the window by scrolling down.

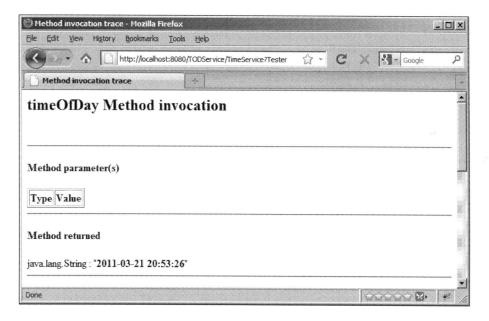

How it works...

The `TimeOfDay` class used a single method, called `timeOfDay`, which returns a string representing the time. To support the formatting of the string we created another string, `DATE_TIME` to hold the string's format pattern. This pattern was used with the `format` method to yield a properly formatted return string.

```
private static final String DATE_TIME = "yyyy-MM-dd HH:mm:ss";
```

The `timeOfDay` method obtained an instance of the `Calendar` class. Its `getTime` method was used to get the current day and time. The `SimpleDateFormat` class along with the `format` method were used to format the string. The string is then returned.

The **@WebService** annotation identifies as a web service provided by the application. This is followed by the class declaration. The `TimeOfDay` object was injected using the **@EJB** annotation. Notice that we used the no-interface view of the `TimeOfDay` EJB. That is, there was no explicit interface defined for the EJB.

The method immediately following the **@WebMethod** annotation is available for use by the client. The `operationName` attribute specified the method name as seen by the client.

The `timeOfDay` method is simple enough. It used the `timeOfDay` method of the `TimeOfDay` object.

There's more...

Notice the URL used to test the application `TODService` contains the context root of the application.

```
http://localhost:8080/TODService/TimeService?Tester
```

This value is configured in the application's `sun-web.xml` file.

```
...
<sun-web-app error-url="">
<context-root>/TODService</context-root>
...
</sun-web-app>
```

Accessing an EJB from a web service (JAX-RS)

Java EE 6 supports **Java API for RESTful Web Services (JAX-RS)**, a **Representational State Transfer** (**RESTful**) web service. This type of service does not require WDSL or XML messages. In this recipe we will create a simple RESTful application, `RESTApplication`, which returns a random tip of the day message.

The beauty of this application is its simplicity and ease of development. We will create two EJBs: one for the application's functionality and a second one to represent the Web Service.

Getting ready

To create a JAX-RS application we need to:

1. Create an EJB to support the functionality of the web service
2. Create a web service EJB annotated with the **@Path** annotation

The use of annotations makes both of these steps easy to do.

How to do it...

Create a new Web Service called `RESTApplication`. In this application we will be adding two stateless session beans: `TipSessionBean` and `TipOfTheDay`.

Next, create a `packt` package for the two stateless EJBs. Follow this by creating a stateless session bean, `TipSessionBean`, to support an application returning a random tip of the day message. Next, we will create the Web Service to access and use the bean.

The `TipSessionBean` is straight forward. The EJB uses an array of strings to hold the tips. The `getTip` method randomly returns a tip from the array.

```
package packt;
import javax.ejb.Stateless;

@Stateless
public class TipSessionBean {
  private final static String tips[] = {
    "I hear and I forget. I see and I remember. I do and
    I understand", "Study the past if you would define
    the future", " Life is simple, it's just not easy."};

  public String getTip() {
    return tips[(int)(Math.random()*tips.length)];
  }

}
```

Now let's turn our attention to the RESTful application. A stateless session bean, called `TipOfTheDay`, is used to represent the service.

```
@Path("tipoftheday")
@Stateless
public class TipOfTheDay {
  @EJB
  TipSessionBean tips;

  @GET
  @Produces("text/html")
  public String processGet() {
    return getTip();
  }

  @POST
  @Produces("text/html")
  public String processPost() {
    return getTip();
  }

  private String getTip() {
    return tips.getTip();
  }

}
```

The service can be tested using an IDE tester or by typing the URL of the service into a browser as illustrated in the following screenshot:

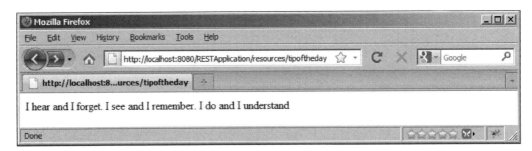

How it works...

At the heart of the `TipSessionBean` is the `getTip` method. This method used the `Math` class' `random` method to return a double number greater than or equal to 0.0 but is less than 1.0. The return value was multiplied by the length of the array, three in this case. This returned a number between 0 and 2.999997. The result was cast to an integer (between 0 and 2 inclusive) and then used to select the tip.

```
public String getTip() {
   return tips[(int)(Math.random()*tips.length)];
}
```

In the `TipOfTheDay` class, the **@Path** annotation used a string to specify the name of the service. This name is part of the URL used by a client. The class itself used the **@EJB** annotation to inject the `TipSessionBean` for the field `tips`.

The **@GET** annotation configured the `processGet` method as the method to use when a HTTP **GET** request is made. The **@Produces** annotation specified the type of output as `text/html`. While we did not actually generate any HTML tags, we could if needed.

Most web applications will support both the **GET** and **POST** operations. However, from a Java EE perspective there is little difference between them. This allows us to create one method which handles both requests in the same way.

The `processGet` method calls a private `getTip` method of the service. A third method, `processPost`, was added to **POST** requests and also called the servlet's `getTip` method. The `getTip` method then used the `Tip's` object to return a tip.

The service can be tested using an IDE tester or typing in the URL of the service into a browser.

There's more...

The actual URL is dependent on the configuration of the application. Consider the URL:

`http://localhost:8080/RESTApplication/resources/tipoftheday`

The context path for the application is `http://localhost:8080/RESTApplication` where `RESTApplication` is the name of the project. The relative URL is **/resources** as specified in the **@ApplicationPath** annotation discussed next. The last part, **tipoftheday**, is specified in the **@Path** annotation.

When a RESTLess application is created in an IDE such as NetBeans, an `ApplicationConfig` class is automatically generated. You may be prompted to choose between various options. Normally, the default option will suffice.

This class, shown below, defines the components used in the application and supplies any metadata needed for the application. The `ApplicationConfig` used for the tip of the day application uses the **@ApplicationPath** annotation to specify the base URI for all of the resources of the application. Notice that annotations can also be written prefixed with the package name as we sometimes do with Java classes.

```
package org.netbeans.rest.application.config;

@javax.ws.rs.ApplicationPath("resources")
public class ApplicationConfig extends javax.ws.rs.core.Application {
}
```

Notice in this example the application path is given as `resources`. This is why the URL used to test the application uses this string in front of the resource name.

Accessing an EJB from an Applet

EJBs can be accessed from a number of different application clients. Here we will see how an EJB can be accessed from an Applet. Applets are still used extensively to provide a richer browser interface than that provided using standard HTML. This includes the use of graphics and animations. Knowing how to access an EJB from an applet gives the applet developer even more opportunities.

Getting ready

Accessing an EJB from an applet uses three steps:

1. Creating an EJB for the actual functionality
2. Creating a remote interface
3. Using JNDI in the applet to obtain a reference to the EJB

The remote interface determines which methods are available to the Applet.

How to do it...

Create two different applications. The first application will be called `CapitalApplication`, packaged as EJB-JAR, and contains an EJB called `CapitalBean`. It possesses a method which, when passed the name of a country, returns its capital. The second is a stand-alone `JApplet` application which uses the `CapitalBean`.

For this recipe, we will create three classes:

- ▸ `CapitalBean` containing the desired functionality
- ▸ `CapitalBeanRemote` exposing the interface used by a client
- ▸ `EJBApplet` using the `CapitalBean`

EJBs used outside of a Java EE application normally need to implement a remote interface. This interface specifies the methods available to a client. The `CapitalBean` EJB implements `CapitalBeanRemote` interface. This interface has a single method called `getCapital`.

```java
package packt;
import javax.ejb.Remote;

@Remote
public interface CapitalBeanRemote {
  public String getCapital(String state);
}
```

The `CapitalBean` implements the `getCapital` method using a `HashMap` initialized with countries and their capitals.

```java
@Stateless
public class CapitalBean implements CapitalBeanRemote {
  private HashMap<String, String> capitals = new HashMap<String,
String>();

  public CapitalBean() {
    capitals.put("United Kingdom", "London");
    capitals.put("Japan", "Tokyo");
    capitals.put("India", "New Delhi");
  }

  @Override
  public String getCapital(String country) {
    return capitals.get(country);
  }
}
```

Create a separate application called `CapitalApplet`. Add a `JApplet` called `EJBApplet`. The applet includes a `JButton` that when pressed will populate a `JTextField` with the capital of Japan.

The applet as shown below includes the following methods:

- ▸ `init`—Executes when the applet starts and calls the `initComponents` method
- ▸ `initComponents`—Sets up the user interface and enables the `JButton`
- ▸ `invokeEJB`—Uses JNDI to access and use the `getCaptial` method of the `CapitalBean`

```java
public class EJBApplet extends JApplet {
    private JButton invokeButton = new JButton("Invoke EJB");
    private JTextField messageTextField = new JTextField("Waiting
        for results");

    public void init() {
      try {
        java.awt.EventQueue.invokeAndWait(new Runnable() {
          public void run() {
            initComponents();
          }
        });
      } catch (Exception ex) {
          ex.printStackTrace();
      }
    }

    private void initComponents() {
      Container container = this.getContentPane();
      container.setLayout(new FlowLayout());
      container.add(invokeButton);
      container.add(messageTextField);

      invokeButton.addActionListener(new
        java.awt.event.ActionListener() {
          public void actionPerformed(java.awt.event.
            ActionEvent evt)
        {
          invokeEJB();
        }
      });
    }

    public void invokeEJB() {
      try {
        InitialContext context =new InitialContext();
        CapitalBeanRemote bean = (CapitalBeanRemote)
        context.lookup(
```

```
              "java:global/CapitalApplication/CapitalBean");
           messageTextField.setText(bean.getCapital("Japan"));
           context.close();

       } catch (Exception e) {
         e.printStackTrace();
       }
     }

   }
```

When setting up the project add libraries for the `CapitalApplication`
(`CapitalApplication.jar`) and for the server (`appserv-rt.jar`). These files
can be added using the properties tab of the `CapitalApplet`.

Most IDEs provide a way of executing an applet without actually creating an HTML page for
the applet. Use the IDE to execute the `EJBApplet`. The applet will appear as shown in the
following screenshot.

How it works...

The `CapitalBean` EJB used a `HashMap` to maintain a list of countries and their capitals. This
`HashMap` was initialized in the constructor. The `getCapital` method was passed the name
of the country and returned the corresponding capital name.

In a `HashMap`, the first string represents a key (which for us is the name of a country), and a
value (which is the country's capital). The `put` method adds the pair to the `HashMap`. The `get`
method returns a value based on a key.

The applet `InitialContext` object bears further explanation. When the applet is created
there are at least two JAR files placed on the application's classpath: the `CapitalBean` EJB
JAR and an `appserv-rt.jar` file.

The EJB JAR contains the class declarations needed for the references to the EJB to be used
correctly within the applet. Without this file, the compiler will be unable to know whether we
are using the `CapitalBean` correctly.

The `appserv-rt.jar` file contains a `manifest.mf` file. This file contains the information needed to configure the client side of JNDI enabling it to successfully locate a resource and return a reference to it. In our case, the client side was our applet. Unless this JNDI information is configured properly, the `InitialContext` object may not be constructed correctly. This often results in an annoying naming exception message.

The declarations for the `JApplet` consisted of a `JButton` and a `JTextField`. The `init` method used a standard Swing technique of creating a thread which works gracefully with the `AWTEvent` thread to call the `initComponents` method. The `initComponents` method created a simple user interface. The `invokeButton` used an anonymous inner class to call the `invokeEJB` method when the button is selected.

The `invokeEJB` method is the interesting part of the applet. An `InitialContext` object was created and used with a global JNDI name to locate and return a reference to the `CapitalBean` EJB.

There's more...

It is sometimes useful to examine the applet JNDI context in more detail. The `InitialContext` object's `getEnvironment` method returns a `Hashtable` we can use to list the environmental properties.

The `Hashtable` consists of key/value pairs which we can iterate through using an `Enumeration` object. The `keys` method of the `Hashtable` returns the `Enumeration`.

```
Hashtable table = context.getEnvironment();
Enumeration<String> enumeration = table.keys();
while (enumeration.hasMoreElements()) {
  String key = enumeration.nextElement();
  System.out.println(key + " - " + table.get(key));
}
```

One possible list may include the following properties and values:

```
java.naming.factory.initial -
  com.sun.enterprise.naming.impl.SerialInitContextFactory
java.naming.factory.url.pkgs - com.sun.enterprise.naming
java.naming.factory.state -
  com.sun.corba.ee.impl.presentation.rmi.JNDIStateFactoryImpl
```

See also

The *Accessing the session bean using JNDI* recipe, discusses the use of JNDI in more detail.

Accessing an EJB from JSP

Yet another way of accessing an EJB is from a **JavaServer Pages** (**JSP**) page. While JSP has largely been supplemented by newer technologies such as **JavaServer Faces** (**JSF**), it is still useful to understand how to incorporate an EJB into a JSP page since you may find yourself maintaining JSP code.

Getting ready

To use an EJB from a JSP client:

1. Create the supporting EJB
2. Use JNDI in the JSP client

JNDI is required because JSP does not support DI.

How to do it...

Create a Java EE application called JSPExample. It should contain both a JSPExample-ejb and a JSPExample-war module. In the JSPExample-ejb module, we will create a remote session bean called ConstantsBean with methods returning common math constants. We will place it in the packt package. The JSPExample-war module has an index.jsp from which we will invoke the EJB.

The ConstantsBean is a remote stateless session bean. The bean extends a remote interface, ConstantsBeanRemote, which defines the methods of the bean. These methods include getPI and getGoldenRatio both returning a double value.

```
@Remote
public interface ConstantsBeanRemote {
  public double getPI();
  public double getGoldenRatio();
}
```

The ConstantsBean implements this interface and is declared as a stateless session bean. The methods return the Math class PI constant and in the case of the golden ratio the actual golden ratio value.

```
@Stateless
public class ConstantsBean implements ConstantsBeanRemote {

  public double getPI() {
    return Math.PI;
  }
```

```
public double getGoldenRatio() {
  return 1.6180339887;
}
}
```

Create an `index.jsp` page in the `JSPExample-war` module. Next, modify the page to invoke and display the result of the EJB's methods.

```jsp
<%@page contentType="text/html" pageEncoding="UTF-8"%>
<!DOCTYPE HTML PUBLIC "-//W3C//DTD HTML 4.01 Transitional//EN"
    "http://www.w3.org/TR/html4/loose.dtd">

<%@ page import="packt.ConstantsBeanRemote" %>
<%@ page import="javax.naming.InitialContext" %>
<%@ page import="javax.naming.Context" %>
<html>
<head><title>Constants</title></head>
<body>
<%!
ConstantsBeanRemote constantsBean;
%>
<%
Context context = null;
try {
  context = new InitialContext();
  constantsBean = (ConstantsBeanRemote) context.lookup(
    "java:global/JSPExample/JSPExample-ejb/ConstantsBean");
}
catch(Exception e) {
  e.printStackTrace();
}
%><p>
<h1>Constants</h1>
PI: <%= constantsBean.getPI() %><br>
Golden Rule: <%= constantsBean.getGoldenRatio() %>
</body>
</html>
```

Execute the application. Its output should be similar to the following screenshot:

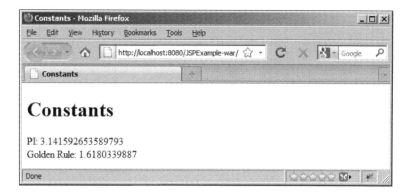

<h2 style="background:#000;color:#fff">How it works...</h2>

The `ConstantsBean` is straight forward; however, the `index.jsp` page requires more explanation. It invoked and displayed the result of the EJB's methods.

There are three sections of the JSP page referencing and using the bean. The first section declared the reference variable `constantsBean`.

```
<%!
ConstantsBeanRemote constantsBean;
%>
```

The second created the initial context and returned a reference to the bean. Notice the global JNDI name was used to locate the bean.

```
<%
Context context = null;
try {
  context = new InitialContext();
  constantsBean = (ConstantsBeanRemote) context.lookup(
    "java:global/JSPExample/JSPExample-ejb/ConstantsBean");
}
catch(Exception e) {
  e.printStackTrace();
}
%>
```

The last section used both methods of the `ConstantsBean`.

```
<h1>Constants</h1>
PI: <%= constantsBean.getPI() %><br>
Golden Rule: <%= constantsBean.getGoldenRatio() %>
```

See also

The *Accessing the session bean using JNDI* recipe, discusses the use of JNDI in more detail.

Calling an EJB from JSF

Java Server Faces (JSF) and Facelets have largely supplemented JSP and permit the use of DI. This simplifies access to the EJB but JNDI can be used if desired. JSF uses the concept of a managed bean to hold business logic. In EJB 3.1 it is not necessary to actually use a managed bean. However, both using an EJB directly and using a managed bean to access an EJB will be presented. Knowing how to use the managed bean approach can be useful especially when reviewing older code.

Getting ready

To access an EJB from a JSF page:

1. Create a supporting EJB
2. Annotate the EJB with the **@Named** annotation

In this example we will also package the beans in the `.war` file to demonstrate this new feature of EJB 3.1. Packaging in `.war` file makes it easier to access EJBs from a web page.

How to do it...

Create a Java EE application called `JSFExample` and include only the `JSFExample-war` module. Be sure to enable contexts and dependency injection when creating the Java EE application. If you don't, you cannot use DI.

We will reuse the `ConstantsBean` from the `JSPExample` application detailed in the *Accessing an EJB from JSP* recipe in this chapter. Create a new package called `packt` and recreate the `ConstantsBean` inside of it. However, do not implement the `ConstantsBeanRemote` interface. Add the following annotation after the **@Stateless** annotation in the `Constantsbean` class. This will make the EJB visible to the JSF client.

```
@Named("constants")
```

Next, create a JSF managed bean called `ConstantsManagedBean`. This class will use DI to create and use the `ConstantsBean`.

```
@ManagedBean
public class ConstantsManagedBean {

    @EJB
    ConstantsBean constants;
```

```
    public ConstantsManagedBean() {
    }

    public double getGoldenRatio() {
      return constants.getGoldenRatio();
    }

    public double getPI() {
      return constants.getPI();
    }


}
```

To demonstrate the use of both the EJB and the JSF-managed bean, create a JSF page titled `index.xhtml`.

```
<?xml version='1.0' encoding='UTF-8' ?>
<!DOCTYPE html PUBLIC "-//W3C//DTD XHTML 1.0 Transitional//EN"
"http://www.w3.org/TR/xhtml1/DTD/xhtml1-transitional.dtd">
<html xmlns="http://www.w3.org/1999/xhtml"
  xmlns:h="http://java.sun.com/jsf/html"
  xmlns:f="http://java.sun.com/jsf/core">
  <h:head>
    <title>Constants</title>
  </h:head>
  <h:body>
    <f:view>
      <h:form>
        <h:outputLabel for="name">
          <h:panelGrid columns="1">
            <h:outputText value="Managed Bean Length:
              #{constantsManagedBean.PI}" />
            <h:outputText value="Managed Bean Status:
              #{constantsManagedBean.goldenRatio}" />
            <h:outputText value="EJB Bean Length:
              #{constants.PI}" />
            <h:outputText value="EJB Bean Status:
              #{constants.goldenRatio}" />
          </h:panelGrid>
        </h:outputLabel>
      </h:form>
    </f:view>

  </h:body>
</html>
```

Execute the application. The following screenshot illustrates its output.

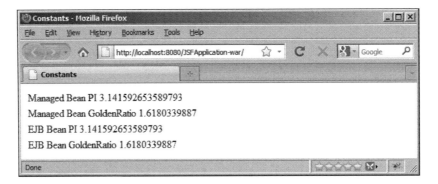

How it works...

The `ConstantsBean` was explained in the previous *Accessing an EJB from JSP* recipe. The JSF managed bean, `ConstantsManagedBean`, was declared as such using the **@ManagedBean** annotation. DI was used to create and use the `ConstantsBean`. The managed bean has two methods, `getGoldenRatio` and `getPI`, which called the corresponding methods of the `ConstantsBean`.

The JSF page used both the `ConstantsBean` directly and the managed bean with `h:outputText` elements. As a developer you can choose to use either technique though the managed bean approach is no longer necessary.

```
<h:outputText value=
    "Managed Bean Length: #{constantsManagedBean.PI}" />
<h:outputText value=
    "Managed Bean Status: #{constantsManagedBean.goldenRatio}" />
<h:outputText value="EJB Bean Length: #{constants.PI}" />
<h:outputText value=
    "EJB Bean Status: #{constants.goldenRatio}" />
```

Accessing an EJB from a Java Application using JNDI

It would be nice if we could use dependency injection outside of a server container. However, this is not possible from a Java SE application unless we use an embeddable container. Using an embeddable container is covered in the next recipe. Here we need to use JNDI. Accessing an EJB from a Java SE application using JNDI is similar to using JNDI in other types of applications.

Getting ready

To use this approach we need:

1. A supporting EJB
2. JNDI code to obtain a reference to the EJB

We will be using the `CapitalApplication` developed in the *Accessing an EJB from an Applet* recipe found in this chapter. This recipe uses a `CapitalBean` to return the name of the capital given a state. Make sure the server and this application are executing before testing the Java application.

How to do it...

The EJB used here is the `CapitalBean`. Create a Java SE application using an IDE of your choice. It does not have to be the same one you used to develop the `CapitalApplication`. In the main method add:

```
try {
   InitialContext context = new InitialContext();
   String name = "java:global/CapitalApplication/CapitalBean";
   CapitalBeanRemote bean =
     (CapitalBeanRemote)context.lookup(name);
   System.out.println(bean.getCapital("India"));
}
catch(javax.naming.NoInitialContextException e) {
   e.printStackTrace();
}
catch (NamingException e) {
   e.printStackTrace();
}
```

Make sure the application's classpath contains `.jar` files for the `CapitalBean` and the `appserv-rt.jar` file.

When executed, the output should appear as:

New Delhi

How it works...

The application JAR file was needed to resolve the class names and the `appserv-rt.jar` file was needed so JNDI could function properly. This file provided the necessary information for JNDI to locate the server and look up the name correctly.

The *Accessing the session bean using JNDI* recipe provides more detail on the use of JNDI.

Accessing an EJB from a Java Application using an embeddable container

The embeddable EJB container allows EJBs to be executed outside of a Java EE environment. Standalone Java SE applications can use the embeddable container to execute EJBs. In addition, it can be used for unit testing of EJBs.

The embeddable container does not require the installation of a server. As a result it has a smaller footprint and will start faster. However, MDBs and inbound **RMI over IIOP (RMI/ IIOP) (Remote Method Invocation (RMI) (Internet Inter-Orb Protocol (IIOP))** calls are not supported. Efficiency features found in the Java EE environment, like clustering, are not available.

How to do it...

Create a standard Java SE application with the following main method.

```
public class Main {

  public static void main(String[] args) {
    try {
      Map properties = new HashMap();
      properties.put(EJBContainer.MODULES, new java.io.File(
        "E:\\Packt\\Projects\\CapitalApplication\\
        build\\classes"));
      properties.put(EJBContainer.APP_NAME,"CapitalApplication");
      EJBContainer ejbC =
        EJBContainer.createEJBContainer(properties);
      Context context = ejbC.getContext();
      String name = "java:global/CapitalApplication/CapitalBean";
      CapitalBeanRemote bean =
        (CapitalBeanRemote)context.lookup(name);
      System.out.println(bean.getCapital("Japan"));

    } catch (NamingException e) {
      e.printStackTrace();
    }
  }

}
```

The Java SE application requires a few JAR files be included in its classpath. These include:

- The embedded EJB container supplied by the server. In the case of GlassFish it is the `glassfish-embedded-static-shell.jar` file.
- The `javax.ejb.jar` file also provided by the server.
- The JAR file containing the `CapitalBean` class.

Use the property window of the application to add these files before executing the application.

How it works...

We declared a `Map` variable called `properties` and assigned to it a new `HashMap`. The variable was used to initialize the `EJBContainer`. This container has a property, `MODULES`, specifying the modules to be used by the container. The `Map` object's `put` method was used to assign the location of the directory containing the `CapitalApplication`'s classes.

The `EJBContainer.APP_NAME` field was used to specify the name of the application. Next, the `EJBContainer` class's static method, `createEJBContainer`, was called with the properties variable as an argument. The `createEJBContainer` method returns an `EJBContainer` object. This class's `getContext` method was used to get a `Context` object. The `Context` object represents the environment needed to find and use the `CapitalBean`.

Next, a portable JNDI name for `CapitalBean` was used as an argument to the `lookup` method. This returned an effective reference to the `CapitalBean`.

The `bean` variable was used to invoke the `getCapital` method and to display the results. The last step caught any exceptions thrown.

The output should appear as:

Tokyo

 The embeddable container is a new EJB 3.1 feature. Not all development environments or servers support this feature. Using NetBeans 6.91 with GlassFish 3.0.1 may not work consistently. However, NetBeans 7 Beta does provide better support.

See also

The previous *Accessing an EJB from a Java Application using JNDI* recipe, provides an alternative technique for accessing EJBs.

Accessing the EJB container

An EJB will always reside inside of an EJB. Normally, this container is part of the server. There are times when it is desirable for the EJB to gain access to this container. This access is provided through an instance of the `EJBContext` interface, which represents the container holding the current bean. The object provides methods to access various aspects of the container including:

- Security issues
- Transactions
- Access to the timer service of the bean
- References to objects available in the JNDI registry
- An object allowing the methods of the bean to be invoked

In this recipe we will obtain a `SessionContext` object for the `Salutation` EJB developed in the *Creating a Simple Session Bean* recipe.

How to do it...

The `Salutation` bean developed in the first recipe will be modified. First, we start to modify the bean by adding a `SessionContext` object. The easiest way of obtaining a `SessionContext` object is to use dependency injection. In order to inject a `SessionContext` object we will need to use the **@Resource** annotation. Both the annotation and the `SessionContext` declaration require imports.

```
import javax.annotation.Resource;
import javax.ejb.SessionContext;
```

Next we add the **@Resource** annotation and declare our `SessionContext` variable `context` as a field of the class.

```
@Stateless
public class Salutation {
...
  @Resource
  private SessionContext context;
...
```

Next, create a `getContextInformation` method returning a string. We can use the `StringBuilder` class to build a string containing context information. There are several `SessionContext` methods available. The result of these methods is appended to `contextInformation` variable.

```
public String getContextInformation() {
   StringBuilder contextInformation = new StringBuilder();
   contextInformation.append(context.toString() + "<br/>");
   try {
      contextInformation.append(
         context.getInvokedBusinessInterface().toString() +
         "<br/>");
   } catch (IllegalStateException e) {
      contextInformation.append(e);
      }
   return contextInformation.toString();
}
```

The simplest way to demonstrate the use of the method is to modify the `SalutationServlet`. Add the `getContextInformation` method call after the statement where the `getFormalGreeting` method is used.

```
out.println("<h1>" +
   salutation.getFormalSalutation("Sherlock Holmes") + "</h1>");
out.println("<h2>" + salutation.getContextInformation() +
   "</h2>");
```

Execute the servlet using the URL `http://localhost:8080/SalutationApplication-war/SalutationServlet` as illustrated in the following screenshot:

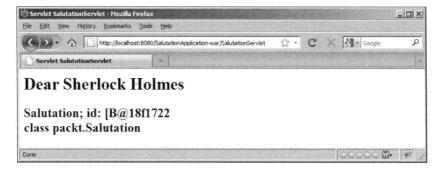

How it works...

The stateless session bean, as we used it, limits the amount of useful context information available. In the example, we only displayed a string to represent the `SessionContext` object and the business interface used by the client, neither of which are terribly exciting. Since the Salutation EJB used a no-interface view, we get back the class name. An EJB not implementing an interface is said to have a no-interface view.

There's more...

The `EJBContext` is the super class for `SessionContext`. It possesses methods common to the three sub-interfaces of the `EBJContext` interface:

- `SessionContext` for Session Beans
- `MessageDrivenContext` for MDB
- `EntityContext` for an Entity

Always choose the corresponding context interface for the EJB or entity in use. The `EJBContext` can be obtained using either dependency inject or JNDI. We have already seen how dependency injection can be used. If we need to use JNDI instead, we need to follow the standard JNDI look up process:

1. Establish an initial context
2. Use the `lookup` method to locate the object
3. Use the methods of the object

```
public String getContextInformationJNDI() {
  SessionContext sctxLookup;
  try {
    InitialContext ic = new InitialContext();
    sctxLookup = (SessionContext)
      ic.lookup("java:comp/EJBContext");
  } catch (NamingException ex) {
      return "NamingException: " + ex.toString();
  }
  return sctxLookup.toString() + "<br/>" +
  sctxLookup.getInvokedBusinessInterface().toString() +
    "<br/>";
}
```

Notice the structure of the JNDI look up string, `java:comp/EJBContext`. It is different from the previous JNDI names we have seen. The `java:comp` prefix is used to allow applications to expose their components. In this case, it specifies the standard name for a `SessionContext`.

2
Session Beans

In this chapter, we will cover:

- ▶ Creating a stateless session bean
- ▶ Creating a stateful session bean
- ▶ Creating a singleton bean
- ▶ Using multiple singleton beans
- ▶ Using container managed concurrency
- ▶ Using bean managed concurrency
- ▶ Controlling the initialization process
- ▶ Using session beans with more than one business interface
- ▶ Understanding parameter behavior and granularity
- ▶ Using an asynchronous method to create a background process

Introduction

The three basic session beans: stateless, stateful, and singleton, are at the heart of most EJB applications. They each differ in their purpose and capabilities. This chapter provides numerous examples of how they can be used and provides insight into how they work.

Many of the examples in this chapter are based on servlets. The use of servlets, specifically the `doGet` and `doPost` methods are detailed in *Chapter 1, Getting Started With EJBs*. When you create your projects, be sure to enable context and dependency injection. The code examples do not include import statements.

Also note that in IDEs such as NetBeans, wizards are frequently used to add elements such as servlets to an application. During this process they will automatically modify the `web.xml` file to map a servlet's name to an URL pattern. If you choose not to use a wizard, you will need to explicitly modify the file itself. Deployment descriptor files are discussed in more detail in *Chapter 11, Packaging the EJB*.

Let's start our discussion with the stateless EJB. This type of session bean has no conversational state. Whenever a client invokes a method of a stateless EJB, it is as if this or any other method of the EJB has never been executed. For example, a method may be passed a height and width to compute the area of a surface and return a result. Any previous height or width values stored with the bean are to be ignored.

Since no state information is maintained, all stateless EJBs of this type are considered to be equivalent by the EJB container. The server's EJB container allocates stateless EJBs and typically reuses them within and between clients. No permanent reference between a client and a stateless EJB is maintained.

A stateful session bean, in contrast, will maintain its state between subsequent client calls. The client uses setter type methods to affect the state of the EJB. Subsequent method calls can use these values to compute and return a value to the client. As such, a stateful bean is not shared between clients. In addition, it can be passivated, that is, temporarily stored between invocations by the server should the server need to remove the bean from memory. Later the bean and its state can be restored as if nothing has happened. A bean may be passivated for a number of reasons. For example, the EJB container may fail yet the server may stay up. When the container is restored the bean can be activated.

A singleton bean is similar to a stateful bean in that state information is maintained between method invocations. However, there is only one singleton bean for the application and it is shared by all of the EJBs and clients of an application. This type of bean provides a convenient means of maintaining the overall state of an application.

The first three recipes illustrate how to create stateless, stateful, and singleton session beans. They further expound upon the behavior of these types of beans.

There is only one instance of a singleton available to an application at a time. However, it is possible to have multiple different singletons in an application. When distributed over multiple Java Virtual Machine (JVM)s, there is only one singleton per JVM.

By default, singletons are not created until a method of the bean is invoked. However, the creation of the singleton can be forced using the **@Startup** annotation. This creation technique is referred to as eager initialization. The effect of most annotations can also be affected using deployment descriptors. The use of deployment descriptors is covered in *Chapter 11, Packaging the EJB*.

There are occasions when it can be advantageous to use multiple singleton beans in the same application. Each singleton can be used to manage a particular aspect of the application. In some applications where multiple singletons are used, the order in which the singletons are created and initialized can be an issue. The **@DependsOn** annotation provides a way of explicitly controlling the order of singleton initialization. The recipe, *Using multiple singleton beans*, addresses this topic.

EJBs can be accessed either locally or remotely. Local access uses a no-interface view or implements a local interface declaration. A no-interface view exposes all of the public methods of an EJB whereas the local and remote interfaces usually expose only a subset of the public methods. Remote EJBs implement a remote interface. The difference between these interfaces involves which methods are made visible and how information is passed between the EJB and a client.

The use of a local interface does not involve a remote procedure call but does require the client to be part of the same JVM process. In addition, parameters are passed by reference. An EJB accessed remotely will use a remote procedure call and parameters are passed by value. That is, only a copy of the object is passed and any modification of the object will not be reflected in the original object. This may be a problem if, for example, the client needs to modify the original object.

The *Using session beans with more than one business interface* and *Understanding parameter behavior and granularity* recipes, address these issues in more detail.

Concurrency is concerned with multiple access of a method by more than one client at a time. If this concurrent access is not planned carefully, data can be corrupted and unpredictable results can occur.

There are two types of locks that can be assigned to an EJB and/or its methods: a read lock and a write lock. When a lock is applied to a class, all of the methods of the class use that locking mechanism. This lock can be overridden by specifying the locking type for an individual method.

A read lock indicates concurrent access to the method is permitted. It is assumed that multiple read operations will not be a problem and will not corrupt the state of the EJB.

A write lock does not permit concurrent access to the method. Once a client begins executing a method marked with a write lock, no other clients are permitted access to the method until the method invocation completes. Other clients are blocked. This is the default concurrent behavior of singletons.

There is nothing the programmer needs to do to enforce concurrent access. However, if more control on the type of concurrent access used is needed, then the programmer can change the type of lock on a method by method basis or use bean-managed concurrency.

The *Using container managed concurrency* and *Using bean managed concurrency* recipes address the concurrency issues.

Sometimes it is desirable to invoke a method of an EJB and not wait for the method to complete its execution. Either the client may not necessarily be concerned with whether the method executes successfully or the client may want to check on its success or failure later. Asynchronous methods provide this capability and the *Using an asynchronous method to create a background process* recipe illustrates this approach.

While it is not obvious from this discussion, EJB 3.1 introduced several new features. For example, there is no need to define explicit interfaces for beans as required in the previous version. Another significant addition is the singleton bean. Prior to EJB 3.1, it was more difficult to implement the singleton design pattern. The ability to invoke session beans asynchronously was also added in this version.

Creating a stateless session bean

In this recipe we will create a stateless session bean called `SphereBean`. This bean will demonstrate the essential elements of a stateless bean and its life cycle. The servlet `SphereServlet` will be used to demonstrate the bean.

Getting ready

Creating a stateless session bean consists of two steps:

1. Annotate the class with the **@Stateless** annotation
2. Add appropriate business methods

Earlier versions of EJB required the use of local and/or remote interfaces. This is no longer necessary.

To use a session bean, inject the EJB into the client using the **@EJB** annotation followed by the declaration of the bean. In this recipe, we will use a servlet to demonstrate this process. It is important to use the **@EJB** annotation, otherwise the bean will not be managed by the EJB container and it will not be able to take advantage of the support provided to EJB such as transaction processing and interceptors.

How to do it...

We will start with an initial version of a stateless session bean called `SphereBean`. From this we will add capability to incrementally demonstrate various aspects of a stateless bean. Start by creating a Java EE application called `StatelessExample`. In the application add a stateless session bean called `SphereBean` in the EJB module under a `packt` package. Add a `HttpServlet` called `SphereServlet` in the WAR module in a `servlet` package.

```
@Stateless
@LocalBean
```

```
public class SphereBean {
  public double computeVolume(double radius) {
    return (4.0/3.0)*Math.PI*(radius*radius*radius);
  }


}
```

Notice the use of the **@LocalBean** annotation. This is the default annotation for a session bean and is normally automatically added by the IDE. However, it is not absolutely required and will often be removed from subsequent examples so as not to distract from the topic at hand.

The SphereServlet illustrates the use of the stateless bean. The SphereServlet invokes computeVolume method and displays the result.

```
public class SphereServlet extends HttpServlet {

  @EJB
  SphereBean sphere;

  protected void processRequest(HttpServletRequest request,
    HttpServletResponse response)
    throws ServletException, IOException {
      response.setContentType("text/html;charset=UTF-8");
      PrintWriter out = response.getWriter();
      try {
        out.println("<html>");
        out.println("<head>");
        out.println("<title>Servlet VolumeServlet</title>");
        out.println("</head>");
        out.println("<body>");
        out.printf("<h3>Volume: %6.2f </h3>",
        sphere.computeVolume(3.0));
        out.println("</body>");
        out.println("</html>");
        out.flush();
      } finally {
        out.close();
      }
  }

  @Override
  protected void doGet(HttpServletRequest request,
    HttpServletResponse response)
    throws ServletException, IOException {
    processRequest(request, response);
```

```
    }

    @Override
    protected void doPost(HttpServletRequest request,
      HttpServletResponse response)
      throws ServletException, IOException {
      processRequest(request, response);
    }

}
```

How it works...

The `SphereBean` possesses a `computeVolume` method that accepts a radius and returns the volume of a sphere with this radius. The session bean is declared as a stateless session bean by using the **@Stateless** annotation. The `SphereBean` implements the formula for calculating the volume of a sphere: Volume = $4/3*PI*radius^3$.

Stateless session beans do not retain state information. The `SphereBean` typifies this type of session bean. In this EJB there are no instance variables and thus no state can be maintained.

Notice the use of the `printf` method used in the `SphereServlet`. This method was introduced in Java SE 6. It mimics the `printf` statement found in the C language. The first argument is a string that provides a format used to display values. These values are the subsequent parameters of the method. In the format string, place holders are used to indicate the type of value to be displayed and any formatting to be applied to the value.

The `printf` statement was used in the servlet to display the volume of the sphere. This statement used a single place holder that corresponds to the second parameter. The place holder was the %6.2f. The %6.2f indicated that a floating point number was to be displayed. In addition, six characters are used to display the number with two digits following the decimal point.

There's more...

There are two other aspects of stateless session beans that should be considered:

- Use of instance variables
- Stateless bean life cycle

Use of Instance variables

It is possible to add instance variables to the session bean. In this version we add a string to the `SphereBean` to specify the measure unit used.

```
@Stateless
public class SphereBean {
  private String unit;

  public String getUnit() {
    return unit;
  }

  public void setUnit(String unit) {
    this.unit = unit;
  }

  ...

}
```

These methods can be used in the `SphereServlet` to set and retrieve the measurement unit.

```
try {
  sphere.setUnit("kilometers");
  ...
    out.printf("<h3>Volume: %6.2f %s</h3>",
      sphere.computeVolume(3.0),
    sphere.getUnit());
  ...
  }
```

Notice the use of two placeholders in this example. The %s field specifies that a string is to be displayed. There is no width specified by the field meaning that the entire string should be displayed.

While the use of these methods is not always desirable, they do illustrate the use of an instance variable within a stateless session bean. **However, there is no guarantee that the same bean instance will be used for these methods**. The EJB container may choose to use different instances of the `SphereBean` for each of these calls resulting in unpredictable behavior. As a result, it is not recommended that stateless session beans be used in this way. Methods of a stateless session bean should be designed to work independently of other method invocations or previous invocations of the same method.

Stateless Bean Life Cycle

The life cycle of a stateless bean supports two call back methods. After the stateless session bean has been constructed, the **@PostConstruct** annotation can be used to designate a method that will be executed before any other methods of the bean are invoked. This method is invoked after all of the bean's dependencies have been resolved. Before the bean is destroyed, the **@PreDestroy** annotated method can likewise be used to designate a method to be executed before the bean goes away.

In this example, the `initialize` method sets a unit value and displays a simple message. In the `destroy` method another message is displayed to indicate that the bean is going away.

```
@Stateless
public class SphereBean {
  private String unit;

  @PostConstruct
  private void initialize() {
    unit = "meters";
    System.out.println("SphereBean initialized");
  }

  @PreDestroy
  private void destroy() {
    System.out.println("Clean up SphereBean");
  }
  ...
}
```

When some sort of initialization or termination action is needed, then these methods can be useful. Normally, most stateless beans do not require such initialization or termination action.

Creating a stateful session bean

In order to illustrate the creation of a stateful EJB, we will use a bean to maintain a list of names. A name will be entered in the `index.jsp` page and passed to a servlet. The servlet will add the name to the stateful bean. Unique to the stateful EJB is the process of passivation. When a stateful bean is experiencing a period of inactivity, the EJB container may decide to remove it from memory temporarily. This process is called passivation. Most of the state of the EJB is saved automatically except for transient fields. When the EJB is restored, the stateless EJB has its original content except for the transient fields.

Getting ready

Creating a stateful session bean requires:

1. Annotating a class with the **@Stateful** annotation
2. Adding appropriate business methods

Earlier versions of EJB required the use of local and/or remote interfaces. This is no longer necessary.

To use a session bean, inject the EJB into the client using the **@EJB** annotation followed by the declaration of the bean. In this recipe, we will use a servlet to demonstrate this process. Remember, it is important to use the **@EJB** annotation, otherwise the bean will not be managed by the EJB container and it will not be able to take advantage of the support provided to EJBs.

How to do it...

Let's start by creating a Java EE application called `StatefulExample`. Add a package called `packt` and a stateful EJB called `NamesBean` to the EJB module. Also, add a package called `servlet` and a servlet called `NamesServlet` to the WAR module.

The `NamesBean` EJB maintains a list of names. Two methods are used. The `addName` method adds a name to the list and the `getNames` method returns a list of names.

```
@Stateful
@LocalBean
public class NamesBean {

  private List<String> names;

  @PostConstruct
  private void initialize() {
    names = new ArrayList<String>();
  }

  public void addName(String name) {
    names.add(name);
  }

  public List<String> getNames() {
    return names;
  }

}
```

The `NamesServlet` injects the `NamesBean` and uses it to add names passed to it.

```java
public class NamesServlet extends HttpServlet {

    @EJB
    private NamesBean names;
    private  List<String> list;

    protected void processRequest(HttpServletRequest request,
       HttpServletResponse response)
       throws ServletException, IOException {
          response.setContentType("text/html;charset=UTF-8");
          PrintWriter out = response.getWriter();
          try {
            names.addName(request.getParameter("name"));
            list = names.getNames();

            out.println("<html>");
            out.println("<head>");
            out.println("<title>NamesServlet</title>");
            out.println("</head>");
            out.println("<body>");
            out.println("<h3>Current List of Names</h3>");
            for(String name: list) {
               out.println(name  + "<br>");
            }
            out.println("</body>");
            out.println("</html>");

        } finally {
            System.out.println("Error");
            out.close();
        }
    }

}
```

A simple implementation of the `index.jsp` pages prompts the user for a name and passes the name to the `NamesServlet`.

```jsp
<%@page contentType="text/html" pageEncoding="UTF-8"%>
<!DOCTYPE HTML PUBLIC "-//W3C//DTD HTML 4.01 Transitional//EN"
    "http://www.w3.org/TR/html4/loose.dtd">

<html>
```

```
<head>
  <meta http-equiv="Content-Type" content="text/html;
    charset=UTF-8">
  <title>Stateful EJB Example</title>
</head>
<body>
  <h1>Names Example</h1>
  <form action="NamesServlet" method="get">
    Name: <input type="text" name="name" /><br />
    <input type="submit" value="Add Name" />
  </form>
</body>
</html>
```

Start the application using the URL provided in the following screenshot. Enter a name and press the **Add Name** button:

When the `index.jsp` page is executed repeatedly, names are added to the list and the `NamesServlet` page displays a list similar to the one shown in the following screenshot:

How it works...

The `NamesBean` class used an `ArrayList` to maintain a list of names. A method was provided to add a name and to return a `List` of the names. The `addName` method used the `add` method of the `List` to add a name. The `getNames` method returned this `ArrayList`. Notice that `names` is a reference to an object that implements the **List** interface. However, an `ArrayList` object was actually assigned. By using the more generic `List` interface, in the future if we change our implementation, calling methods are not affected.

In the `NamesServlet`, the `getParameter` method returned a value associated with the parameter `name`. Notice this name was declared in the `input` tag of the `index.jsp` file. The value entered by the user was passed to the servlet using this parameter.

There's more...

When the stateful EJB is passivated, it is sometimes necessary for the EJB to perform additional actions. For example, certain resources, such as database connections may need to be closed. Likewise, when the EJB is restored the resources may need to be restored. The **@PrePassivate** and **@PostActivate** methods are used to designate which methods need to be executed when passivation or restoration occurs.

```
@PrePassivate
private void prepareForPassivation() {
  // Perform prepassivation tasks
}

@PostActivate
private void restoreFromPassivation() {
  // Restore stateful EJB
}
```

Creating a singleton bean

We will use a singleton to support a game application. A `PlayerBean` will be created to support the attributes of a player. We will assume that our game will never have more than one player so a singleton is an appropriate choice for this type of bean.

Getting ready

The process of creating a singleton bean uses two steps:

1. Use the **@Singleton** annotation to designate the bean as a singleton
2. Add appropriate methods to the class

These methods will reflect the functionality desired for the singleton.

How to do it...

Begin this recipe by creating a Java EE application called `SingletonExample`. Within the EJB module, create a package called `packt` and add the singleton `PlayerBean`. In the WAR module, create a `servlet` package and add a `GameServlet` servlet.

Let's start with the game bean which is declared as a singleton using the **@Singleton** annotation. This version of the bean maintains only the name of the player.

```
@Singleton
public class PlayerBean {
  private String name;
  public String getName() {
    return name;
  }

  public void setName(String name) {
    this.name = name;
  }

}
```

Add the `GameServlet` that follows. It is assumed that the `GameServlet` is invoked from an HTML page that passes the player's name as a request parameter. The use of request parameters will be demonstrated after the servlet has been explained. The name passed is used to set the `PlayerBean's` name and later is retrieved and displayed.

```
public class GameServlet extends HttpServlet {
  @EJB
  private PlayerBean player;

  protected void processRequest(HttpServletRequest request,
    HttpServletResponse response)
    throws ServletException, IOException {
      response.setContentType("text/html;charset=UTF-8");
      PrintWriter out = response.getWriter();
      try {
        player.setName(request.getParameter("name"));
        out.println("<html>");
        out.println("<head>");
        out.println("<title>Servlet GameServlet</title>");
        out.println("</head>");
        out.println("<body>");
```

```
        out.println("<h3>Name: " + player.getName() + "</h3>");
        out.println("</body>");
        out.println("</html>");

    } finally {
        out.close();
    }
}
```

Execute the servlet using the URL found in the following screenshot. It will invoke the servlet with **"Edison"** as its argument.

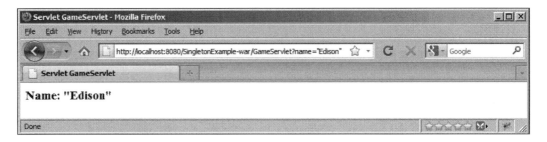

How it works...

The servlet was able to access parameters sent using the HttpServletRequest object's getParameter method. In this example the name parameter was identified using the word name. The name of the player returned from the getParameter method was then used as the argument to the PlayerBean class' setName method. Next, the PlayerBean class' getName method was used to retrieve the name and then displayed.

There's more...

The singleton session bean also supports the **@PostConstruct** and **@PreDestroy** annotations. The **@PostConstruct** annotation specifies which method to invoke after the bean has been instantiated but before any business methods are invoked. The **@PreDestroy** annotation designates the method to execute before the bean is destroyed.

In this example we assumed that a support file or possible database entry needs to be created before any of the singleton's methods are executed. In the initialize method these files or database operations are performed. Likewise, in the destroy method, any cleanup operations are performed.

```
@Singleton
public class PlayerBean {
    String name;

    @PostConstruct
```

```
private void initialize() {
  this.name = "Ultimate Software Warrior";
  // Initialize player file/database
  System.out.println("PlayerBean initialized " + this.name);
}

@PreDestroy
private void destroy() {
  // Clean up player files/database
  System.out.println("PlayerBean destroyed " + this.name);
}
...


}
```

See also

The next recipe shows how multiple singletons are used in an application. In addition, the *Container Managed Concurrency* recipe illustrates the use of singletons.

Using multiple singleton beans

Multiple singletons can be useful when it becomes necessary or desirable to represent multiple objects in an application that need to be shared across the application. In this recipe, we will expand upon the previous recipe's SingletonExample application by adding a GameBean.

The second singleton is called GameBean and maintains the state of the game. It is assumed that player information maintained in the PlayerBean and this EJB, and its supporting files, need to be created before the GameBean is created. The GameBean will use the player files or initialized database to support the game.

Getting ready

Adding multiple singleton session beans to an application generally requires:

1. Adding multiple beans annotated with the **@Singleton** annotation
2. Specifying interdependencies between the beans using the **@DependsOn** annotation

The **@DependsOn** annotation is added to the dependent bean. That is the bean that is to be created last.

How to do it...

In this recipe, we will reuse the `SingletonExample` application. Start by adding a second singleton to the `packt` package called `GameBean` as listed below. We will follow this with modifications to the application's servlet.

```
@Singleton
@Startup
@DependsOn("PlayerBean")
public class GameBean {
  private String state;

  @PostConstruct
  private void initialize() {
    // Use player files/database to initialize the state of the game
    playerState = "Initilizing";
    System.out.println("GameBean initialized");
  }

  public String getState() {
    return state;
  }

  public void setState(String state) {
    this.state = state;
  }

}
```

Modify the `GameServlet` to use the `GameBean` and retrieve the state of the player.

```
public class GameServlet extends HttpServlet {
  @EJB
  private GameBean game;

  protected void processRequest(HttpServletRequest request,
    HttpServletResponse response)
    throws ServletException, IOException {
      response.setContentType("text/html;charset=UTF-8");
      PrintWriter out = response.getWriter();
      try {

        out.println("<html>");
        out.println("<head>");
        out.println("<title>Servlet GameServlet</title>");
```

```
            out.println("</head>");
            out.println("<body>");
            out.println("<h3>State: " + game.getState() + "</h3>");
            out.println("</body>");
            out.println("</html>");

        } finally {
            out.close();
        }
    }
    ...
}
```

Execute the servlet using the URL shown in the following screenshot:

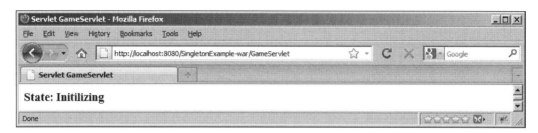

How it works...

The `GameBean` used the **@Singleton** annotation to designate the bean as a singleton. The **@Startup** annotation was used to force the creation of the bean as soon as the application started. The **@DependsOn** annotation specified that the `PlayerBean` must be created first.

The `GameServlet` wass simple. DI is used to inject a `GameBean` and then it used the `getState` method to retrieve its state.

There's more...

More than one singleton bean can be used in the **@DependsOn** annotation with their names separated by commas. However, the actual order of construction of the dependent beans is indeterminate. If the order of singleton creation is important, then multiple **@DependsOn** annotations are needed.

For example, if we introduce a third singleton called, `EnemyBean`, we may want to force the `PlayerBean` and the `EnemyBean` to be created before the creation of the `GameBean`. This is done in the **@DependsOn** annotation by listing the two dependent beans separated by a comma.

```
@DependsOn("PlayerBean, EnemyBean")
public class GameBean {
```

This declaration will force the creation of the `PlayerBean` and the `EnemyBean` first but it does not specify the order in which these two EJBS will be created. When it is desirable to create the `PlayerBean` first followed by the `EnemyBean`, and then finally the `GameBean`, the **@DependsOn** annotation will need to be used with both the `GameBean` and `EnemyBean` singletons.

```
@DependsOn("EnemyBean")
public class GameBean {...}

@DependsOn("PlayerBean ")
public class EnemyBean {...}

public class PlayerBean {...}
```

Using container managed concurrency

Concurrent access to a singleton EJB is by default controlled by the container. Both read and write access to a singleton is limited to one client at a time. However, it is possible to provide a finer level of concurrency control through the use of annotations. In this recipe we will examine how this is done.

Getting ready

The steps used to incorporate container managed concurrency involve:

1. Specify the currency approach using the **@ConcurrencyManagement** annotation
2. Annotate each method with the **@Lock** annotation

The concurrency management approach used by an EJB is specified using the **@ConcurrencyManagement** annotation. Its argument determines whether concurrency management is maintained by the container, or as we will see in the next recipe, by the bean.

Once this annotation has been added, methods of the EJB are annotated with the **@Lock** annotation. Its argument determines the type of concurrency access permitted for the method.

How to do it...

Start by creating a Java EE application called `ConcurrencyExample`. Add a singleton EJB called `SimulationContainerManaged` to the EJB module under a package named `packt`. In the WAR module add a package called `servlet` and a servlet named `ConcurrencyServlet`.

The `SimulationContainerManaged` singleton uses an enumeration to maintain the state of the application. A get and set method is provided to access and change the state.

```
@Singleton
@ConcurrencyManagement(ConcurrencyManagementType.CONTAINER)
public class SimulationContainerManaged {
  public enum State {PAUSED, RUNNING, TERMINATED};
  private State state;

  @Lock(LockType.READ)
  public State getState() {
    return state;
  }

  @Lock(LockType.WRITE)
  public void setState(State state) {
    this.state = state;
  }

}
```

To demonstrate the use of this EJB we will use the `ConcurrencyServlet`. This servlet uses dependency injection for the `SimulationContainerManaged` EJB. It then invokes the `setState` and `getState` methods of the singleton. There is nothing in the invocation of the get or set methods that suggests a locking mechanism is used. The behavior of the locking mechanism is hidden from the client.

```
public class ConcurrencyServlet extends HttpServlet {

  @EJB
  SimulationContainerManaged simulationContainerManaged;

  protected void processRequest(HttpServletRequest request,
    HttpServletResponse response)
    throws ServletException, IOException {
      response.setContentType("text/html;charset=UTF-8");
      PrintWriter out = response.getWriter();
      try {
        simulationContainerManaged.setState(
          SimulationContainerManaged.State.PAUSED);
        out.println("<html>");
        out.println("<head>");
        out.println("<title>Servlet ConcurrencyServlet</title>");
        out.println("</head>");
        out.println("<body>");
```

```
        out.println("<h3>Simulation Container Managed State: " +
           simulationContainerManaged.getState() + "</h3>");
        out.println("</body>");
        out.println("</html>");

    } finally {
        out.close();
    }
}
```

Execute the application using the URL specified in the following screenshot. It will show the application in a paused state:

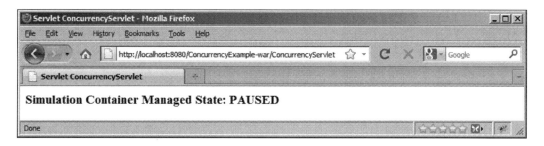

How it works...

The **@ConcurrencyManagement** annotation was used to explicitly denote the concurrency management scheme used. **ConcurrencyManagementType.CONTAINER** was used to specify that the EJB container will manage concurrency. This statement was not necessary as this is the default type of concurrency management. However, it never hurts to be clear about our intentions.

The SimulationContainerManaged singleton used an enumeration to maintain the state of the application. A read lock was specified for the getState method and a write lock was used for the setState method. The **@Lock** annotation with either a **LockType.READ** or **LockType.WRITE** is used to specify a read lock or a write lock respectively.

There's more...

When a lock is obtained for a method, it is possible to specify how long to wait for the method. If it takes too long then it may be desirable to throw an exception. The **@AccessTimeout** annotation is used to specify the timeout limit.

The timeout is specified in milliseconds. To specify a timeout of five seconds, use 5000 as the argument of the annotation.

```
@AccessTimeout(5000)
```

If a value of 0 is used then concurrent access is not permitted. Should a client attempt a concurrent access to the method, a `javax.ejb.ConcurrentAccess` exception is thrown.

A value of -1 indicates that the client will wait as long as necessary. A value of less than -1 is not permitted. If the timeout limit is exceeded a `javax.ejb.ConcurrentAccessTimeoutException` is thrown.

Note that concurrency can also be controlled through deployment descriptors.

See also

The *Using bean managed concurrency* recipe that follows addresses bean managed concurrency.

Using bean managed concurrency

While concurrency of a singleton is container managed by default, the developer can elect to manage the concurrency directly. The techniques used for this effort are illustrated in this recipe.

Getting ready

The steps used to incorporate bean managed concurrency involve:

1. Specify the currency approach using the **@ConcurrencyManagement** annotation
2. Designate critical methods with the Java `synchronized` keyword

Critical methods are those methods which allow only a single thread at a time to use it.

How to do it...

We will reuse the `ConcurrencyExample` application developed in the previous recipe to illustrate bean-managed concurrency. In the EJB module add a singleton EJB to the `packt` package called `SimulationBeanManaged`. Use the **@ConcurrencyManagement** annotation with an argument of **ConcurrencyManagementType.BEAN** to designate the EJB as a bean-managed EJB.

```java
@Singleton
@ConcurrencyManagement(ConcurrencyManagementType.BEAN)
public class SimulationBeanManaged {
  public enum State {PAUSED, RUNNING, TERMINATED};
  private State state;

  public State getState() {
```

```
            return state;
      }

      public synchronized void setState(State state) {
         this.state = state;
      }
}
```

Modify the `ConcurrencyServlet` servlet to use the `SimulationBeanManaged` bean instead of the `SimulationContainerManaged` bean. From the client perspective there is no indication of how concurrency is supported.

```
public class ConcurrencyServlet extends HttpServlet {

   @EJB
   SimulationBeanManaged simulationBeanManaged;

   protected void processRequest(HttpServletRequest request,
      HttpServletResponse response)
   throws ServletException, IOException {
   ...
      simulationBeanManaged.setState(
         SimulationBeanManaged.State.PAUSED);
   ...
      out.println("<h3>Simulation Bean Managed State: " +
         simulationBeanManaged.getState() + "</h3>");
   ...
   }
```

Execute the application using the URL found in the following screenshot. It will show the application in a paused state.

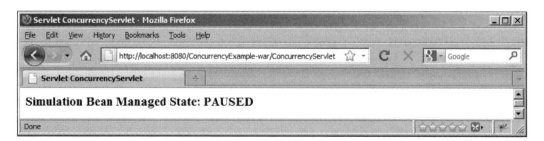

How to do it...

The `SimulationBeanManaged` EJB used an enumeration to reflect the state of the application with a get and set method to control the state. The `synchronized` keyword was used for the `setState` method. This restricted access to the method to one client at a time. It has the same effect as the **@Write** annotation used with container-managed concurrency.

The `getState` method is not synchronized thus allowing concurrent access to the method. For a get method, this should not be a problem since it is a read type operation.

There's more...

The **synchronized** keyword was also be used on a block of code instead of a method. The following rewrite of the `setState` method illustrates how to synchronize a block. Concurrent access is restricted when a thread enters the synchronized block. That is, no other methods are allowed to access the object while the current thread is in the block.

```java
public void setState(State state) {
  synchronized  (this) {
    this.state = state;
  }
}
```

A Java compiler may use various optimization techniques to speed up the execution of an application. Some optimization techniques may move the value of a variable into a register to increase the speed of execution. However, when this occurs, changes to the original variable may not necessarily be reflected in the register. To avoid this problem the `volatile` keyword was introduced. The `volatile` keyword is used as part of the declaration of a class' instance variable.

```java
private volatile int serverID;
```

The `volatile` keyword guarantees that any thread that accesses the variable will get the most current value. When synchronizing EJB methods using bean-managed concurrency, it may be necessary to use this keyword.

See also

The previous recipe, *Using container managed concurrency*, illustrates how to use the EJB container to manage concurrency.

Controlling the initialization process

In this recipe, we will examine how the initialization and termination of a singleton is controlled. We will use the **@Startup** annotation to force eager initialization of the singleton. The annotation does not have any arguments and is simple to use. We will use the **@PostConstruct** annotation to illustrate the process.

How to do it...

Create a Java EE application called `ApplicationIntializationExample`. In the EJB module add a package called `packt` and a singleton bean called `ApplicationStateBean`. In the WAR module create a package called `servlet` and add a servlet called `ApplicationServlet`.

Create the `ApplicationStateBean` EJB and add the **@Startup** annotation to the EJB as shown below. This results in the singleton being created as soon as the application starts up. The `ApplicationStateBean` uses an enumeration variable called `state` to store the state of the application. Add an initialize and a terminate method:

```
@Singleton
@Startup
public class ApplicationStateBean {
    public enum States {PENDING, STARTED, PAUSED, TERMINATING};
    private States state;

    @PostConstruct
    public void initialize() {
        state = States.PENDING;
        // Perform intialization
        state = States.STARTED;
        System.out.println("---ApplicationStateBean Started");
    }

    @PreDestroy
    public void terminate() {
        state = States.TERMINATING;
        // Perform termination
        System.out.println("---ApplicationStateBean Terminating");
    }

    public States getState() {
        return state;
    }
}
```

```
      public void setState(States state) {
        this.state = state;
      }

  }
```

Next, create the `ApplicationServlet` as shown below. An `ApplicationStateBean` is injected and used to get the state of the application.

```
  public class ApplicationServlet extends HttpServlet {

    @EJB
    ApplicationStateBean state;

    protected void processRequest(HttpServletRequest request,
      HttpServletResponse response)
      throws ServletException, IOException {
      response.setContentType("text/html;charset=UTF-8");
        PrintWriter out = response.getWriter();
        try {

          out.println("<html>");
          out.println("<head>");
          out.println("<title>Servlet ApplicationServlet</title>");
          out.println("</head>");
          out.println("<body>");
          out.println("<h3>" + state.getState() + "</h3>");
          out.println("</body>");
          out.println("</html>");
        } finally {
          out.close();
        }
    }

  }
```

Deploy your application. The `initialize` method will execute and the console window will produce the following output. Note, that the **INFO** prefix is appended to the output by NetBeans.

INFO: ---ApplicationStateBean Started

Next, execute the servlet using the URL shown in the following screenshot:

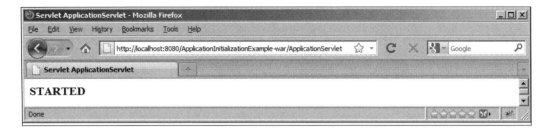

When the application terminates, such as when it is redeployed, the console will reflect the execution of the `terminate` method as shown here:

INFO: ---ApplicationStateBean Terminating

How it works...

Let's examine the `ApplicationStateBean` first. The assumption is that we need to maintain state information about the application and the singleton needs to be initialized before other EJBs in the application are used.

The `initialize` method was annotated with the **@PostConstruct** annotation. This means the method was executed as soon as the bean was created. The state variable was set to `STARTED`.

The `terminate` method was annotated with **@PreDestroy.** This marks the `terminate` method as the method to execute immediately before the singleton is destroyed. In this method any cleanup activities should be executed.

See also

The Using *multiple singleton beans* recipe is also concerned with the initialization process.

Using session beans with more than one business interface

A session bean can use more than one business interface. In this recipe we will use multiple interfaces to illustrate how a subset of methods can be exposed to a client while providing a larger set of methods to the beans of the application. An account EJB is used exposing the discount rates based on the type of client.

Getting ready

The process of adding more than one business interface involves two steps:

1. Defining the interfaces
2. Implementing the interfaces in the EJB.

Each of these steps is not difficult. However, the implementation of the business methods can be a different matter.

How to do it...

Start by creating a Java EE application called `MultipleInterfacesExample`. In the EJB module add a `packt` package with two interfaces and one class:

- `AccountBeanRemote` interface
- `AccountBeanLocal` interface
- `AccountBean` stateless session bean

In the WAR module add an `index.jsp` file if your IDE does not automatically add one for you. When the file is created, select a **JavaServer Faces (JSF)** page or later add a JSF framework to the module. Failure to do this may result in a run-time exception.

Create an `AccountBeanLocal` interface that exposes getters and setters for both a corporate and a non-profit discount rate. Use the **@Local** annotation to designate this as a local interface.

```
@Local
public interface AccountBeanLocal {
   public float getCorporateDiscount();
   public void setCorporateDiscount(float corporateDiscount);
   public float getNonProfitDiscount();
   public void setNonProfitDiscount(float nonProfitDiscount);
}
```

Next, create an `AccountBeanRemote` interface that exposes only get methods for the discounts. This can be used to restrict access to the implementing class. Use the **@Remote** annotation to designate this as a remote interface.

```
@Remote
public interface AccountBeanRemote {
   public float getCorporateDiscount();
   public float getNonProfitDiscount();
}
```

The next step is to implement these interfaces. Add the `AccountBean` such that it implements both of these interfaces. The implementation below is simple and uses different percentages for the two types of discounts.

```java
@Stateless
@Named("account")
public class AccountBean implements AccountBeanRemote,
AccountBeanLocal {
  private float corporateDiscount;
  private float nonProfitDiscount;

  @PostConstruct
  public void initialize() {
    corporateDiscount = 0.15f;
    nonProfitDiscount = 0.25f;
  }
  public float getCorporateDiscount() {
    return corporateDiscount;
  }

  public void setCorporateDiscount(float corporateDiscount) {
    this.corporateDiscount = corporateDiscount;
  }

  public float getNonProfitDiscount() {
    return nonProfitDiscount;
  }

  public void setNonProfitDiscount(float nonProfitDiscount) {
    this.nonProfitDiscount = nonProfitDiscount;
  }


}
```

To demonstrate the use of these interfaces, create an `index.jsp` file that displays the corporate and non-profit discount rates. Notice this implementation uses JSF. When creating this file, or once it has been created, make sure it is associated with a JSF framework. From NetBeans this can be accomplished by modifying the properties of the WAR module and adding a JSF framework.

```jsp
<%@page contentType="text/html" pageEncoding="UTF-8"%>
<!DOCTYPE HTML PUBLIC "-//W3C//DTD HTML 4.01 Transitional//EN"
  "http://www.w3.org/TR/html4/loose.dtd">
```

```
<%@taglib prefix="f" uri="http://java.sun.com/jsf/core"%>
<%@taglib prefix="h" uri="http://java.sun.com/jsf/html"%>
<f:view>
  <html>
  <head>
    <meta http-equiv="Content-Type" content="text/html;
      charset=UTF-8">
    <title>Account</title>
  </head>
  <body>
    <h1>Discount Rates</h1>
    <h:form>
      <h:outputText value="Corporate Discount:
        #{account.corporateDiscount}"/><br/>
      <h:outputText value="Non-Profit Discount:
        #{account.nonProfitDiscount}"/><br/>
    </h:form>
  </body>
  </html>
</f:view>
```

The following screenshot shows the two discount rates available:

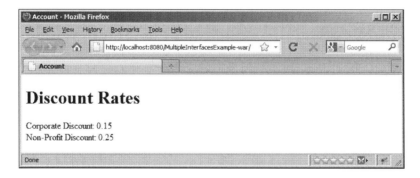

How it works...

Notice the use of the **@Named** annotation with the `AccountBean`. It was used to associate the name "account" with this EJB when used within a JSF page. In the `index.jsp` page, this name was followed by a period and either `corporateDiscount` or `nonProfitDiscount`. This had the effect of invoking the corresponding `getCorporateDiscount` and `getNonProfitDiscount` methods of the `AccountBean`. There was no need to use the get prefix as this is a feature of JSF.

In this application, a client that is not part of the application is only able to access the getter methods. This effectively limits its access to the full capabilities of the EJB. As we will see in *Chapter 7, EJB Security*, there are other techniques based on the credentials of the actual user, which can be used to limit access to an EJB's methods. These techniques can be used to provide a finer grained way of limiting access to an EJB's methods.

Understanding parameter behavior and granularity

It is important to invoke the methods of a remote EJB in an efficient manner. This recipe illustrates how to return data from a remote EJB using a coarse-grained approach. This is then contrasted with a fine-grained approach to accessing the elements of an EJB which is less efficient.

The position of a satellite in orbit can be specified using a set of six orbital parameters. For the interested reader, a good discussion of these parameters is found in the Wikipedia article at http://en.wikipedia.org/wiki/Orbital_elements. We will create the class PositionBean to hold these parameters. We will also use an OrbitalElements EJB to return an instance of the PositionBean using a remote interface. A client can directly access the PositionBean in a fine-grained manner or access the PositionBean from the OrbitalElements bean in a coarse-grained manner.

Getting ready

This technique is about how to organize your code. You can return information as a single object or you provide methods to return individual elements one at a time. Either approach is valid. However, the latter approach will not be as efficient.

The approach illustrated here uses an interface to define methods to access elements of an object. The object is returned as a single object and its methods permit access to the information of interest.

How to do it...

Let's begin by creating a Java Web application called ParameterExample. Add a packt package with the following EJBs and interfaces:

- OrbitalElements – A singleton EJB
- OrbitalElementsRemote – An interface
- PositionBean – A stateless EJB
- PositionBeanRemote – An interface

Also create a second package called servlet and add a servlet called PositionServlet.

Beginning with the `PositionBeanRemote` interface, this simple interface has only get type methods.

```
package packt;

public interface PositionBeanRemote {
  public double getArgumentOfPeriapsis();
  public double getEccentricity();
  public double getInclination();
  public double getLongitudeOfTheAscendingNode();
  public double getMeanAnomaly();
  public double getSemimajorAxis();
}
```

Next, the `PositionBean` implements the remote interface methods and in this example only initializes the eccentricity instance variable. In a more sophisticated version of the application, other fields of the `PositionBean` would be initialized.

```
@Stateless
@Remote
@Startup
public class PositionBean implements PositionBeanRemote{

  private double eccentricity;
  private double semimajorAxis;
  private double inclination;
  private double longitudeOfTheAscendingNode;
  private double argumentOfPeriapsis;
  private double meanAnomaly;

  //@PostConstruct
  public PositionBean() {
    eccentricity = 1.0;
  }

  public double getArgumentOfPeriapsis() {
    return argumentOfPeriapsis;
  }

  public double getEccentricity() {
    System.out.println("--- Return eccentricity");
    return eccentricity;
  }

  public double getInclination() {
```

```
      return inclination;
    }

    public double getLongitudeOfTheAscendingNode() {
      return longitudeOfTheAscendingNode;
    }

    public double getMeanAnomaly() {
      return meanAnomaly;
    }

    public double getSemimajorAxis() {
      return semimajorAxis;
    }

}
```

To illustrate the use of the `PositionBean` the `PostionServlet` declares an instance of the bean and uses the `getEccentricity` method. This technique illustrates a fine-grained approach.

```
public class PositionServlet extends HttpServlet {

  @EJB
  PositionBeanRemote position;

  protected void processRequest(HttpServletRequest request,
    HttpServletResponse response)
    throws ServletException, IOException {
      response.setContentType("text/html;charset=UTF-8");
      PrintWriter out = response.getWriter();
      try {

        out.println("<html>");
        out.println("<head>");
        out.println("<title>Servlet PositionServlet</title>");
        out.println("</head>");
        out.println("<body>");
        out.println("<h3>Eccentricity: " +
          position.getEccentricity() + "</h3>");
        out.println("</body>");
        out.println("</html>");

      } finally {
          out.close();
        }
    }

}
```

The `OrbitalElements` EJB implements the `OrbitalElementsRemote` interface with a single method, `getPosition`, returning a `PositionBean`. This technique illustrates a coarse-grained approach.

```
@Remote
public interface OrbitalElementsRemote {
    public PositionBean getPosition();
}
```

The `OrbitalElements` EJB creates an instance of the `PositionBean` and then returns the bean. This example did not provide a means of initializing the `PositionBean` to unique values or perhaps treating the bean as a singleton. Its actual type and creation will depend on the needs of the application.

```
@Singleton
public class OrbitalElements implements OrbitalElementsRemote {
  public PositionBean getPosition() {
    return new PositionBean();
  }

}
```

In the `PostionServlet` declare a reference to the `OrbitalElementsRemote` interface and use the `getPosition` method to return an instance of the `PositionBean`.

```
public class PositionServlet extends HttpServlet {

  @EJB
  PositionBeanRemote position;
  @EJB
  OrbitalElementsRemote orbitalElements;

  protected void processRequest(HttpServletRequest request,
    HttpServletResponse response)
    throws ServletException, IOException {
      response.setContentType("text/html;charset=UTF-8");
      PrintWriter out = response.getWriter();
      try {

        out.println("<html>");
        out.println("<head>");
        out.println("<title>Servlet PositionServlet</title>");
        out.println("</head>");
        out.println("<body>");
        out.println("<h3>Eccentricity: " +
          position.getEccentricity() + "</h3>");
```

```
        out.println("<h3>Eccentricity: " +
          orbitalElements.getPosition().getEccentricity() + "</h3>");
        out.println("</body>");
        out.println("</html>");

    } finally {
        out.close();
    }
}
```

Execute the servlet using the URL shown in the following screenshot:

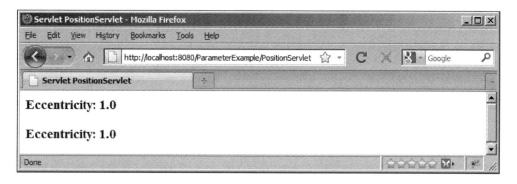

How it works...

Notice the creation of the `PositionBean` using the `new` keyword in the `OrbitalElements` EJB. This illustrates an easily made potential problem. The object created is not managed by the EJB container. As a result, the benefits of an EJB such as security and transaction management are not supported. This may not be a problem depending on the intended use of the object. Use dependency injection if the object needs to be managed by the EJB container.

There's more...

Local beans execute in the same JVM as the client. This type of access is typically faster than using remote access which occurs when the client is in a different JVM. There is less communication overhead required to execute a method and to pass parameters. However, there are times when it is necessary to access an EJB in a remote fashion. Be aware that some servers are able to optimize such access and avoid the overhead costs.

Consider a class with several private instance variables. If individual calls are made to access each variable one at a time, then this requires repeated method invocations. This type of access is referred to as fine-grained access.

In contrast, when the entire object is passed, only a single remote method invocation is needed. This is called coarse-grained access. It will still be necessary to invoke the individual methods, but these are local to the client. Fine-grained access becomes more of a problem when the client resides on a different JVM.

One coarse-grained remote procedure call followed by multiple "local" method calls in the client is more efficient than multiple fine-grained remote procedure calls. If it is necessary to modify the original object, then fine-grained access for the setter type methods is required along with its performance penalties.

When passing or returning an object in a different JVM, the object is passed by value. That is, a copy of the object is passed to the client. Should the client attempt to modify the object, only the copy of the object is modified. The original object is not touched.

When passing an object by value it is a good idea to pass an immutable object so as to make it clear that it cannot be modified. The creation of an immutable object means at minimum the class should not have setter type methods.

Using an asynchronous method to create a background process

Accessing an EJB synchronously allows the client to continue its work without having to wait for the EJB to return. This can be used in one of two ways. The first technique is done in an "invoke and forget" manner where the request is made of the EJB and the client is not concerned about the success or failure of the request. The second technique invokes the method but does not wait for the method to complete. The method returns a `Future` object. This object is used later to determine the result of the request.

In this recipe, we will develop a stateless `PrintServlet` EJB with two methods: `printAndForget` and `printAndCheckLater`, used to demonstrate the use of asynchronous methods.

How to do it...

Create a Java EE application called `AsynchronousExample`. Add a `packt` package to the EJB module and a stateless EJB called `PrintBean`. Add a `servlet` package to the WAR module and a servlet called `PrintServlet`. The `PrintServlet` uses the `PrintBean` to simulate the printing of a message.

First, let's start with the `PrintBean`. Create the stateless session bean with two methods: `printAndForget` and `printAndCheckLater`, as shown here:

```
@Stateless
@LocalBean
public class PrintBean {
```

```
@Asynchronous
public void printAndForget() {
   System.out.println("***printAndForget  ***");
}

@Asynchronous
public Future<String> printAndCheckLater() {
   System.out.println("***printAndCheckLater ***");
   return new AsyncResult<String>("OK");
}

}
```

Next, in the `PrintServlet` create an instance of `PrintBean` and use the two asynchronous methods. The `printAndCheckLater` method will return the value assigned to the `AsyncResult` object. Later, the `futureResult` instance's `get` method returns the results.

```
public class PrintServlet extends HttpServlet {

@EJB
PrintBean printBean;

protected void processRequest(HttpServletRequest request,
   HttpServletResponse response)
   throws ServletException, IOException {
      response.setContentType("text/html;charset=UTF-8");
      PrintWriter out = response.getWriter();
      try {
        printBean.printAndForget();

        out.println("<html>");
        out.println("<head>");
        out.println("<title>Servlet PrintServlet</title>");
        out.println("</head>");
        out.println("<body>");
        out.println("<h3>printAndForget executed</h3>");
        Future<String> futureResult = printBean.printAndCheckLater();
        String result = "";
        try {
          result = futureResult.get();
        } catch (InterruptedException ex) {
            Logger.getLogger(PrintServlet.class.getName()).
              log(Level.SEVERE, null, ex);
          } catch (ExecutionException ex) {
```

```
                    Logger.getLogger(PrintServlet.class.getName()).
                        log(Level.SEVERE, null, ex);
                }
            out.println("<h3>printAndCheckLater executed - Result: " +
                result + "</h3>");
            out.println("</body>");
            out.println("</html>");

        } finally {
            out.close();
        }
    }

}
```

When executed, the `printAndForget` method does exactly that. The
`printAndCheckLater` method returns as "**OK**", as seen in the following screenshot.

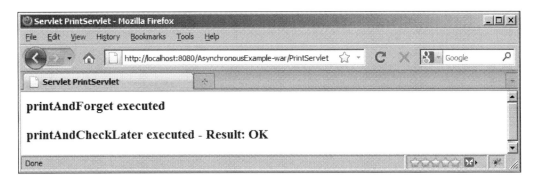

How it works...

Let's examine the `printAndForget` method first. The method was preceded with the
@Asynchronous annotation. This designated the method as an asynchronous method. Since
the method returns **void**, the method was not obligated to return the success or failure of
the request to the client. In addition, the use of the **@Asynchronous** annotation means the
method will return immediately and not block until the completion of the method.

The `printAndCheckLater` method, in contrast, returned a **Future** object. This object was
used later in the servlet to obtain the results of the `printAndCheckLater` execution. An
`AsyncResult` is a class that implements the `Future` interface. It is not used directly by
the client but is a way of associating the result of the method with the `Future` object that is
returned immediately.

There's more...

The `Future` object can be used not only to get the results but also to cancel an asynchronous invocation in some situations or determine if the invocation is complete. The `Future` object's `cancel` method is used to cancel the task. The `isCancelled` and `isDone` methods return **Boolean** values reflecting whether the task has been cancelled or whether it is done respectively.

3

Message-Driven Beans

In this chapter, we will cover:

- ▸ Handling a text-based message
- ▸ Handling a byte-based message
- ▸ Handling a stream-based message
- ▸ Handling a map-based message
- ▸ Handling an object-based message
- ▸ Using MDB in a publish-and-subscribe application
- ▸ Using MDB in a point-to-point application
- ▸ Specifying which types of messages to receive using the message selector
- ▸ Browsing messages in a message queue

Introduction

A **Message-Driven Bean (MDB)** implements business logic in an asynchronous fashion. The client does not receive a response to the message from the MDB. A client will send a message to a queue or topic. The message is then retrieved and processed by the MDB. A queue differs from a topic in that a message in a queue is sent to a single MDB. In contrast, a message in a topic will be sent to each MDB that is registered with that topic.

From the client's perspective, the MDB is anonymous. There is no way for the client to identify or otherwise select a specific MDB. The EJB container decides which MDB object to use in response to a request. In order to send a message to an MDB, the client can use dependency injection or JNDI lookup to locate the queue or topic.

MDBs are managed by the server EJB container. The EJB container will treat all instances of the same MDB class identically. A message will be delivered to the next available instance of the MDB. The container will create and destroy MDBs as necessary. While an MDB has no conversational state, instance variables in an MDB may hold information needed to work correctly. This can include database connection and references to other EJBs.

An MDB may use a `MessageDrivenContext` to obtain information regarding the server's EJB container. This interface is based on the `EJBContext` interface that deals with transaction and security issues among other things. The `MessageDrivenContext` will be addressed in other chapters.

The Java EE server uses **Java Message Service (JMS)** to support MDBs. Many of the details of JMS are hidden, making the use of MDBs easier. As a result, MDBs should not attempt to use the JMS to acknowledge the receipt of messages. This type of response is handled by the container. While not covered here, MDBs can be driven by other connector-driven technologies. For example, the **Java EE Connector Architecture (JCA)** provides a means of interfacing with **Enterprise Information Systems (EIS)**. These types of technologies can expand the potential uses of MDBs.

The creation of an MDB involves three tasks:

1. Using the **@MessageDriven** annotation to designate the class as an MDB
2. Implementing the `javax.jms.MessageListener` interface for JMS-driven beans
3. Overriding the `onMessage` method

The MDB must be defined as public and cannot be declared as final or abstract. In addition, it needs a public default constructor and cannot have a `finalize` method.

The `javax.jms.MessageListener` interface has a single method, `onMessage`. This method is passed a `javax.jms.Message` object. Five sub-interfaces exist based on the Message interface:

- `TextMessage` – A Java `String` object
- `BytesMessage` – An unformatted stream of bytes
- `StreamMessage` – A stream of bytes based on primitive Java data types
- `MapMessage` – A set of key/value pairs
- `ObjectMessage` – Contains a Java object

When a message is sent to the `onMessage` method, the message is cast to one of these interface types and processed.

There are two life cycle call back methods used with MDBs: `PostConstruct` and `PreDestroy`. The `PostConstruct` annotated method will be invoked after the MDB has been created and before any business methods of the MDB are used (and after dependency injection has been done). The `PreDestroy` annotated method will be called before the MDB is destroyed. The `PreDestroy` method may not be invoked if the EJB container crashes or a system exception is thrown by the MDB.

When a method of an MDB instance is invoked, it will be executed to completion before that instance of the MDB is called again. This means that MDBs do not have to be re-entrant. The calls to an MDB are done in a serial fashion. However, if a client sends out multiple messages to the server containing an MDB, there is no guarantee the same MDB instance will be used for each message or that the messages will be processed in the same order the client sent them. This means that the application should be designed to handle messages arriving out of order.

For example, an MDB may be created to receive a bill and then process the bill. If the order in which the bills are processed is important, then special processing may be required to ensure they are handled in the correct order. If an MDB is designed to receive commands and then add a command entry in a log, the command to close the log may arrive before a message to append an entry.

As mentioned before, there are several types of messages that can be sent to an MDB. In this chapter, we will compare and contrasts these types by developing five different applications using the five different types of messages to send an order to an MDB for processing. An order will consist of a part number (12345), a weight (12.5f) and a quantity (50). Each application will use a servlet to compose the message but will send it with a different `Message` derived interface.

Each servlet uses the same structure as illustrated below. Both `doGet` and `doPost` methods are used to call a common `processRequest` method that contains the code for the client.

```
public class ServletName extends HttpServlet {

    @Resource(mappedName="jms/SomeMessageFactory")
    private QueueConnectionFactory queueConnectionFactory;
    @Resource(mappedName="jms/SomeMessageQueue")
    private Queue queue;
    protected void processRequest(HttpServletRequest request,
      HttpServletResponse response)
      throws ServletException, IOException {
        response.setContentType("text/html;charset=UTF-8");
        PrintWriter out = response.getWriter();
        try {

          Connection connection;
          try {
```

```
        connection = queueConnectionFactory.createConnection();
        Session session = connection.createSession(false,
            Session.AUTO_ACKNOWLEDGE);
        MessageProducer messageProducer = (MessageProducer)
            session.createProducer(queue);
        // Create message
        // Initialize message

        messageProducer.send(SomeMessage);
        System.out.println("---> Text Message Sent");
      } catch (JMSException ex) {
          Logger.getLogger(TextServlet.class.getName()).
          log(Level.SEVERE, null, ex);
      }

      // HTML output
    } finally {
        out.close();
    }
  }
}

@Override
protected void doGet(HttpServletRequest request,
  HttpServletResponse response)
  throws ServletException, IOException {
    processRequest(request, response);
}

@Override
protected void doPost(HttpServletRequest request,
  HttpServletResponse response)
  throws ServletException, IOException {
    processRequest(request, response);
}
```

The servlet is declared and a `queueConnectionFactory` and `queue` variables are injected using the **@Resource** annotation. In this example, the **mappedName** attribute was assigned a value of `jms/SomeMessageFactory` and `jms/SomeMessageQueue` for the `queueConnectionFactory` and `queue` variables respectively. The creation of the queue and factory along with the assignment of their names will need to be done using the EE server. In GlassFish, this is done from the administration console under JMS Resources. You can use whatever naming convention you want, just be consistent.

In the servlet's `processRequest` method, a `Connection` variable is declared. A try block is used to catch `javax.jms.JMSException`.

The process of connecting to a queue and sending a message to the queue involves:

1. Establishing a connection using the `Connection` object
2. Creating a `Session` object that represents the communications between the servlet and the queue. It is also used to send the message.
3. Creating a `MessageProducer` object to create the Message

The connection to the queue/topic is established using the `QueueConnectionFactory` interface's `createConnection` method. Once a connection is made, a `Session` object is declared and initialized using the connection.

The first parameter of the `createSession` method determines whether the connection needs to support transactions. We used false since we are not using transactions in this chapter. The second parameter specifies the acknowledge mode used. For this chapter we will use auto-acknowledge.

Before a message can be created, the `Session` object creates a `MessageProducer` object. At this point, we can use any one of several `MessageProducer` create type methods to create the message type of interest.

This code is followed by a message-type specific sequence of statements used to create and initialize the message. The last part of the try block will use the `Session` object to send the message to the destination queue/topic.

The actual MDB is annotated with **@MessageDriven**. The following illustrates a typical MDB structure. Notice the implementation of the `MessageListener` interface and the presence of the `onMessage` method.

```
@MessageDriven(mappedName = "jms/MapQueue",
  activationConfig =  {
    @ActivationConfigProperty(propertyName = "acknowledgeMode",
    propertyValue = "Auto-acknowledge"),
    @ActivationConfigProperty(propertyName = "destinationType",
    propertyValue = "javax.jms.Queue")
  })
public class SampleMDB implements MessageListener {
  . . .
  public void onMessage(Message message) {
    . . .
  }
}
```

The **@MessageDriven** annotation uses a **mappedName** element and an **activationConfig** element to declare the class. The **mappedName** element is assigned the name of the queue to associate with this MDB. In this example the queue name is `jms/MapQueue`. The **mappedName** attribute is vendor-specific and is frequently a JNDI name.

The **activationConfig** element is a bit more complex. In this example, two **@ActivationConfigProperty** annotations are used to further define the characteristics of the MDB. The first one establishes how JMS is to acknowledge the receipt of a message from a client. The second one indicates the destination type. The acknowledgement is auto-acknowledge and the destination is a JMS Queue.

There are two common techniques for structuring an MDB application:

- ▸ Point-to-Point – One or more producers will send messages to a queue. These messages are then consumed by one or more consumers (MDBs). Once removed from a queue it is no longer available to other consumers.

- ▸ Publish/Subscribe – One or more producers will send messages to a topic. Each message in the topic will then be sent to each consumer (MDB) that is currently subscribing to the topic.

When a message is placed in a queue it will remain there until it is removed and sent to an MDB. The `QueueBrowser` class provides a way of determining the messages currently in a queue. The *Browsing messages in a message queue* recipe illustrates the use of the `QueueBrowser`.

Sometimes messages of a similar type are sent to the same queue. However, it may be desirable that the messages be sent to different MDBs based on these differences in message type. A message selector enables this behavior. The approach is sometimes called "message filtering" and is illustrated in the *Specifying which types of messages to receive using the message selector* recipe.

Handling a string-based message

In this recipe, we will use a `TextMessage` to send an order to an MDB. The `TextMessage` interface uses a `String` object to hold the order. We will use the `java.util.Scanner` class to parse the order information from this string.

Getting ready

The essential structure of a servlet used to generate a message was introduced in the introduction. Here we will address the unique elements of creating and using a `TextMessage` which include:

1. Creating a `TextMessage` using the `createTextMessage` method
2. Creating a string containing the message
3. Sending the message

How to do it...

Create a Queue named jms/TextQueue and a QueueConnectionFactory named jms/ TextFactoryPool as described in the introduction. Next, create a Java EE application called TextMessageApplication. In the EJB module, add a package called packt with an MDB called TextBean. In the WAR module add a package called servlet and a servlet called TextServlet.

Create the TextServlet as follows. The doGet and doPost methods are not listed here.

```java
public class TextServlet extends HttpServlet {

    @Resource(mappedName="jms/TextFactoryPool")
    private QueueConnectionFactory queueConnectionFactory;
    @Resource(mappedName="jms/TextQueue")
    private Queue queue;

    protected void processRequest(HttpServletRequest request,
      HttpServletResponse response)
      throws ServletException, IOException {
        response.setContentType("text/html;charset=UTF-8");
        PrintWriter out = response.getWriter();
        try {

          Connection connection;

          try {
            connection = queueConnectionFactory.createConnection();
            Session session = connection.createSession(false,
              Session.AUTO_ACKNOWLEDGE);
            MessageProducer messageProducer = (MessageProducer)
              session.createProducer(queue);
            TextMessage textMessage = session.createTextMessage();

          // Part number - 12345
          // Weight - 12.5f
          // Quantity - 50
            String message = "12345 12.5 50";
            textMessage.setText(message);
            messageProducer.send(textMessage);
            System.out.println("---> Text Message Sent");
          } catch (JMSException ex) {
              Logger.getLogger(TextServlet.class.getName()).
                log(Level.SEVERE, null, ex);
          }
```

```
                    out.println("<html>");
                    out.println("<head>");
                    out.println("<title>Servlet TextServlet</title>");
                    out.println("</head>");
                    out.println("<body>");
                    out.println("<h1>Servlet TextServlet at " +
                       request.getContextPath () + "</h1>");
                    out.println("</body>");
                    out.println("</html>");

            } finally {
                    out.close();
                }
        }

    }
```

Next, let's look at the `TextBean`. Use the **@MessageDriven** annotation to designate the EJB as an MDB. Be sure to implement the `MessageListener` interface and add the `onMessage` method.

```
@MessageDriven(mappedName = "jms/TextQueue", activationConfig = {
    @ActivationConfigProperty(propertyName = "acknowledgeMode",
    propertyValue = "Auto-acknowledge"),
    @ActivationConfigProperty(propertyName = "destinationType",
    propertyValue = "javax.jms.Queue")
})
public class TextBean implements MessageListener {

    public TextBean() {
}

    public void onMessage(Message message) {
      TextMessage textMessage = (TextMessage) message;
      try {
        Scanner scanner = new Scanner(textMessage.getText());
        System.out.println("---> Part Number: " + scanner.nextInt());
        System.out.println("---> Weight: " + scanner.nextFloat());
        System.out.println("---> Quantity: " + scanner.nextInt());
        System.out.println("---> TextMessage Received");
      } catch (JMSException ex) {
          Logger.getLogger(TextBean.class.getName()).log(Level.SEVERE,
          null, ex);
      }
    }

    }
```

Execute the servlet. The server's log will display the output of the `println` methods.

INFO: ---> Text Message Sent

INFO: ---> Part Number: 12345

INFO: ---> Weight: 12.5

INFO: ---> Quantity: 50

INFO: ---> TextMessage Received

How it works...

In the `TextServlet`, the **@Resource** annotation injected a `QueueConnectionFactory` and a `Queue`. The general details of connecting to a `Queue` are detailed in the introduction. Notice that we used the `jms/TextQueue` in this example.

In the `processRequest` method, the `TextMessage` was created using the session's `createTextMessage` method. A string was declared to hold the parts information (part number, weight, and quantity) and was then assigned to the `TextMessage` with the `setText` method. Next, the `MessageProducer` object's `send` method transferred the message to the queue.

The `TextBean` started with the **@MessageDriven** annotation and used the **mappedName** attribute to specify the queue used. Two **@ActivationConfigProperty** elements were used to specify the acknowledgement mode and that the destination is a queue.

The `Message` received in the `onMessage` method was cast to a `TextMessage`. A `Scanner` object was created to retrieve the individual elements of the order. Using the `nextInt` and `nextFloat` methods, the elements of the message were easily extracted and displayed.

There's more...

Once the `TextMessage` object has been created in the servlet, writing to and reading from `TextMessage` is permitted. When it is received by the MDB, it is in a read-only mode. Attempts to write to the message will result in a `javax.jms.MessageNotWriteableException`. However, the `clearBody` method in the MDB can be used to permit subsequent writing and reading of the message. Normally, this is not necessary.

This example illustrates a simple use of the `TextMessage`. Using an `ObjectMessage` may be the best approach for handling orders or similar object-oriented requests. However, the `TextMessage` is well suited for XML type messages.

See also

The first five recipes present alternative techniques for sending messages.

Handling a byte-based message

Sometimes it is necessary to send an unformatted stream of bytes as a message. This recipe illustrates this process using the `BytesMessage` interface. However, when possible, other message types such as string and objects should be used.

The advantages of using an unformatted stream of bytes include ease of read and write operations and a fixed size message. When data is written or read using the `BytesMessage` methods, it is stored using the appropriate primitive data format. For example, when an integer is written, it will be stored as a 32-bit two's complement number. The size of the number will always be four bytes regardless of the number of digits comprising the number.

Getting ready

The essential structure of a servlet used to generate a message was introduced in the introduction. Here we will address the unique elements of creating and using a `BytesMessage` which include:

1. Creating a `BytesMessage` using the `createBytesMessage` method
2. Writing values to the `BytesMessage`
3. Sending the message

How to do it...

Create a `Queue` named `jms/PartsQueue` and a `QueueConnectionFactory` named `jms/PartsFactory` as described in the introduction. Next, create a Java EE application called `BytesMessageApplication`. In the EJB module add a package called `packt` and then an MDB called `PartsBean`. In the WAR module create a package called `servlet` with a servlet called `PartsServlet`.

Create the `PartsServlet` as follows. The `doGet` and `doPost` methods are not listed here.

```
public class PartsServlet extends HttpServlet {
  @Resource(mappedName="jms/PartsFactory")
  private QueueConnectionFactory queueConnectionFactory;
  @Resource(mappedName="jms/PartsQueue")
  private Queue queue;

  protected void processRequest(HttpServletRequest request,
    HttpServletResponse response)
```

```
    throws ServletException, IOException {
      response.setContentType("text/html;charset=UTF-8");
      PrintWriter out = response.getWriter();
      try {
        Connection connection;

        try {
          connection = queueConnectionFactory.createConnection();
          Session session = connection.createSession(false,
            Session.AUTO_ACKNOWLEDGE);
          MessageProducer messageProducer = (MessageProducer)
            session.createProducer(queue);
          BytesMessage bytesMessage = session.createBytesMessage();
          bytesMessage.writeInt(12345);    // part number
          bytesMessage.writeFloat(12.5f); // weight
          bytesMessage.writeInt(50);       // quantity
          messageProducer.send(bytesMessage);
          System.out.println("---> comment sent");
        } catch (JMSException ex) {
            Logger.getLogger(PartsServlet.class.getName()).
              log(Level.SEVERE, null, ex);
        }
        out.println("<html>");
        out.println("<head>");
        out.println("<title>Servlet PartsServlet</title>");
        out.println("</head>");
        out.println("<body>");
        out.println("<h1>Servlet PartsServlet at " +
          request.getContextPath () + "</h1>");
        out.println("</body>");
        out.println("</html>");

      } finally {
          out.close();
      }
    }
```

The `PartsBean` starts with the **@MessageDriven** annotation where we specify we want to listen to the `jms/PartsQueue`. The `onMessage` method receives a `BytesMessage` and is displayed.

```
@MessageDriven(mappedName = "jms/PartsQueue", activationConfig = {
  @ActivationConfigProperty(propertyName = "acknowledgeMode",
  propertyValue = "Auto-acknowledge"),
  @ActivationConfigProperty(propertyName = "destinationType",
  propertyValue = "javax.jms.Queue")
```

```
})
public class PartsBean implements MessageListener {

  public PartsBean() {
  }

  public void onMessage(Message message) {
    BytesMessage bytesMessage = (BytesMessage) message;
    try {
      System.out.println("Part Numer: " + bytesMessage.readInt());
      System.out.println("Weight: " + bytesMessage.readFloat());
      System.out.println("Quantity: " + bytesMessage.readInt());
    } catch (JMSException ex) {
      Logger.getLogger(PartsBean.class.getName()).log(Level.SEVERE,
        null, ex);
    }
    System.out.println("---> parts received");
  }

}
```

Execute the `PartsServlet`. The output will appear as follows:

INFO: ---> comment sent

INFO: Part Numer: 12345

INFO: Weight: 12.5

INFO: Quantity: 50

INFO: ---> parts received

How it works...

In the `PartsServlet`, the **@Resource** annotation injected a `QueueConnectionFactory` and a `Queue`. This chapter's introduction details the process for establishing a connection to a queue. In this application we use the `jms/PartsQueue`.

The interesting part is the creation and use of the `BytesMessage`. The `Session` object's `createByteMessage` method returns a `BytesMessage` object. The methods available to this object are similar to those used by the `java.io.DataOutputStream`. In this example, we wrote the order's parts ID number, weight, and quantity to the `BytesMessage` object using the `writeInt` and `writeFloat` methods. As the method's names imply, one writes out an integer and the other a float. Once all needed information was written, the message was sent to the `jms/PartsQueue` using the send method.

The `PartsBean` started with the **@MessageDriven** annotation and used the **mappedName** attribute to specify the queue used. Two **@ActivationConfigProperty** elements were used to specify the acknowledgement mode and that the destination was a queue.

The `Message` received in the `onMessage` method was cast to a `BytesMessage`. The `BytesMessage` object's methods are similar to that of the `java.io.DataInputStream`. Using the `readInt` and `readFloat` methods, the elements of the message were easily extracted and displayed.

There's more...

Note that it is possible to write data out as one data type and read it in using a different type. For example, an integer is written out as a four byte two's complement number. On the receiving end, the same four byte quantity can be read as two short values. While this is possible, it does not make sense to interpret the data using different data types in most situations.

When the `BytesMessage` object is first created it is placed in a write-only mode. The client is able to write to it. Once the message is received, the message is in a read-only mode.

The `Message` object's `clearBody` method has the effect of clearing out the contents of the message and placing the message in a write-only mode. It is possible for the client to send the message and then continue writing to the `BytesMessage` object. However, subsequent writing does not affect the message previously sent. The `BytesMessage` object can be sent multiple times if necessary.

There are several methods of the `BytesMessage` object that permit the writing and reading of Java's primitive data types and strings along with the writing of an unsigned byte and short value. In addition, the `getBodyLength` returns the length of the message body. This method is only available when the message is in the read-only mode.

See also

The `StreamMessage`, as described in the next recipe, is similar to the `BytesMessage` interface. However, it requires that for each write operation of a specific data type, the corresponding read data type operation be performed on the receiving end.

Handling a stream-based message

Sometimes it is desirable to send a stream of primitive values as a message. This recipe illustrates this process using the `StreamMessage` interface.

The advantages of using a stream of bytes are essentially the same as those for the BytesMessage: ease of read and write operations and a fixed size message. Data is written or read by storing the data in primitive format. In addition, information about the type of data written is also stored. This means that if an integer is written then only a corresponding integer read operation can be used against the data.

The StreamMessage interface differs from the BytesMessage in that data stored using StreamMessage interface incorporates information about the data type. This prevents mismatched read/write operations that can occur in BytesMessage message.

Getting ready

The essential structure of a servlet used to generate a message was introduced in the introduction. Here we will address the unique elements of creating and using a StreamMessage which include:

1. Creating a StreamMessage using the createStreamMessage method
2. Writing values to the BytesMessage
3. Sending the message

How to do it...

Create a Queue named jms/ItemsQueue and a QueueConnectionFactory named jms/ItemsFactory as described in the introduction. Next, create a Java EE application called StreamMessageApplication. In the EJB module add a package called packt and then an MDB called ItemBean. When creating the MDB use a queue named jms/ItemsQueue. In the WAR module add a package called servlet with a servlet called ItemsServlet.

The ItemsServlet follows. The doGet and doPost methods are not listed here.

```
public class ItemsServlet extends HttpServlet {

    @Resource(mappedName="jms/ItemsFactory")
    private QueueConnectionFactory queueConnectionFactory;
    @Resource(mappedName="jms/ItemsQueue")
    private Queue queue;

    protected void processRequest(HttpServletRequest request,
      HttpServletResponse response)
      throws ServletException, IOException {
        response.setContentType("text/html;charset=UTF-8");
        PrintWriter out = response.getWriter();
        try {
          Connection connection;
```

```
            try {
              connection = queueConnectionFactory.createConnection();
              Session session = connection.createSession(false,
                Session.AUTO_ACKNOWLEDGE);
              MessageProducer messageProducer = (MessageProducer)
                session.createProducer(queue);
              StreamMessage streamMessage =
                session.createStreamMessage();
              streamMessage.writeInt(12345);    // part number
              streamMessage.writeFloat(12.5f); // weight
              streamMessage.writeInt(50);       // quantity
              messageProducer.send(streamMessage);
              System.out.println("---> Item sent");
            } catch (JMSException ex) {
                Logger.getLogger(ItemsServlet.class.getName()).
                  log(Level.SEVERE, null, ex);
            }
            out.println("<html>");
            out.println("<head>");
            out.println("<title>Servlet ItemsServlet</title>");
            out.println("</head>");
            out.println("<body>");
            out.println("<h1>Servlet ItemsServlet at " +
              request.getContextPath () + "</h1>");
            out.println("</body>");
            out.println("</html>");

        } finally {
              out.close();
        }
    }
```

Next, create the `ItemBean`. Notice that `jms/ItemsQueue` is used in the **@MessageDriven** annotation. In the `onMessage` method, the message elements are retrieved and displayed.

```
@MessageDriven(mappedName = "jms/ItemsQueue", activationConfig = {
  @ActivationConfigProperty(propertyName = "acknowledgeMode",
  propertyValue = "Auto-acknowledge"),
  @ActivationConfigProperty(propertyName = "destinationType",
  propertyValue = "javax.jms.Queue")
})
public class ItemBean implements MessageListener {

  public ItemBean() {
  }
```

```
public void onMessage(Message message) {
  StreamMessage streamMessage = (StreamMessage) message;
  try {
    System.out.println("Part Number: " + streamMessage.readInt());
    System.out.println("Weight: " + streamMessage.readFloat());
    System.out.println("Quantity: " + streamMessage.readInt());
  } catch (JMSException ex) {
      Logger.getLogger(ItemBean.class.getName()).log(Level.SEVERE,
        null, ex);
  }
  System.out.println("---> Item received");
}

}
```

Execute the `PartsServlet`. The output will appear as follows:

INFO: ---> Item sent

INFO: Part Number: 12345

INFO: Weight: 12.5

INFO: Quantity: 50

INFO: ---> Item received

How it works...

In the `ItemsServlet`, the **@Resource** annotation injected a `QueueConnectionFactory` and a `Queue`. This chapter's introduction details the process for establishing a connection to a queue.

The `Session` object's `createStreamMessage` method returns a `StreamMessage` object. As with the `BytesMessage`, the read/write methods result in the data being stored using primitive data format. In this example, we wrote a parts ID number, weight, and quantity to order to the `streamMessage` object using the `writeInt` and `writeFloat` methods. Once all needed information was written, the message was sent to the `jms/ItemsQueue` using the `send` method.

Let's examine the `ItemBean` next. In the **@MessageDriven** annotation the `mappedName` was set to `jms/ItemsQueue`. In the `onMessage` method, the message received was cast to a `StreamMessage` and read type methods were used to extract the part information.

There's more...

When the `StreamMessage` object is first created it is placed in a write-only mode. The client is able to write to it. Once the message is received, the message is in a read-only mode.

As with the `BytesMessage`, it is possible for the client to send the message and then continue writing to the `StreamMessage` object. Subsequent writing does not affect the message previously sent. Sending the `StreamMessage` object to the queue multiple times is permitted.

There are other methods available to write and read primitive data. In addition, the `getBodyLength` returns the length of the message body. However, this method is only available when the message is in the read-only mode.

See also

The `BytesMessage` is similar to the `StreamMessage` interface except that it does not require that for each write operation of a specific data type, the corresponding read data type operation be performed. See the *Handling byte-based message* recipe.

Handling a map-based message

The `MapMessage` interface supports a message consisting of a set of mapped key/value pairs. This is similar to the Java `HashMap` class where a key, such as a name, can be assigned a value, such as a telephone number. It allows this type of information to be transferred as a set of key/value pairs. In this recipe we will develop an application that illustrates their use.

Getting ready

The essential structure of a servlet used to generate a message was introduced in the introduction. Here we will address the unique elements of creating and using a `MapMessage` which include:

1. Creating a `MapMessage` using the `createMapMessage` method
2. Writing key/value pairs to the `MapMessage`
3. Sending the message

How to do it...

Create a `Queue` named `jms/MapQueue` and a `QueueConnectionFactory` named `jms/MapFactory` as described in the introduction. Next, create a Java EE application called `MapMessageApplication`. In the EJB module add a package called `packt` and then an MDB called `MapBean`. When creating the MDB use a queue named `jms/MapQueue`. In the WAR module add a `package` called `servlet` with a servlet called `MapServlet`.

The `MapServlet` follows. The `doGet` and `doPost` methods are not listed here.

```java
public class MapServlet extends HttpServlet {

  @Resource(mappedName="jms/MapFactory")
  private QueueConnectionFactory queueConnectionFactory;
  @Resource(mappedName="jms/MapQueue")
  private Queue queue;

  protected void processRequest(HttpServletRequest request,
    HttpServletResponse response)
    throws ServletException, IOException {
      response.setContentType("text/html;charset=UTF-8");
      PrintWriter out = response.getWriter();
      try {
        Connection connection;

        try {
          connection = queueConnectionFactory.createConnection();
          Session session = connection.createSession(false,
            Session.AUTO_ACKNOWLEDGE);
          MessageProducer messageProducer = (MessageProducer)
            session.createProducer(queue);
          MapMessage mapMessage = session.createMapMessage();
          mapMessage.setInt("PartNumber",12345);
          mapMessage.setFloat("Weight",12.5f);
          mapMessage.setInt("Quantity",50);
          messageProducer.send(mapMessage);
          System.out.println("---> mapMessage sent " +
            mapMessage.getInt("PartNumber"));
        } catch (JMSException ex) {
          Logger.getLogger(MapServlet.class.getName()).
            log(Level.SEVERE, null, ex);
        }

        out.println("<html>");
        out.println("<head>");
```

```
        out.println("<title>Servlet MapServlet</title>");
        out.println("</head>");
        out.println("<body>");
        out.println("<h1>Servlet MapServlet at " +
           request.getContextPath () + "</h1>");
        out.println("</body>");
        out.println("</html>");

    } finally {
        out.close();
    }
  }
```

The MapBean uses the jms/MapQueue. In the onMessage method the message is cast to a MapMessage and its paired key/values are retrieved and displayed.

```
@MessageDriven(mappedName = "jms/MapQueue", activationConfig =  {
  @ActivationConfigProperty(propertyName = "acknowledgeMode",
  propertyValue = "Auto-acknowledge"),
  @ActivationConfigProperty(propertyName = "destinationType",
  propertyValue = "javax.jms.Queue")
    })
public class MapBean implements MessageListener {

  public MapBean() {
  }

  public void onMessage(Message message) {
    MapMessage mapMessage = (MapMessage) message;
    try {
      System.out.println("Part Number: " +
        mapMessage.getInt("PartNumber"));
      System.out.println("Weight: " + mapMessage.getFloat("Weight"));
      System.out.println("Quantity: " +
        mapMessage.getInt("Quantity"));

    } catch (JMSException ex) {
        Logger.getLogger(MapBean.class.getName()).log(Level.SEVERE,
          null, ex);
    }
    System.out.println("---> map message received");
  }

}
```

Execute the `MapServlet`. The output will appear as follows:

INFO: ---> mapMessage sent 12345

INFO: Part Number: 12345

INFO: Weight: 12.5

INFO: Quantity: 50

INFO: ---> map message received

How it works...

In the `MapServlet`, the **@Resource** annotation injected a `QueueConnectionFactory` and a `Queue`. This chapter's introduction discusses the process for establishing a connection to a queue.

Once a `MapMessage` object was created, a series of set methods were used to store the order information. The argument of each method used a set of key/value pair representing the order's fields. The key was a string and the value was either a Java primitive data type or a string. Null keys and values are not permitted. The message was then sent.

In the `MapBean`, the **@MessageDriven** annotation used the **mappedName** attribute to specify the queue used. Two **@ActivationConfigProperty** elements were used to specify the acknowledgement mode and that the destination was a queue.

The `MapBean` received the message and cast it to a `MapMessage` in the `onMessage` method. A series of get methods were used to retrieve the order information. Each method argument corresponded to the key of the map values.

There's more...

When an instance of the `MapMessage` is created in the `MapServlet`, key/value pairs can be written to the message and read from the message. Normally, only write operations are used here. When `MapMessage` is received by an MDB it is in a read-only mode.

The `itemExists` method accepts a string and returns a boolean value indicating whether that key specified by its argument exists in the map. This can be useful in determining whether a message has assigned a particular key to a message.

The `getMapNames` method returns a `java.util.Enumeration` object. This method allows the retrieval of all key/value pairs without necessarily knowing what pairs make up the map. If we wanted to list all of the key/value pairs we could use the Enumeration's `hasMoreElements` and `nextElement` methods to traverse the enumeration. It is necessary to cast the return of the `nextElement` method to `String` because they are stored in the map as an object.

```
System.out.println("List of key/value pairs");
Enumeration enumeration = mapMessage.getMapNames();
while(enumeration.hasMoreElements()) {
  String key = (String)enumeration.nextElement();
  System.out.println(key + ": " +
    mapMessage.getString(key));
}
```

The output of this code sequence, when added to the end of the try block in the `onMessage` method, follows:

INFO: List of key/value pairs

INFO: Quantity: 50

INFO: Weight: 12.5

INFO: PartNumber: 12345

Notice that only string keys and primitive values can be used. It is possible to use a `setBytes` and a `setObject` method to construct a message. However, the `setObject` method only works for primitive data types such as Integer. As a result, serialization of the key/value pairs is not an issue.

See also

The first five recipes present alternative techniques for sending messages.

Handling an object-based message

This is the last in the series of recipes illustrating how to send an order type message. In this recipe we will use a simple Java class called `Order` to represent the order and an `ObjectMessage` object to encapsulate the `Order` object. Since an order is best represented as a class, the `ObjectMessage` is the preferred technique for sending an order.

Getting ready

The essential structure of a servlet used to generate a message was introduced in the introduction. Here we will address the unique elements of creating and using an `ObjectMessage` which include:

1. Creating an `ObjectMessage` using the `createObjectMessage` method
2. Attaching the object to the `ObjectMessage` using the `setObject` method
3. Sending the message

How to do it...

Create a `Queue` named `jms/OrderQueue` and a `QueueConnectionFactory` named `jms/OrderFactory` as described in the introduction. Next, create a Java EE application called `ObjectMessageApplication`. In the EJB module add a package called `packt` with an MDB called `OrderBean`. Also, add a Java class called `Order`. In the WAR module add a package called `servlet` and a servlet called `OrderServlet`.

Let's start with the `Order` class which, as its names implies, encapsulates an order. It holds the part number, weight, and quantity as private variables. The `Order` class needs to implement the `Serializable` interface. Otherwise, it would not be possible to send it across the network. Setter/getter methods are provided to facilitate access to the member variables.

```java
package packt;

import java.io.Serializable;

public class Order implements Serializable {
  private int partNumber;
  private float weight;
  private int quantity;

  public Order(int partNumber, float weight, int quantity) {
    this.partNumber = partNumber;
    this.weight = weight;
    this.quantity = quantity;
  }

  public int getPartNumber() {
    return partNumber;
  }

  public void setPartNumber(int partNumber) {
    this.partNumber = partNumber;
  }

  public int getQuantity() {
    return quantity;
  }

  public void setQuantity(int quantity) {
    this.quantity = quantity;
  }

  public float getWeight() {
```

```
      return weight;
   }

   public void setWeight(float weight) {
      this.weight = weight;
   }

}
```

Next, add the `OrderServlet`. Once again, the `doGet` and `doPost` methods are not shown.

```
public class OrderServlet extends HttpServlet {

   @Resource(mappedName="jms/OrderFactoryPool")
   private QueueConnectionFactory queueConnectionFactory;
   @Resource(mappedName="jms/OrderQueue")
   private Queue queue;

   protected void processRequest(HttpServletRequest request,
     HttpServletResponse response)
     throws ServletException, IOException {
       response.setContentType("text/html;charset=UTF-8");
       PrintWriter out = response.getWriter();
       try {
         Connection connection;

         try {
           connection = queueConnectionFactory.createConnection();
           Session session = connection.createSession(false,
             Session.AUTO_ACKNOWLEDGE);
           MessageProducer messageProducer = (MessageProducer)
             session.createProducer(queue);
           ObjectMessage objectMessage =
             session.createObjectMessage();
           objectMessage.setObject(new Order(1234,12.5f,50));
           messageProducer.send(objectMessage);
           System.out.println("---> objectMessage sent ");
         } catch (JMSException ex) {
             Logger.getLogger(OrderServlet.class.getName()).
               log(Level.SEVERE, null, ex);
           }


           out.println("<html>");
           out.println("<head>");
```

```
            out.println("<title>Servlet OrderServlet</title>");
            out.println("</head>");
            out.println("<body>");
            out.println("<h1>Servlet OrderServlet at " +
               request.getContextPath () + "</h1>");
            out.println("</body>");
            out.println("</html>");

        } finally {
            out.close();
        }
    }
```

Add the `OrderBean` as shown below:

```
    @MessageDriven(mappedName = "jms/OrderQueue", activationConfig = {
       @ActivationConfigProperty(propertyName = "acknowledgeMode",
       propertyValue = "Auto-acknowledge"),
       @ActivationConfigProperty(propertyName = "destinationType",
       propertyValue = "javax.jms.Queue")
       })
    public class OrderBean implements MessageListener {

        public OrderBean() {
        }

        @Override
        public void onMessage(Message message) {
          try {
            ObjectMessage objectMessage = (ObjectMessage) message;
            Order order = (Order)objectMessage.getObject();
            System.out.println("Part Number: " + order.getPartNumber());
            System.out.println("Weight: " + order.getWeight());
            System.out.println("Quantity: " + order.getQuantity());
            System.out.println("Order Received");

          } catch (JMSException ex) {
             Logger.getLogger(OrderBean.class.getName()).log(Level.SEVERE,
                null, ex);
          }
        }

    }
```

Execute the application using the `OrderServlet`. The output will reflect the sending and reception of the message.

INFO: ---> objectMessage sent

INFO: Part Number: 1234

INFO: Weight: 12.5

INFO: Quantity: 50

INFO: Order Received

How it works...

In the `OrderServlet`, the **@Resource** annotation injected a `QueueConnectionFactory` and a `Queue`. This chapter's introduction details the process for establishing a connection to a queue.

The `ObjectMessage` object was created using the `createObjectMessage` method. Next, an `Order` object was created, initialized with the order information and assigned to the `ObjectMessage` using the `setObject` method. The message was then sent to the queue.

In the `OrderBean`, the **@MessageDriven** annotation used the **mappedName** to associate the MDB with the `jms/OrderQueue`. The primary aspect of the `OrderBean` of interest is the object's `onMessage` method which received a message from the `jms/OrderQueue`. The message was cast to an `ObjectMessage` to obtain the `Order` object. The values of the `Order` object were then processed using the getter methods of the `Order` class.

See also

The first five recipes present alternative techniques for sending messages.

Using an MDB in a point-to-point application

The first five recipes are point-to-point applications. They represent a simple type of point-to-point application as there is only one producer of information, a servlet, and only a single consumer, the MDB. In this recipe, we will further develop this type of application by reusing the `ObjectMessageApplication` developed in the previous recipe.

Getting ready

Make sure you are familiar with the `ObjectMessageApplication`. We will add a minimal amount of code to illustrate variations of the point-to-point application architecture. This type of application is sometimes referred to as a producer-consumer application. One or more producers will generate messages which are placed in a queue. One or more consumers will retrieve and process the messages.

How to do it...

In the figure that follows, one or more producers will create items such as a purchase order and place them in a queue. At a later time, one or more consumers may pull an item off of the queue and process it. This decouples the production and consumption of items and can result in performance enhancements.

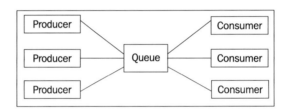

The `ObjectMessageApplication` creates an order that is placed in a queue. More than one servlet, or other types of client, can generate an order. A single MDB will handle only a single request at a time. However, with multiple MDBs available in the container, multiple messages can be consumed concurrently.

A variation of this architecture is where an MDB consumes and sends messages to the queue. For example, the `OrderBean` may receive an order and based on factors, such as the customer's purchase history, decide to provide an additional "bonus" order as thanks for their patronage. The MDB may then place an additional order as a bonus and add this new order to the queue.

The following is a modified version of the `OrderBean`. The **@Resource** annotations have been added as instance variables to permit the MDB to send messages to the queue. The `onMessage` method has been modified to send a message to the queue under certain circumstances.

```
@MessageDriven(mappedName = "jms/OrderQueue", activationConfig = {
    @ActivationConfigProperty(propertyName = "acknowledgeMode",
    propertyValue = "Auto-acknowledge"),
    @ActivationConfigProperty(propertyName = "destinationType",
    propertyValue = "javax.jms.Queue")
    })
```

```java
public class OrderBean implements MessageListener {

  // These declarations are used to send out a thank you order
  @Resource(mappedName="jms/OrderFactoryPool")
  private QueueConnectionFactory queueConnectionFactory;
  @Resource(mappedName="jms/OrderQueue")
  private Queue queue;

  public OrderBean() {
  }

  @Override
  public void onMessage(Message message) {
    try {
      ObjectMessage objectMessage = (ObjectMessage) message;
      Order order = (Order)objectMessage.getObject();
      System.out.println("Part Number: " + order.getPartNumber());
      System.out.println("Weight: " + order.getWeight());
      System.out.println("Quantity: " + order.getQuantity());
      System.out.println("Order Received");

      // Send out a thank you order
      if(order.getQuantity() > 40) {
        Connection connection;

        try {
          connection = queueConnectionFactory.createConnection();
          Session session = connection.createSession(false,
            Session.AUTO_ACKNOWLEDGE);
          MessageProducer messageProducer = (MessageProducer)
            session.createProducer(queue);
          objectMessage = session.createObjectMessage();
          objectMessage.setObject(new Order(54321,5.5f,1));
          messageProducer.send(objectMessage);
          System.out.println("---> Thank you order sent ");
        } catch (JMSException ex) {
            Logger.getLogger(OrderBean.class.getName()).
              log(Level.SEVERE, null, ex);
          }
      }

    } catch (JMSException ex) {
        Logger.getLogger(OrderBean.class.getName()).log(Level.SEVERE,
        null, ex);
      }
  }

}
```

Execute the application and observe that the order has been placed from the MDB.

INFO: ---> Thank you order sent

INFO: Part Number: 54321

INFO: Weight: 5.5

INFO: Quantity: 1

INFO: Order Received

How it works...

To send a message from an MDB we use essentially the same code as that found in the servlet. The **@Resource** annotations have been added to allow us to send a message.

A test was made in the `onMessage` method to determine if the bonus order should be placed. This was accomplished by determining if the order's quantity was greater than 40. If this was the case, then a new connection and message was created and sent to the queue.

There's more...

Another version of the architecture uses more than one queue. In some situations the consumer of the message may need to validate or otherwise process the order. Once the validation is complete, then it is sent to a second queue. Messages from the second queue are consumed by another MDB that may actually place the order. The figure below illustrates this process.

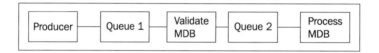

The advantage of this approach is that the number of MDBs required to perform the validation versus the order placement can be controlled and administered separately. The time it takes to validate an order can be more or less than it takes to place the order. Splitting the work across multiple queues and MDBs provides more flexibility in administrating the overall application.

See also

The next recipe illustrates another common architecture for MDBs.

Using MDB in a publish-and-subscribe application

The publish-and-subscribe architecture can be useful in keeping track of the availability of individuals. In this recipe, we will develop an application that uses a topic to monitor and record when a person is available. That is, when a person is at his/her desk, logged on to a computer or otherwise able to respond to requests.

Getting ready

A topic is similar to a queue. Messages are sent to a topic just as they are sent to a queue. However, once there they may be accessed by more than one consumer. The essential structure of a servlet used to generate a message was introduced in the introduction. Here we will address the unique elements of creating and using a topic to support a publish-and-subscribe application which include:

1. Creating a message and sending it to the topic
2. Registering a subscriber for the topic
3. Receiving and processing the message

How to do it...

Create a `Topic` named `jms/AvailabilityTopic` and a `TopicConnectionFactory` named `jms/AvailabilityFactoryPool` as described in the introduction. Next, create a new Java EE application called `PublishAndSubscribeApplication`. In the EJB module add a package called `packt` and three classes:

▶ `Availability` – a simple Java class representing the availability of an individual

▶ `LoggingBean` – an MDB that logs a person's availability

▶ `SubscriberBean` – an MDB that may be interested in whether someone is available or not

In the WAR module add a package called `servlet` with a servlet called `AvailabilityServlet`.

The `Availability` class associates a name with that person's availability. It consists of a string variable for a name and a Boolean variable to indicate whether they are available or not. The class must implement the `Serializable` interface otherwise the object cannot be sent as part of a message.

```
import java.io.Serializable;

public class Availability implements Serializable {
```

```
    private String name;
    private boolean available;

    public Availability(String name, boolean available) {
      this.name = name;
      this.available = available;
    }

    public boolean isAvailable() {
      return available;
    }

    public String getName() {
      return name;
    }

}
```

Next, create the `AvailabilityServlet` as listed below. The `doGet` and `doPost` methods are not shown.

```
public class AvailabilityServlet extends HttpServlet {

    private Availability availability;
    @Resource(mappedName="jms/AvailabilityFactoryPool")
    private TopicConnectionFactory topicConnectionFactory;
    @Resource(mappedName="jms/AvailabilityTopic")
    private Topic topic;

    protected void processRequest(HttpServletRequest request,
      HttpServletResponse response)
      throws ServletException, IOException {
        response.setContentType("text/html;charset=UTF-8");
        PrintWriter out = response.getWriter();
        try {

          Connection connection;
          availability = new Availability("Tom",true);

            try {
              connection = topicConnectionFactory.createConnection();
              Session session = connection.createSession(false,
                Session.AUTO_ACKNOWLEDGE);
              MessageProducer messageProducer = (MessageProducer)
                session.createProducer(topic);
```

```
        ObjectMessage availabilityMessage =
          session.createObjectMessage(availability);
        availabilityMessage.setStringProperty("test", "tested");
          messageProducer.send(availabilityMessage);
        System.out.println("---> availability status sent");
      } catch (JMSException ex) {
        Logger.getLogger(AvailabilityServlet.class.getName()).
          log(Level.SEVERE, null, ex);
      }

      out.println("<html>");
      out.println("<head>");
      out.println("<title>Servlet
        AvailabilityServlet</title>");
      out.println("</head>");
      out.println("<body>");
      out.println("<h1>Servlet AvailabilityServlet at " +
        request.getContextPath () + "</h1>");
      out.println("</body>");
      out.println("</html>");

    } finally {
      out.close();
    }
  }
```

We will use two MDBs. The `LoggingBean` EJB logs an individual's availability for later analysis. The `SubscriberBean` EJB listens to the messages and indicates it has received the message.

Add the `LoggingBean` as follows:

```
@MessageDriven(mappedName = "jms/AvailabilityTopic",
  activationConfig = {
    @ActivationConfigProperty(propertyName = "acknowledgeMode",
    propertyValue = "Auto-acknowledge"),
    @ActivationConfigProperty(propertyName = "destinationType",
    propertyValue = "javax.jms.Topic"),
    @ActivationConfigProperty(propertyName =
    "subscriptionDurability", propertyValue = "Durable"),
    @ActivationConfigProperty(propertyName = "clientId",
    propertyValue = "LoggingBean"),
    @ActivationConfigProperty(propertyName = "subscriptionName",
    propertyValue = "LoggingBean")
})
public class LoggingBean implements MessageListener {
```

```
    public LoggingBean() {
    }

    public void onMessage(Message message) {
      ObjectMessage objectMessage = (ObjectMessage) message;
      try {
        Availability availability = (Availability)
          objectMessage.getObject();
        if(availability.isAvailable()) {
          Logger.getLogger(LoggingBean.class.getName()).
            log(Level.SEVERE,
            availability.getName() + " is available");
        } else {
            Logger.getLogger(LoggingBean.class.getName()).
              log(Level.SEVERE,
            availability.getName() + " is not available");
          }
          System.out.println("---> logging ");
      } catch (JMSException ex) {
          Logger.getLogger(LoggingBean.class.getName()).
          log(Level.SEVERE, null, ex);
        }
    }
}
```

Create the `SubscriberBean` next.

```
    @MessageDriven(mappedName = "jms/AvailabilityTopic",
      activationConfig =  {
      @ActivationConfigProperty(propertyName = "acknowledgeMode",
      propertyValue = "Auto-acknowledge"),
      @ActivationConfigProperty(propertyName = "destinationType",
      propertyValue = "javax.jms.Topic"),
      @ActivationConfigProperty(propertyName = "subscriptionDurability",
      propertyValue = "Durable"),
      @ActivationConfigProperty(propertyName = "clientId",
      propertyValue = "SubscriberBean"),
      @ActivationConfigProperty(propertyName = "subscriptionName",
      propertyValue = "SubscriberBean")
    })
    public class SubscriberBean implements MessageListener {

      public SubscriberBean() {
      }

      public void onMessage(Message message) {
        System.out.println("---> subscriber ");
      }

    }
```

Execute the `AvailabilityServlet`. You will observe the following output in the console window:

INFO: ---> availability status sent

INFO: ---> subscriber

SEVERE: Jonathan is available

INFO: ---> logging

How it works...

The `AvailabilityServlet` created a message that was sent to a topic. The **@Resource** annotation injected a `TopicConnectionFactory` and a `Topic`. This chapter's introduction discusses the process for establishing a connection to a queue. The approach is essentially the same for a topic except a topic is used instead of a queue.

Notice how the `Availability` object was created and sent. An `ObjectMessge` was used for the message and is discussed in the *Handling an object-based message* recipe earlier in this chapter.

The `LoggingBean` is responsible for maintaining a log of the availability of individuals. The **@MessageDriven** annotation used the **mappedName** attribute to specify the topic used. Two **@ActivationConfigProperty** elements were used to specify the acknowledgement mode and that the destination was a topic. In addition, three other **@ActivationConfigProperty** elements were set for the topic:

- ▶ `subscriptionDurability` – Durable
- ▶ `clientId` – LoggingBean
- ▶ `subscriptionName` – LoggingBean

A durable message is held in the topic temporarily if the subscriber happens to become temporarily unavailable. It is sent to the subscriber once the subscriber is able to receive the message. However, it is necessary for the subscriber to register with the topic using a unique `clientId` and `subscriptionName` as affected by the **@ActivationConfigProperty** annotation.

The `onMessage` method retrieved the `Availability` object and used the `isAvailable` method to determine whether the individual was available or not. It then logged a message to that effect.

The `SubscriberBean` represents an individual or entity that is interested in knowing whether someone is available or not. Its **@MessageDriven** annotation is similar to the `LoggingBean`. The `onMessage` implementation simply displayed a message indicating the subscriber has handled the message.

See also

The *Using an MDB in a point-to-point application* recipe illustrates another common strategy for using MDBs. Also, the *Handling an object-based message* recipe details the use of the `ObjectMessage`.

Specifying which types of message to receive using the message selector

A message selector is a string containing an expression used to control which messages are consumed by which MDBs. The application used in this recipe submits different messages to the same queue. The messages are then sent to different MDBs based on their message selector settings.

Getting ready

The essential structure of a servlet used to generate a message was introduced in the introduction. We will be using a `TextMessage` to demonstrate the message selection process. This message type is discussed earlier in this chapter under the *Handling a text-based message* recipe. Here we will address the unique elements of creating and using a `TextMessage` to support a message selector which include:

1. Creating a message and assigning a type to it
2. Sending the message
3. Specifying the MDB's property to select based on the type message

How to do it...

Create a `Queue` named `jms/PostingsQueue` and a `QueueConnectionFactory` named `jms/PostngsQueueFactory` as described in the introduction. Next, create a Java EE application called `MessageSelectorApplication`. In the EJB module create a `packt` package and two MDBs: `PublicPostingBean` and `PrivatePostingBean`. In the WAR module add a `servlet` package and a servlet called `PostingServlet`.

The `PostingServlet` follows without its `doGet` and `doPost` methods. Two `TextMessages` are created and sent to the queue.

```
public class PostingServlet extends HttpServlet {

    @Resource(mappedName="jms/PostingsQueueFactory")
    private QueueConnectionFactory queueConnectionFactory;
    @Resource(mappedName="jms/PostingsQueue")
    private Queue queue;
```

```
protected void processRequest(HttpServletRequest request,
  HttpServletResponse response)
  throws ServletException, IOException {
    response.setContentType("text/html;charset=UTF-8");
    PrintWriter out = response.getWriter();
    try {
      Connection connection;

      try {
        connection = queueConnectionFactory.createConnection();
        Session session = connection.createSession(false,
          Session.AUTO_ACKNOWLEDGE);
        MessageProducer messageProducer = (MessageProducer)
          session.createProducer(queue);
        TextMessage textMessage = session.createTextMessage();

        textMessage.setText("For your eyes only");
        textMessage.setStringProperty("PostingType", "private");
        messageProducer.send(textMessage);
        System.out.println("---> Public textMessage sent");

        textMessage.setText("Distribute freely");
        textMessage.setStringProperty("PostingType", "public");
        messageProducer.send(textMessage);
        System.out.println("--->Private textMessage sent");

      } catch (JMSException ex) {
          Logger.getLogger(PostingServlet.class.getName()).
            log(Level.SEVERE, null, ex);
        }

        out.println("<html>");
        out.println("<head>");
        out.println("<title>Servlet PostingServlet</title>");
        out.println("</head>");
        out.println("<body>");
        out.println("<h1>Servlet PostingServlet at " +
          request.getContextPath () + "</h1>");
        out.println("</body>");
        out.println("</html>");

    } finally {
        out.close();
      }
}
```

The `PublicPostingBean` is created to handle public messages. The selection of public versus private messages is specified in the **@MessageDriven** annotation.

```java
@MessageDriven(mappedName = "jms/PostingsQueue",
    activationConfig =   {
    @ActivationConfigProperty(propertyName = "acknowledgeMode",
    propertyValue = "Auto-acknowledge"),
    @ActivationConfigProperty(propertyName = "destinationType",
    propertyValue = "javax.jms.Queue"),
    @ActivationConfigProperty(propertyName = "messageSelector",
    propertyValue = "PostingType = 'public'")
    })
public class PublicPostingBean implements MessageListener {

    public PublicPostingBean() {
    }

    public void onMessage(Message message) {
        TextMessage textMessage = (TextMessage)message;
        try {
            System.out.println("Public Post Received - " +
                textMessage.getText());
        } catch (JMSException ex) {
            Logger.getLogger(PublicPostingBean.class.getName()).
                log(Level.SEVERE, null, ex);
        }
    }

}
```

The `PrivatePostingBean` is very similar to the `PublicPostingBean` except it is configured to handle private messages.

```java
@MessageDriven(mappedName = "jms/PostingsQueue",
    activationConfig =   {
    @ActivationConfigProperty(propertyName = "acknowledgeMode",
        propertyValue = "Auto-acknowledge"),
        @ActivationConfigProperty(propertyName = "destinationType",
        propertyValue = "javax.jms.Queue"),
        @ActivationConfigProperty(propertyName = "messageSelector",
        propertyValue = "PostingType = 'private'")
    })
public class PrivatePostingBean implements MessageListener {

    public PrivatePostingBean() {
    }
```

```
    public void onMessage(Message message) {
      TextMessage textMessage = (TextMessage)message;
      try {
        System.out.println("Private Post Received - " +
          textMessage.getText());
      } catch (JMSException ex) {
          Logger.getLogger(PublicPostingBean.class.getName()).
            log(Level.SEVERE, null, ex);
        }
    }

  }
```

Execute the `PostingServlet`. Your output should appear as follows:

INFO: ---> Public textMessage sent

INFO: --->Private textMessage sent

INFO: Private Post Received - For your eyes only

INFO: Public Post Received - Distribute freely

How it works...

The `PostingServlet` was associated with the `jms/PostingsQueueFactory` and `jms/PostingsQueue` factory and queue. This chapter's introduction discusses the process for establishing a connection to a queue.

After the connection and session had been established, two `TextMessages` were created. The first one was a private message. The `TextMessage` object's `setStringProperty` method assigned a value of `private` to the `PostingType` property. It is this string property that is ultimately used to determine which MDB will receive the message. The message was then sent.

This was followed by the creation of a public message and setting the `PostingType` property to `public`. The `setStringProperty` method was used to assign a value to a message. A message selector is a string. The string contains an expression whose syntax is based on SQL92. This means that more complex message selectors can be defined to meet the needs of an application.

Next, let's examine the two MDBs. The **@ActivationConfigProperty** element of the **@MessageDriven** annotation limits messages received by an MDB. This element has a **propertyName** and a **propertyValue** field. The **propertyName** was set to `messageSelector` and the **propertyValue** was set to a string used to limit the messages that the MDB receives. In this recipe, the value used a `PostingType` field that was assigned a value of either `public` or `private`. For the `PublicPostingBean` it was set to `public`. The `onMessage` method then received and processed the message.

The `PrivatePostingBean` used the same approach for messages marked as `private`. Like the `PublicPostingBean`, the `PostingType` setting restricted the message that the MDB received.

Browsing messages in a message queue

The JMS queue can contain a number of messages that have not been processed. It is possible to use the `QueueBrowser` class to examine the contents of a queue. This recipe will build upon the `MessageSelectorApplication` to illustrate how the `QueueBrowser` is used.

Getting ready

We will reuse the `MessageSelectorApplication` as found in the *Specifying which types of messages to receive using the message selector* recipe.

How to do it...

In the `MessageSelectorApplication`, modify the `PostingServlet` to send a "protected" message and to incorporate the `QueueBrowser` as shown below:

```java
public class PostingServlet extends HttpServlet {
  @Resource(mappedName="jms/PostingsQueueFactory")
  private QueueConnectionFactory queueConnectionFactory;
  @Resource(mappedName="jms/PostingsQueue")
  private Queue queue;

  protected void processRequest(HttpServletRequest request,
    HttpServletResponse response)
    throws ServletException, IOException {
    response.setContentType("text/html;charset=UTF-8");
    PrintWriter out = response.getWriter();
    try {
      Connection connection;

      try {
        connection = queueConnectionFactory.createConnection();
        Session session = connection.createSession(false,
          Session.AUTO_ACKNOWLEDGE);
        MessageProducer messageProducer = (MessageProducer)
          session.createProducer(queue);
        TextMessage textMessage = session.createTextMessage();

        textMessage.setText("For your eyes only");
```

```java
        textMessage.setStringProperty("PostingType", "private");
        messageProducer.send(textMessage);
        System.out.println("---> Public textMessage sent");

        textMessage.setText("Distribute freely");
        textMessage.setStringProperty("PostingType", "public");
        messageProducer.send(textMessage);
        System.out.println("--->Private textMessage sent");

        // Used by Browsing Messages in a Message Queue recipe
        textMessage.setText("Distribute in house only");
        textMessage.setStringProperty("PostingType", "protected");
        messageProducer.send(textMessage);

        QueueBrowser queueBrowser = session.createBrowser(queue);
        Enumeration messages = queueBrowser.getEnumeration();
        while(messages.hasMoreElements()) {
          TextMessage message = (TextMessage) messages.nextElement();
          System.out.println("Message: " + message.getText());
        }

    } catch (JMSException ex) {
        Logger.getLogger(PostingServlet.class.getName()).
          log(Level.SEVERE, null, ex);
    }

    out.println("<html>");
    out.println("<head>");
    out.println("<title>Servlet PostingServlet</title>");
    out.println("</head>");
    out.println("<body>");
    out.println("<h1>Servlet PostingServlet at " +
      request.getContextPath () + "</h1>");
    out.println("</body>");
    out.println("</html>");

  } finally {
      out.close();
    }
}
```

Execute the `PostingServlet`. Repeated execution of the servlet will result in a number of protected messages being sent to the queue as shown below. They will remain in the queue until they expire.

INFO: Message: Distribute in house only

INFO: Message: Distribute in house only

INFO: Message: Distribute in house only

INFO: Message: Distribute in house only

INFO: Message: Distribute in house only

INFO: Message: Distribute in house only

INFO: Message: Distribute in house only

How it works...

Code was added to send a "Distribute in house only" message to the queue so the `QueueBrowser` has something to display. Since there are no MDBs to process this type of message, they will sit there. The `QueueBrowser` object was obtained using the `Session` object's `createBrowser` method. The `getEnumeration` method returns a `java.util.Enumeration` object. This object was then used to list or otherwise process the messages in the queue.

There's more...

The `createBrowser` method also accepts a second argument specifying a message selector. The message selector will narrow down the messages returned by the `QueueBrowser`.

Messages will stay in a queue indefinitely. However, if the useful lifetime of a message is limited, the `MessageProducer` object's `setTimeToLive` method takes a long argument to specify when the message will expire. In addition, the overloaded `send` method has a version that specifies the expiration time.

```
producer.send(message, DeliveryMode.NON_PERSISTENT, 3, 10000);
```

The second argument specifies the delivery mode. The third specifies the message's priority and the last argument is the timeout.

4
EJB Persistence

In this chapter, we will cover:

- ▶ Creating an entity
- ▶ Creating an entity facade
- ▶ Using the EntityManager
- ▶ Controlling the Object-Relationship Mapping (ORM) process
- ▶ Using embeddable classes in entities
- ▶ Using application-managed persistence
- ▶ Validating persistent fields and properties
- ▶ Validating null fields
- ▶ Validating string fields
- ▶ Validating temporal fields
- ▶ Validation using regular expressions
- ▶ Validating Boolean fields
- ▶ Validating Integer fields
- ▶ Using the Validator class

Introduction

Most applications have a need to store and retrieve data. The data may be stored in a file or other location such as a database. This location is sometimes referred to as the backing store. This need is also present for object-oriented applications. The Java class provides a convenient unit for organizing data and is a natural place to start when saving and retrieving data. There are technologies that persist data in the form of an object to a data store. For us, the **Java Persistence API (JPA)** provides the underlying mechanism in support of this approach. JPA usage is not restricted to EJBs but can be used in other Java applications including SE applications.

An entity is a class representing data persisted to a backing store using JPA. The **@Entity** annotation designates a class as an entity. It can also be declared in an `orm.xml` file. In addition to the **@Entity** annotation, there is a series of annotations to further define and tie the class to a backing store. In general, and for our purposes, we will assume the data store will be a relational database. While entity classes are quite useful, they are sometimes hidden behind a facade to facilitate their use. The *Creating an entity facade* recipe illustrates the use of facades.

To actually use the entity with the backing store, a persistence unit, persistence context, and an `EntityManager` is needed. The persistence unit defines mapping between the entity and the data store. A persistence context is a set of entities. Each entity within the set is unique. The persistence context keeps track of the state and changes made to its entities. When an `EntityManager` is created it is associated with a persistence context. The `EntityManager` manages the entities and their interaction with the data store. The use of the `EntityManager` to persist the entity is covered in the *Using the EntityManager* recipe.

Object-Relationship Mapping (ORM) is the process of mapping an object to a database. Most servers, in conjunction with IDEs, provide means of performing this mapping automatically. However, there exist a number of annotations that can provide more information to guide the mapping.

The *Creating an entity* recipe details how to declare an entity. The actual relationship between an entity and the database is explained in the *Controlling the Object-Relationship Mapping (ORM) process* recipe. When one class is used as a field of a second class, this relationship is referred to as composition. This relationship is supported using embeddable classes and is discussed in the *Using embeddable classes in entities* recipe.

Normally, persistence is accomplished using what is known as container-managed persistence. In certain circumstances it can be desirable to allow the application to exercise more control over the persistence process. This technique is addressed in the *Using application-managed persistence* recipe.

An important issue in most applications is the validation of the data. Before data is saved to a database, it is usually a good idea to ensure its correctness and conformity to any rules governing its values. The Java API for JavaBean Validation API provides a way of validating fields of a class. As with the JPA API, the use of the JavaBean Validation API is not restricted to JBs. The use of this validation technique for entities is covered in the *Validating persistent fields and properties* recipe.

Creating an entity

The creation of a simple entity is not difficult and is accomplished using the **@Entity** annotation. The essence of the process is demonstrated here and elaborated upon in subsequent recipes.

Getting ready

The creation of an entity involves two steps:

1. Annotating a class with the **@Entity** annotation
2. Adding methods to provide access to the fields of the entity

An entity is frequently added using a wizard provided by an IDE. This frequently involves specifying a primary key and the creation of a persistence unit. The primary key is used to optimize access to the underlying database table and the persistence unit provides mapping from the entity to the underlying data store.

How to do it...

Create a Java EE application called `EntityBeanApplication`. In the EJB module, add a package called `packt` with an entity called `PartsBean`. While we will use the EJB module, EJB components do not have to be packaged in the EJB jar but can now be packaged as part of the WAR file in EJB 3.1.

The `PartsBean` is intended to represent a part. The initial version of the class has fields for:

- `name` – The part's name
- `partNumber` – A part number
- `weight` – The weight of a part
- `quantity` – The quantity on hand

The first step is to declare the class an entity using the **@Entity** annotation. If an entity is passed by value then it must implement the `Serializable` interface. We implement the interface here in case we need to pass the entity later.

```java
@Entity
public class PartsBean implements Serializable {
  @Id
  @GeneratedValue(strategy = GenerationType.AUTO)
  private Long id;

  public Long getId() {
    return id;
  }
  private String name;
  private int partNumber;
  private float weight;
  private int quantity;

  public String getName() {
    return name;
  }

  public void setName(String name) {
    this.name = name;
  }

  public int getPartNumber() {
    return partNumber;
  }

  public void setPartNumber(int partNumber) {
    this.partNumber = partNumber;
  }

  public int getQuantity() {
    return quantity;
  }

  public void setQuantity(int quantity) {
    this.quantity = quantity;
  }

  public float getWeight() {
    return weight;
  }
}
```

```
    public void setWeight(float weight) {
      this.weight = weight;
    }

  }
```

How it works...

Each entity has a unique key used to identify it. For the `PartsBean` we used a long value called `id`. The **@Id** annotation identified the field as a primary key. The use of the **@GeneratedValue** field with the strategy of **GeneratationType.AUTO**, means the key will be generated automatically. A get method was provided for the field. We cannot change the primary key so we did not provide a set method for it.

Since the `id` field was auto-generated, when an entity is created the value assigned may differ from what is shown in the examples in this chapter. The number provided depends on the actual generator and the number of entities of that type created.

There's more...

The class developed so far represents a minimal entity. However, there are other methods proven to be useful for an entity. Two commonly provided methods include: `equals` and `toString`. Both of these methods override the base class object.

The `equals` method is used to compare the equality of two entities. It first determines whether the object it is being compared to is an actual `PartsBean`. If so, it verifies that the `id` fields are the same.

```
    @Override
    public boolean equals(Object object) {
      if (!(object instanceof PartsBean)) {
        return false;
      }
      PartsBean other = (PartsBean) object;
      if ((this.id == null && other.id != null) || (this.id != null &&
        !this.id.equals(other.id))) {
        return false;
      }
      return true;
    }
```

The implementation of this `toString` method returns a String containing the `id` of the `PartsBean`.

```
@Override
public String toString() {
    return "packt.PartsBean[id=" + id + "]";
}
```

See also

The next recipe illustrates the persistence of the `PartsBean`.

Creating an entity facade

A building facade is a false front to a building. Movie sets frequently use facades to give the appearance of an actual building avoiding the cost of a real building. In programming, a facade is an object which provides an interface to another class to make the hidden class easier to use or reduce dependencies among classes.

Getting ready

We will build upon the `EntityBeanApplication` application from the previous recipe. We will be adding to the EJB module two new classes to the `packt` package: `AbstractFacade` and `PartsBeanFacade`.

An entity facade is commonly used to hide the entity class. A typical approach is to create a base class encapsulating much of the common functionality of an entity and then extend this class with one providing specific entity support. For example, NetBeans provides a wizard which creates an abstract class possessing a number of useful methods:

- ▶ `getEntityManager` – Returns a reference to the `EntityManager` for the persistence unit containing the entity
- ▶ `create` – Persists an object
- ▶ `edit` – Modifies an existing entry in the database
- ▶ `remove` – Removes an entry from the database
- ▶ `find` – Finds a specific entry
- ▶ `findAll` – Returns a **List** of all entries
- ▶ `findRange` – Returns a **List** of entries within a specified range

How to do it...

First, create an abstract `AbstractFacade` class to support the basic persistence methods listed previously.

```
package packt;

import java.util.List;
import javax.persistence.EntityManager;

public abstract class AbstractFacade<T> {
  private Class<T> entityClass;

  public AbstractFacade(Class<T> entityClass) {
    this.entityClass = entityClass;
  }

  protected abstract EntityManager getEntityManager();

  public void create(T entity) {
    getEntityManager().persist(entity);
  }

  public void edit(T entity) {
    getEntityManager().merge(entity);
  }

  public void remove(T entity) {
    getEntityManager().remove(getEntityManager().merge(entity));
  }

  public T find(Object id) {
    return getEntityManager().find(entityClass, id);
  }

  public List<T> findAll() {
    javax.persistence.criteria.CriteriaQuery cq =
      getEntityManager().getCriteriaBuilder().createQuery();
    cq.select(cq.from(entityClass));
    return getEntityManager().createQuery(cq).getResultList();
  }

  public List<T> findRange(int[] range) {
```

```
        javax.persistence.criteria.CriteriaQuery cq =
          getEntityManager().getCriteriaBuilder().createQuery();
        cq.select(cq.from(entityClass));
        javax.persistence.Query q = getEntityManager().createQuery(cq);
        q.setMaxResults(range[1] - range[0]);
        q.setFirstResult(range[0]);
        return q.getResultList();
      }

    public int count() {
        javax.persistence.criteria.CriteriaQuery cq =
          getEntityManager().getCriteriaBuilder().createQuery();
        javax.persistence.criteria.Root<T> rt = cq.from(entityClass);
        cq.select(getEntityManager().getCriteriaBuilder().count(rt));
        javax.persistence.Query q = getEntityManager().createQuery(cq);
        return ((Long) q.getSingleResult()).intValue();
      }


    }
```

Next, create the `PartsBeanFacade` class and extend the `AbstractFacade` class. To associate this class with an underlying database, use the **@PersistenceContext** annotation. Notice in its default constructor the `PartsBean` class is specified as the entity class to be managed.

Most IDEs provide a means of creating the persistence unit when a facade type class is used. In NetBeans, the wizard used to create an entity provides the option to create a persistence unit in the first step. In the second step, a name is automatically generated but can be changed. Also the persistence provided and data source can be selected. If you are using NetBeans accept the default persistence provider and use **jdbc/__default** as the data source.

```
    package packt;

    import javax.ejb.Stateless;
    import javax.persistence.EntityManager;
    import javax.persistence.PersistenceContext;

    @Stateless
    public class PartsBeanFacade extends AbstractFacade<PartsBean> {
      @PersistenceContext(unitName = "EntityBeanApplication-ejbPU")
      private EntityManager em;

      protected EntityManager getEntityManager() {
        return em;
      }
```

```
    public PartsBeanFacade() {
        super(PartsBean.class);
    }

}
```

How it works...

The `AbstractFacade` class uses several base `EntityManager` methods in support of the entity. Most of these are straightforward mapping of an `EntityManager` method to an `AbstractFacade` method. However, for the `create` method the `EntityManager` class method `persist` was used and `merge` was used for `edit`.

The `AbstractFacade` class is a generic class capable of being used with a number of different entities. A specific entity is assigned and retrieved using the `AbstractFacade`'s constructor and its `getEntityManager` method. Notice that this method is abstract in `AbstractFacade` and was implemented in `PartsBeanFacade`.

The `AbstractFacade` class's `findAll`, `findRange`, and `count` methods do not map directly to an `EntityManager` method. Instead, they provide additional capabilities often needed by an entity.

All of these methods use `CriteriaQuery` interface methods to return either a list of entities or a count of the number of entities available. This interface is discussed in more detail in *Chapter 5, Querying Entities using JPQL and the Criteria API*.

The `PartsBeanFacade` class associated the `PartsBean` with a persistence unit using the **@PersistenceContext**. This annotation injected the entity manager for the persistence unit. It used the attribute, `unitName`, to specify the name of the persistence unit.

The `PartsBeanFacade` class overrode one method, `getEntityManager`. This method returned a reference to the `EntityManager` used with the `PartsBean`.

See also

The *Using the EntityManager* recipe illustrates the use of these facade classes.

Using the EntityManager

The entity is used in conjunction with an `EntityManager` to persist and otherwise ensure the state of the entity is consistent with the database. In this recipe we will examine the use of the `PartsBeanFacade` class.

Getting ready

To use the entity in a client we need to:

1. Inject the session facade EJB into the client
2. Use the methods of the facade

We will build upon the `EntityBeanApplication` application developed in the first recipe.

How to do it...

Add a package called `servlet` and a servlet called `PartsServlet` to the WAR module. The `PartsBeanFacade` class extends the `AbstractFacade` class as developed in the *Creating an entity facade* recipe. It is associated with a persistence unit through the use of the **@PersistenceContext** annotation. We will use this as a part of a servlet to manage the underlying `PartsBean`.

Within the `PartsServlet` servlet we will use two instances of the `PartsBean` and a single instance of the `PartsBeanFacade` to manage instances of the entity.

```
public class PartsServlet extends HttpServlet {

    @EJB
    PartsBeanFacade partsFacade;

    PartsBean parts;
    PartsBean otherParts;
```

Add a `processRequest` method to create a `PartsBean` and use the `PartsBeanFacade` class method to persist the entity. The servlet's `doGet` and `doPost` methods are not shown here.

```
protected void processRequest(HttpServletRequest request,
    HttpServletResponse response)
    throws ServletException, IOException {
        response.setContentType("text/html;charset=UTF-8");
        PrintWriter out = response.getWriter();
        try {

            parts = new PartsBean();
            parts.setName("Traverse Gear");
            parts.setPartNumber(12345);
            parts.setWeight(2.54f);
            parts.setQuantity(2);
```

```java
            partsFacade.create(parts);

            parts = new PartsBean();
            parts.setName("Differential Axle");
            parts.setPartNumber(90334);
            parts.setWeight(12.35f);
            parts.setQuantity(1);

            partsFacade.create(parts);

            otherParts = partsFacade.find(parts.getId());

            out.println("<html>");
            out.println("<head>");
            out.println("<title>Servlet PartsServlet</title>");
            out.println("</head>");
            out.println("<body>");
            out.println("<h1>Servlet PartsServlet at " +
              otherParts.getName() +
              " id: " + otherParts.getId()+ "</h1>");
            out.println("</body>");
            out.println("</html>");

        } finally {
            out.close();
        }
    }
```

Execute the `PartsServlet` using the URL shown in the following screenshot:

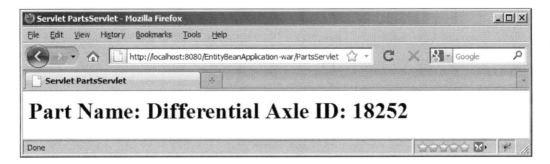

How it works...

The PartsBeanFacade was injected using the **@EJB** annotation. Notice since the PartsBeanFacade did not implement an interface we used the no-interface client view which is new in EJB 3.1.

Two PartsBean reference variables were declared: parts and otherParts. The parts variable was used to create two PartsBean and assign values to its fields. The PartsFacade class's create method was used to persist the two entities.

To verify a part had actually been created in the database, the find method retrieved the last part created and displayed its name and ID using otherParts.

There's more...

There is a lot that's going on in this servlet. When we use the create method, JPA is using the PartsBean we created and persisting it to some data store. In this case, it is persisted to a database (Derby if you are using NetBeans) represented by persistence unit EntityBeanApplication-ejbPU we created in the *Creating an entity facade* recipe. A table within the database representing the entity was updated using a **Java DataBase Connectivity (JDBC)** driver.

Controlling the Object-Relationship Mapping (ORM) process

Object-Relationship Mapping (ORM) is concerned with persisting an object to a database. There exist a number of annotations which provide information to guide the mapping process. The uses of these annotations are illustrated in this recipe.

Getting ready

When we persist an entity it is sometimes desirable to exercise more control over which table in a database should be used. In addition, we may want to specify the field names to use within the table. ORM allows us to control these factors by using the **@Table** and **@Column** annotations. The use of these annotations will be demonstrated by expanding upon the previous recipe and augmenting the EntityBeanApplication application.

How to do it...

The PartsBean developed so far provides little guidance in terms of which database table to use or how the fields of the object are mapped to columns of a table. The first thing we will look at is how to specify the database to be used for the PartsBean.

This database is specified in the `persistence.xml` file which we created using an IDE wizard in the *Creating an Entity Facade* recipe. This file is found in the EJB module and should appear as shown below. The presentence unit `EntityBeanApplication-ejbPU` is declared as and is associated with the database `jdbc/__default`.

```xml
<?xml version="1.0" encoding="UTF-8"?>
<persistence version="2.0" xmlns="http://java.sun.com/xml/ns/
persistence" xmlns:xsi="http://www.w3.org/2001/XMLSchema-instance"
xsi:schemaLocation="http://java.sun.com/xml/ns/persistence http://
java.sun.com/xml/ns/persistence/persistence_2_0.xsd">
  <persistence-unit name="EntityBeanApplication-ejbPU"
    transaction-type="JTA">
    <provider>org.eclipse.persistence.jpa.PersistenceProvider
      </provider>
    <jta-data-source>jdbc/__default</jta-data-source>
    <properties>
      <property name="eclipselink.ddl-generation"
        value="create-tables"/>
    </properties>
  </persistence-unit>
</persistence>
```

Having specified the database, we will probably want to specify the table to use. If we don't explicitly choose a table, one is automatically provided by the server. To specify the table we use the **@Table** annotation. We could have also modified the `orm.xml` file to achieve the same effect. Modify the `PartsBean` to add the **@Table** annotation. The **name** attribute of the annotation specifies the database table to use.

```java
@Entity
@Table(name="PARTS")
public class PartsBean implements Serializable {
```

Next, add a series of **@Column** annotations to the entity as shown here:

```java
@Column(name="NAME")
private String name;

@Column(name="PARTNUMBER")
private int partNumber;

@Column(name="WEIGHT")
private float weight;

@Column(name="QUANTITY")
private int quantity;
```

The persistence of the `PartsBean` is performed as illustrated in the *Using the EntityManager* recipe. The use of these annotations does not require modification of the `PartsServlet`.

How it works...

Notice for the `EntityBeanApplication`, the source was specified in the `<jta-data-source>` element. The value, `jdbc/__default`, specified the database to use. The available databases are a function of the Java EE server and its configuration. This application was developed using Glassfish. The `jdbc/__default` database was one of the available options. Using a different server or adding a different data store to a server will provide you with other options. Also, note that the database table's catalog and schema can also be specified using the **catalog** and **schema** elements.

Specific fields of an entity are mapped to columns of a table using the **@Column** annotation. The **name** element of the annotation determines the name to be used for the table column. In this example we used the same name as the field and in all caps. However, you can always use fields and naming conventions appropriate for your application.

There's more...

There are other elements of the **@Column** annotation which control the configuration of a column including but not limited to:

- **unique** – Specifies whether the column represents a unique key
- **nullable** – The column can or cannot hold a null value
- **length** - The length of a string column
- **precision** – The precision of a decimal column

We will not discuss these options here.

So far the fields of the `PartsBean` have been simple Java primitives or the `String` class. If we need to use a collection, such as a `Map` or `Set` of basic types, then the **@ElementCollection** annotation can be used.

To illustrate this annotation, add an enumeration called `ColorEnumeration` to the class. Next, declare a `Set` of this type called `colors`. This field is intended to allow us to specify the available part's colors. Also add a get and set method for `colors`.

```
public enum ColorEnumeration {RED, GREEN, BLUE}
@ElementCollection
private Set<ColorEnumeration> colors;

public Set<ColorEnumeration> getColors() {
  return colors;
}

public void setColors(Set<ColorEnumeration> colors) {
  this.colors = colors;
}
```

The **@ElementCollection** annotation has two attributes: `targetClass` used with collections of basic or embeddable classes; and `fetch` which specifies either a **LAZY** or **EAGER** retrieval of the field. The `fetch` attribute controls when the field is retrieved. With a lazy retrieval, the value for the field is not retrieved until it is needed. An eager fetch will retrieve the value immediately. If a generic class is used, as was the case with the set of colors above, the `targetClass` attribute is not required.

Modify the `PartsServlet` to create a set of objects and then populate the set with various colors.

```
parts = new PartsBean();
...
HashSet<PartsBean.ColorEnumeration> colors = new
  HashSet<PartsBean.ColorEnumeration>();
colors.add(PartsBean.ColorEnumeration.RED);
colors.add(PartsBean.ColorEnumeration.BLUE);
parts.setColors(colors);
partsFacade.create(parts);
```

See also

The *Using the EntityManager* recipe illustrates the complete process to persist a `PartsBean`.

Using embeddable classes in entities

A common relationship between classes is composition. One class may declare and use another class as a field to support some common functionality. For example, the `PartsBean` may have a need to maintain the location of the part using some sort of bin location scheme. This scheme may also be used for classes other than a part. This need is addressed for entities using the **@Embeddable** and **@Embedded** annotations.

Getting ready

The steps to embed a class within another class involves:

1. Designating the class that can be embedded with the **@Embeddable** annotation
2. Embedding the embeddable class into the other class using the **@Embedded** annotation

We will expand upon the previous recipe and augment the `EntityBeanApplication` application.

How to do it...

The **@Embeddable** annotation is used to declare a class which can be embedded within
another class. Add the `BinLocation` class to the `EntityBeanApplication` application
as part of the `packt` package. This class possesses `aisle` and `level` fields to specify the
location of an item. Add get and set methods for these fields.

```
@Embeddable
public class BinLocation implements Serializable {
    private int aisle;
    private int level;

    public int getAisle() {
        return aisle;
    }

    public void setAisle(int aisle) {
        this.aisle = aisle;
    }

    public int getLevel() {
        return level;
    }

    public void setLevel(int level) {
        this.level = level;
    }

}
```

The next step is to embed the `BinLocation` class into the `PartsBean`. The
@Embedded annotation designates a class as one which will be included in the class.
Modify the `PartsBean` class by adding a reference variable to this class using the
@Embedded annotation.

```
@Embedded
BinLocation binLocation;
```

Add get and set methods to allow modification of the bin location. We could have also added
individual methods for the aisle and level.

```
public BinLocation getBinLocation() {
    return binLocation;
}

public void setBinLocation(BinLocation binLocation) {
    this.binLocation = binLocation;
}
```

Modify the `PartsServlet` to create and use a new `BinLocation` object as follows:

```
parts = new PartsBean();
...
BinLocation binLocation = new BinLocation();
binLocation.setAisle(12);
binLocation.setLevel(3);
parts.setBinLocation(binLocation);
partsFacade.create(parts);
```

How it works...

The `BinLocation` class is simple. In order to use it in the `PartsBean` we used the **@Embedded** annotation. However, to make this object available to users of `PartsBean` we had to add the `getBinLocation` and `setBinLocation` methods to the entity. In the `PartsServlet`, we created a new `BinLocation` object and set aisle and level values for a part. The `setBinLocation` method was used to associate the `BinLocation` object with the `PartsBean` instance.

See also

The *Using the EntityManager* recipe illustrates the complete process to persist a `PartsBean`.

Using application-managed persistence

Application-managed persistence is useful when special handling of persistence is required such as the explicit management of an `EntityManager` life cycle or more explicit control over **Java Transaction API (JTA)** transactions is needed. Application-managed persistence is the focus of this recipe.

Getting ready

The essential process for using application-managed persistence involves:

1. Injecting an `EntityManagerFactory` to provide a means to create an `EntityManager`
2. Creating the `EntityManager` to control the persistence process
3. Using the `EntityManager` method to manage the entity

How to do it...

Create a new Java EE application called `ApplicationManagedPersistenceApplication`. In this application we will only use the WAR module. Add a `packt` package and a `servlet` package to the module. Add a `RegistrationBean` to the `packt` package and a `RegistrationServlet` to the servlet package.

We will use a `RegistrationBean` to illustrate application-managed persistence. This entity represents a registration for some event and includes fields for:

- `name` – The name of the participant
- `company` – The name of the participant's company
- `session` – An integer representing the session to be attended

Add the `RegistrationBean` along with an `id` field and getters and setters.

```java
@Entity
public class RegistrationBean implements Serializable {
  private String name;
  private String company;
  private int session;

  public String getCompany() {
    return company;
  }

  public void setCompany(String company) {
    this.company = company;
  }

  public String getName() {
    return name;
  }

  public void setName(String name) {
    this.name = name;
  }

  public int getSession() {
    return session;
  }

  public void setSession(int session) {
    this.session = session;
```

```
    }


    private static final long serialVersionUID = 1L;
    @Id
    @GeneratedValue(strategy = GenerationType.AUTO)
    private Long id;

    public Long getId() {
      return id;
    }

...
  }
```

Next add the `RegistrationServlet` as shown below. The `doGet` and `doPost` methods are not shown.

```
public class RegistrationServlet extends HttpServlet {

  @PersistenceUnit(unitName =
    "ApplicationManagedPersistenceApplication-warPU")
  EntityManagerFactory entityManagerFactory;

  protected void processRequest(HttpServletRequest request,
    HttpServletResponse response)
    throws ServletException, IOException {
      RegistrationBean registration;
      RegistrationBean secondRegistration;
      EntityManager entityManager;

      response.setContentType("text/html;charset=UTF-8");
      PrintWriter out = response.getWriter();
      try {
        try {

          registration = new RegistrationBean();
          registration.setName("Steve Best");
          registration.setCompany("Grey Beard Software");
          registration.setSession(10);

          entityManager = entityManagerFactory.createEntityManager();
          entityManager.persist(registration);

          secondRegistration = entityManager.find(
```

```
                    RegistrationBean.class, registration.getId());
                out.println("<html>");
                out.println("<head>");
                out.println("<title>Servlet RegistrationServlet</title>");
                out.println("</head>");
                out.println("<body>");
                out.println("<h1>" + secondRegistration.getName()
                    + " ID: " + secondRegistration.getId()+ "</h1>");
                out.println("</body>");
                out.println("</html>");
                entityManager.close();

            } catch (SecurityException ex) {
                Logger.getLogger(RegistrationServlet.class.getName()).
                    log(Level.SEVERE, null, ex);
                } catch (IllegalStateException ex) {
                    Logger.getLogger(RegistrationServlet.class.getName()).
                        log(Level.SEVERE, null, ex);
                }

        } finally {
            out.close();
        }
    }
}
```

Next, execute the application using the URL shown in the following screenshot:

How it works...

The RegistrationServlet began with the insertion of the EntityManagerFactory object as a persistence unit. Since we are executing as a client, an EntityManagerFactory is needed to create the EntityManager.

In this example, two `RegistrationBeans` variables were defined: `registration` and `secondRegistration`. Next, a `RegistrationBean` was created and its fields were assigned values for a name, company, and a session. The `EntityManagerFactory` class's `createEntityManager` method created an instance of an `EntityManager`. The `EntityManager` was used to persist the `RegistrationBean`.

In order to verify the entity was actually saved, `secondRegistration` was used to hold a reference to the entity retrieved from the table. The `secondRegistration` variable's `name` and `id` fields were then displayed. The `close` method was used to close the `EntityManager` as it was not longer needed. This is a good practice as it helps free up database connections.

There's more...

With application-managed persistence, the management of transactions is delegated to the application. In this example we did not use transactions. However, this topic is addressed in *Chapter 6, Transaction Processing*.

Validating persistent fields and properties

The integrity of most, if not all, applications depend on the correctness of its data. The Java API for JavaBeans Validation provides a means to validate data through the use of annotations.

This recipe explains this technique by introducing a driver's license entity. The next set of recipes illustrates how to specify constraints on several different types of fields. The last recipe pulls these techniques together and illustrates the use of the `javax.validation.Validator` class to determine if the constraints were met.

Getting ready

First we will create an entity representing a driver's license and its supporting classes. Once this is working we will enhance the entity to incorporate validation annotations.

How to do it...

Create a Java EE application named `ValidationApplication`. In the EJB module add a package called `packt` and an entity called `LicenseBean`. In addition, add an `AbstractFacade` and `LicenseBeanFacade` as illustrated in the *Creating an Entity Facade* recipe. In the WAR module add a package called `servlet`. To this package add a servlet called `LicenseServlet`.

Create an entity representing a driver's license called `LicenseBean`. Its attributes include:

- ▸ `name` – The name of the driver
- ▸ `dateOfBirth` – The birth date (`java.util.Date`)
- ▸ `restrictions` – A field to hold any restrictions
- ▸ `monthsToExpire` – The duration of the license in months

We will use these fields to demonstrate how validation can be performed.

```
@Entity
public class LicenseBean implements Serializable {

  private String name;
  @Temporal(javax.persistence.TemporalType.DATE)
  private Date dateOfBirth;
  private String restrictions;
  private int monthsToExpire;

  public Date getDateOfBirth() {
    return dateOfBirth;
  }

  public void setDateOfBirth(Date dateOfBirth) {
    this.dateOfBirth = dateOfBirth;
  }

  public int getMonthsToExpire() {
    return monthsToExpire;
  }

  public void setMonthsToExpire(int monthsToExpire) {
    this.monthsToExpire = monthsToExpire;
  }

  public String getName() {
    return name;
  }

  public void setName(String name) {
    this.name = name;
  }

  public boolean isResident() {
    return resident;
```

```
  }

  public void setResident(boolean resident) {
    this.resident = resident;
  }
  public String getRestrictions() {
    return restrictions;
  }

  public void setRestrictions(String restrictions) {
    this.restrictions = restrictions;
  }

  private static final long serialVersionUID = 1L;
  @Id
  @GeneratedValue(strategy = GenerationType.AUTO)
  private Long id;

  public Long getId() {
    return id;
  }

  ...

}
```

We will use the AbstractFacade class developed in the *Creating an entity facade* recipe and derive the LicenseBeanFacade class from it.

```
@Stateless
public class LicenseBeanFacade extends AbstractFacade<LicenseBean> {
  @PersistenceContext(unitName = "ValidationApplication-ejbPU")
  private EntityManager em;

  protected EntityManager getEntityManager() {
    return em;
  }

  public LicenseBeanFacade() {
    super(LicenseBean.class);
  }

}
```

The `LicenseServlet` demonstrates the use of these classes.

```java
public class LicenseServlet extends HttpServlet {

    @EJB
    LicenseBeanFacade licenseBeanFacade;


    LicenseBean license;

    protected void processRequest(HttpServletRequest request,
      HttpServletResponse response)
      throws ServletException, IOException {
        response.setContentType("text/html;charset=UTF-8");
        PrintWriter out = response.getWriter();
        try {
          license = new LicenseBean();
          license.setName("Pax Maxwell");
          Calendar calendar = Calendar.getInstance();
          calendar.set(1981, 4, 18);
          license.setDateOfBirth(calendar.getTime());
          license.setMonthsToExpire(24);
          license.setResident(true);
          license.setRestrictions("C6");

          licenseBeanFacade.create(license);

          out.println("<html>");
          out.println("<head>");
          out.println("<title>Servlet LicenseServlet</title>");
          out.println("</head>");
          out.println("<body>");
          out.println("<h1>Name: " +license.getName() + " -
            License ID: "  + license.getId() + "</h1>");
          out.println("</body>");
          out.println("</html>");

        } finally {
            out.close();
        }
    }
```

Execute the application using the URL shown in the following screenshot:

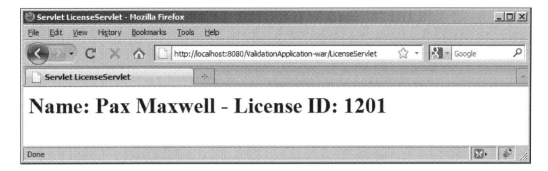

How it works...

This recipe sets up the `LicenseBean` and `LicenseServlet` for use in this chapter's remaining recipes. The `LicenseBean` maintains information regarding a license. Notice the use of the **@Temporal** annotation in the `LicenseBean`. When a time-based field, such as the `java.util.Date` class is used, this annotation is required.

In the `LicenseServlet`, a license was created and then persisted using the `LicenseBeanFacade` instance. In later recipes we will modify the `LicenseBean` and `LicenseServlet` to demonstrate various validation techniques.

See also

The remaining recipes build upon this entity and illustrate various validation techniques.

Validating null fields

Object references are used extensively in Java. Assigning a null value is not an uncommon practice though they need to be assigned a value before a method can be executed against it. Fields of a database may or may not be allowed to contain a null value. The **@Null** and **@NotNull** annotations can be used to indicate whether a reference field can be assigned a null value or not.

Getting ready

We will use the `LicenseBean` and `LicenseBeanFacade` classes from the `ValidationApplication` as discussed in the *Validating persistent fields and properties* recipe.

How to do it...

If we want to prevent a column of a database from being assigned a value of null, then we can enforce this with the **@NotNull** annotation.

```
@NotNull
private String name;
```

If the field must contain a null, then the **@Null** annotation is used.

```
@Null
private String name;
```

How it works...

These annotations are used to control the assignment of null values to fields. The `Validator` class is used in conjunction with these annotations to detect and handle violations. This technique is illustrated in the *Using the Validator class* recipe

See also

The *Using the Validator class* recipe illustrates the use of this annotation.

Validating string fields

Strings are used extensively in many Java applications. When strings are persisted to a database, the database column may be restricted in size. The entity can use annotations to enforce a size constraint of these fields.

Getting ready

We will use the `LicenseBean` and `LicenseBeanFacade` classes from the `ValidationApplication` as discussed in the *Validating persistent fields and properties* recipe.

How to do it...

We can specify the size of a **String** using the **@Size** annotation. This annotation has a `min` and a `max` attribute. The `min` attribute specifies the minimum length allowed while the `max` attribute specifies the upper bound on the length of the string. Here we specify a minimum length of 12 characters and a maximum length of 36 characters for the string field name.

```
@Size(min=12, max=36)
private String name;
```

The `min` and `max` attributes can be used together or by themselves. Here, only the minimum length is specified. There is no upper bound on the length of the string.

```
@Size(min=12)
private String name;
```

Using only the **max** attribute indicates an upper bound. The string can have a zero length.

```
@Size(max=36)
private String name;
```

The **@Size** annotation can also be used with the **@Null** or **@NotNull** annotations.

```
@Size(min=12, max=36)
@NotNull
private String name;
```

How it works...

By assigning a value to the `min` or `max` fields, these annotations are used to control the assignment the number of characters assigned to a `String` field. The `Validator` class is used in conjunction with these annotations to detect and handle violations. This technique is illustrated in the *Using the Validator class* recipe

See also

The *Using the Validator class* recipe illustrates the use of this annotation.

Validating temporal fields

The `java.util.Date` and `java.util.Calendar` classes can be used to represent time in Java. If these classes are used for fields of an entity, the **@Temporal** annotation needs to be used. In addition, the **@Future** or **@Past** annotations are used to specify constraints on the relationship of the assigned date to the current time.

Getting ready

We will use the `LicenseBean` and `LicenseBeanFacade` classes from the `ValidationApplication` as discussed in the *Validating persistent fields and properties* recipe.

The **@Temporal** annotation designates a field as a time unit. JPA permits three basic mappings:

- **TemporalType.DATE** – `java.util.Date`
- **TemporalType.CALENDAR** – `java.util.Calendar`
- **TemporalType.TIMESTAMP** – `java.sql.Timestamp`

How to do it...

This annotation is used to annotate a `Date` or `Calendar` field as temporal data for a database column.

```
@Temporal(javax.persistence.TemporalType.DATE)
private Date dateOfBirth;
```

The **@Temporal** annotation can be used in conjunction with the **@Future** or **@Past** annotations to establish a constraint on the value of a field. The **@Future** requires the value of the field to be in the future. The use of the **@Past** requires the value of the field to be in the past which is expected for a field such as a birth date.

```
@Past
@Temporal(javax.persistence.TemporalType.DATE)
private Date dateOfBirth;
```

Below, we use the **@Future** annotation with the `dateOfBirth` field. While we would normally use the **@Past** annotation for this type of field, we will use it to illustrate a temporal constraint violation in the *Using Validator class* recipe.

```
@Future
@Temporal(javax.persistence.TemporalType.DATE)
private Date dateOfBirth;
```

How it works...

These annotations are used to control the assignment of temporal values to time-based fields. The `javax.validation.Validator` class is used in conjunction with these annotations to detect and handle violations. This technique is illustrated in the *Using the Validator class* recipe.

See also

The *Using the Validator class* recipe illustrates the use of this annotation.

Validating using regular expressions

Regular expressions provide a powerful technique for validating fields. Phone numbers and Zip codes can be easily verified using regular expressions. The **@Pattern** annotation allows us to use a regular expression to verify the correct usage of these types of fields.

Getting ready

We will use the `LicenseBean` and `LicenseBeanFacade` classes from the `ValidationApplication` as discussed in the *Validating persistent fields and properties* recipe.

In order to illustrate the use of regular expressions we need to define allowable values for the restrictions field. This field may hold a combination of values reflecting driving constraints such as:

- C – Requires the use of corrective lenses
- A – Must be accompanied by an adult driver
- 6 – Limited to vehicles with 6 or less axles
- N – Not permitted to drive at night

How to do it...

The **@Pattern** annotation uses a `regexp` argument to define a regular expression. The regular expression is applied to the field declaration that follows it. Regular expressions follow the convention as defined in `java.util.regex.Pattern`.

Let's start by using a simple regular expression to test for patterns which meet these restrictions. The "??" regular expression qualifiers specify that the preceding character will appear once or not all.

```
@Pattern(regexp="C??A??6??N??")
private String restrictions;
```

More sophisticated regular expressions can be developed. For example, a `zipCode` field might be defined as follows:

```
@Pattern(regexp="\\d{5}(-\\d{4})?")
private String zipCode;
```

How it works...

Regular expressions provide a powerful, if not sometimes cryptic, technique for validating more complex string patterns. It is not possible to adequately cover regular expression in this recipe. There are a number of books that are devoted entirely to this topic.

The `Validator` class is used in conjunction with this annotation to detect and handle violations. This technique is illustrated in the *Using the Validator Class* recipe

See also

The *Using the Validator class* recipe illustrates the use of this annotation.

Validating Boolean fields

Some fields are Boolean. If we want to ensure the field will be assigned a true value in some situations and a false in others, the **@AssertTrue** and **@AssertFalse** annotations can be used.

Getting ready

We will use the `LicenseBean` and `LicenseBeanFacade` classes from the `ValidationApplication` as discussed in the *Validating persistent fields and properties* recipe.

How to do it...

Here, the **@AssertTrue** annotation is used to indicate that the license holder should be a resident. This means the `resident` field must be true.

```
@AssertTrue
private boolean resident;
```

The **@AssertFalse** annotation means that the field should be assigned a false value.

```
@AssertFalse
private boolean resident;
```

How it works...

These annotations are used to control the assignment of Boolean values to fields. The `Validator` class is used in conjunction with these annotations to detect and handle violations. This technique is illustrated in the *Using the Validator class* recipe.

See also

The *Using the Validator class* recipe illustrates the use of this annotation.

Validating Integer fields

Integers are widely used in most applications. When these variables are persisted, it is useful to be able to limit their values to a specific range. The **@Min** and **@Max** annotations are used for this purpose.

Getting ready

We will use the `LicenseBean` and `LicenseBeanFacade` classes from the `ValidationApplication` as discussed in the *Validating persistent fields and properties* recipe.

How to do it...

The size of an integer field can also be validated using the **@Min** and **@Max** annotations. The `monthsToExpire` field in the following declaration must have a value between 12 and 48 inclusive to avoid a constraint violation.

```
@Min(12)
@Max(48)
private int monthsToExpire;
```

The **@Min** or **@Max** annotations can be used without the other one. In such situations, there is no lower or upper bound depending on which annotation is not used.

How it works...

These annotations are used to control the assignment of integer values to fields. The `Validator` class is used in conjunction with these annotations to detect and handle violations. This technique is illustrated in the *Using the Validator class* recipe

See also

The *Using the Validator class* recipe illustrates the use of this annotation.

Using the Validator class

Before the `create` method of a facade class is used to add the license to the database, we need to validate the values for the fields. The `Validator` class provides this capability. It allows an object to be checked to see if any of the fields have failed to meet its validation criteria.

Getting ready

We will use the `LicenseBean` and `LicenseBeanFacade` classes from the `ValidationApplication` as discussed in the *Validating persistent fields and properties* recipe.

How to do it...

In order to demonstrate this approach we need to modify both the `LicenseBean` and the `LicenseServlet`. First, modify the field declarations of the `LicenseBean` as shown here:

```
public class LicenseBean implements Serializable {

    @Size(min=12)
    @NotNull
    private String name;

    @Future
    @Temporal(javax.persistence.TemporalType.DATE)
    private Date dateOfBirth;

    @Pattern(regexp="C??A??6??N??")
    private String restrictions;

    @AssertFalse
    private boolean resident;

    @Min(12)
    @Max(48)
    private int monthsToExpire;

    . . .
}
```

Next, replace the try block in the `LicenseServlet` with the following code:

```
try {

  out.println("<html>");
  out.println("<head>");
  out.println("<title>Servlet LicenseServlet</title>");
  out.println("</head>");
  out.println("<body>");
  license = new LicenseBean();
  license.setName("Pax Maxwell");
  Calendar calendar = Calendar.getInstance();
  calendar.set(1981, 4, 18);
  license.setDateOfBirth(calendar.getTime());
  license.setMonthsToExpire(50);
  license.setResident(true);
  license.setRestrictions("CT6");

  Validator validator =
    Validation.buildDefaultValidatorFactory().getValidator();
  Set constraintViolations = validator.validate(license);
  Iterator iter = constraintViolations.iterator();
  if (iter.hasNext()) {
    while (iter.hasNext()) {
      ConstraintViolation constraintViolation =
        (ConstraintViolation) iter.next();
      out.println("<h3>Message: " +
        constraintViolation.getMessage());
      out.println(" however value given was: " +
        constraintViolation.getInvalidValue() + "</h3>");
    }
  } else {
      licenseBeanFacade.create(license);
      out.println("<h1>Name: " + license.getName() + " -
        License ID: " + license.getId() + "</h1>");

  }

  out.println("</body>");
  out.println("</html>");

} finally {
    out.close();
  }
```

Execute the application using the URL found in the following screenshot:

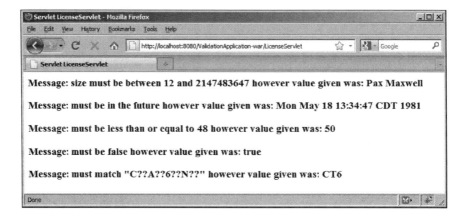

How it works...

The `LicenseBean` class's declarations have been annotated to use various validators illustrated in the previous set of validation recipes. For example, the minimum of the `name` field is 12. The reader is encouraged to experiment with other settings.

In the `LicenseServlet`, a `Validator` instance was obtained using the static `buildDefaultValidatorFactory` method to return an instance of a `ValidatorFactory` interface. In this example, the object returned was not explicitly saved, but was chained with its `getValidator` method to return a `Validator` object.

The `Validator` uses a `validate` method which is passed the object to be validated and returns a `Set` of `ConstraintViolations`. Using the `ConstraintViolation` object, an `Iterator` object was returned from the set. If it was not empty, then the constraint violations were displayed. Otherwise, the servlet continued normally.

There were two `ConstraintViolation` methods used to display the violations:

- `getMessage` – This returned a message describing the violation
- `getInvalidValue` – Returned the value which caused the violation

They can be used to display information about the violations or used to isolate and deal with violations.

In this simple application, we dealt with the violations by displaying them. In a more robust application we would need to determine and act upon each violation in a more user friendly fashion.

5
Querying Entities using JPQL and the Criteria API

In this chapter, we will cover:

- ▶ Populating the Patient and Medication tables
- ▶ Using the Select clause
- ▶ Using the Where clause
- ▶ Controlling the number of entities returned by a select query
- ▶ Using the Delete query
- ▶ Using the Update query
- ▶ Using parameters in a query
- ▶ Using a named query
- ▶ Using the Criteria API

Introduction

There are two primary Java EE technologies for querying a database: **Java Persistence Query Language (JPQL)** and the Criteria API. JPQL is similar in appearance and usage to SQL while the Criteria API provides a more type-safe and object-oriented entity querying capability.

When using EJB 2.0, developers used EJB QL as the query language. With the introduction of J2EE 5.0, JPQL was introduced and replaced EJB QL. JPQL is based on the **Hiberate Query Language (HQL)** and is a subset of HQL. It is portable and allows queries to be executed against different data stores. This is in contrast to the use of a native query where the query is expressed in the native SQL of the data store. Another older, yet still viable technique is the Java database classes and interfaces found in the `java.sql` package. In this chapter we will focus on JPQL and the Criteria API.

JPQL statements are similar to those of SQL and are written as a string. However, JPQL is not type-safe. When the query is processed its string representation is evaluated and executed. If there are any errors in the query, they cannot be caught at compile-time and cannot be handled very easily during run-time. Another difference between JPQL and SQL is the focus of the languages. JPQL deals with entities while SQL is concerned with records.

The Criteria API offers better performance than JPQL but it is more verbose and difficult to use. It is essentially another Java API that has the benefit of being type-safe. Exceptions occurring during execution are more easily handled. The *Using the Criteria API* recipe provides an introduction to the Criteria API.

There are two types of JPQL queries: dynamic and static. A dynamic query is used as an argument of the **Query**'s `createQuery` method. A static query is also called a named query. A named query is declared as part of an entity class and used with the `createNamedQuery` method. Static queries are more efficient and are detailed in the *Using a Named query* recipe. Most of the recipes used in this chapter are dynamic queries as they simplify the presentation of the various JPQL techniques. Regardless of the type of query used, JPQL works in the same manner.

The recipes found in this chapter are built around two tables: Patient and Medication. The Patient table maintains information about patients such as the patient's name and medications. The Medication table maintains information about a specific medication a patient is taking such as its name and dosage level. These two tables are related. One Patient may have zero or more medications. This is reflected in the methods of the two entity classes and the **@OneToMany** and **@ManyToOne** annotations used in defining the entity classes.

We will create two facade classes for these entity classes: **PatientFacade** and **MedicationFacade**. Both of these use the **AbstractFacade** as their base class. These entities, facades and their relational mapping are explained in the *Populating the Patient and Medication tables* recipe.

By the way, these tables are used throughout the recipes addressed in this chapter. We will populate the database in the **PatientServlet**. Populating the tables in code does not impose on the reader the need to import or otherwise use an existing database. The execution of multiple queries against a table will result in a table whose state may be different from what we expect. If we always execute queries against a table with the same initial state we can more easily understand and verify the results. This is the approach we will use in this chapter.

To create a query we need to use an instance of the **EntityManager** class. The entity facade classes expose the **EntityManager** class. This means we should normally execute our queries as a method of the facade class.

The JPQL language is similar to SQL. However, the parts of the query are expressed using the entity's names and its fields as opposed to specifying tables and columns. These fields are selected using an identification variable as illustrated in the *Using the Select query* recipe. One nice benefit of this approach is if the table or column names are changed, it does not affect the query. However, if we modify the entities then this may affect the JPQL queries.

There are three basic types of queries supported by JPQL.

- ▸ Select
- ▸ Update
- ▸ Delete

In addition, the Where clause is frequently used in conjunction with these queries. This clause provides considerable control over which entities will be affected by a query. The *Using the Where clause* recipe covers this clause.

Populating the Patient and Medication tables

In this recipe, we will learn how to create and populate the Patient and a Medication table. These tables will be used for the other recipes in this chapter. This approach means you do not have to import or otherwise use an existing database. The process of creating these tables is facilitated through several helper methods. Upon completion of this recipe, you will have the base for learning how to use JPQL as illustrated in the remaining recipes.

Getting ready

The process of creating this application consists of:

1. Creating five classes
   - ❑ `Patient` – An entity representing a patient
   - ❑ `Medication` – An entity representing the medications used by a patient
   - ❑ `AbstractFacade` – A base class used by the next two classes
   - ❑ `PatientFacade` – A facade class for the `Patient` entity
   - ❑ `MedicationFacade` – A facade class for the `Medication` entity

2. Creating a servlet to populate and demonstrate the use of JPQL

We will start with the description of a patient and a medication entity. The facade classes are then defined and a servlet will be created to actually use the facade classes to populate the tables.

The `Patient` class represents a patient with several attributes:

- `id` – A long integer automatically generated
- `firstName` – A simple string
- `lastName` – A simple string
- `sex` – A character
- `dateOfBirth` – An instance of the `java.util.Date` class
- `medications` – A collection of medication for the patient

The `Medication` class represents a medication with several attributes:

- `name` – The name of the drug
- `type` – The type of the drug
- `dosage` – The dosage level
- `frequency` – The frequency the medication is taken
- `patient` – A reference to the patient using this medication

How to do it...

Create a new Java EE application called `PatientApplication`. Add a package called `packt` to the EJB module and a package called `servlet` to the WAR module.

We will create two entity classes that deal with patients and their medications; `Patient` and `Medication`. A patient can have zero or more medications. This relationship between the entities is called a One-To-Many relationship.

Create the `Patient` entity in the package `packt`. The creation of an entity is detailed in the *Chapter 4, Creating an entity* recipe. We will augment this entity with the **@Table** annotation to associate the entity with the table PATIENT. Add fields for the patient attributes listed previously along with getter and setter methods. The fields are annotated with **@Column** which specifies the field name for the corresponding table. In addition, we will need constructors and two methods: `addMedication` and `removeMedication` which associates a medication with a patient. Until the `Medication` class is added, these methods will result in a syntax error.

```
@Entity
@Table(name="PATIENT")
public class Patient implements Serializable {
```

```
@Column(name="FIRSTNAME")
private String firstName;

@Column(name="LASTNAME")
private String lastName;

@Column(name="SEX")
private char sex;

@Column(name="DATEOFBIRTH")
@Temporal(javax.persistence.TemporalType.DATE)
private Date dateOfBirth;

@OneToMany(mappedBy="patient")
private Collection<Medication> medications;

@Id
@GeneratedValue(strategy = GenerationType.AUTO)
private Long id;

public Patient() {

}

public Patient(String firstName, String lastName, char sex,
  Date dob) {
  this.firstName = firstName;
  this.lastName = lastName;
  this.sex = sex;
  this.dateOfBirth = dob;
}
public void addMedication(Medication medication) {
  medications.add(medication);
}

public Medication removeMedication(Medication medication) {
  medications.remove(medication);
  medication.setPatient(null);
  return medication;
}
```

Next, add the `Medication` entity to the `packt` package. Use the **@Table** annotation to associate this entity with the MEDICATION table. Add getter and setter methods to the class for the fields listed earlier. Also add a default and four argument constructor to facilitate the construction of a `Medication` instance.

```
@Entity
@Table(name = "MEDICATION")
public class Medication implements Serializable {

    @ManyToOne
    private Patient patient;

    @Column(name = "NAME")
    private String name;

    @Column(name = "TYPE")
    private String type;

    @Column(name = "DOSAGE")
    private int dosage;

    @Column(name = "FREQUENCY")
    private int frequency;

    @Id
    @GeneratedValue(strategy = GenerationType.AUTO)
    private Long id;

    public Medication() {
}

    public Medication(String medication, String type, int dosage,
        int frequency) {
      this.patientId = patientId;
      this.name = medication;
      this.type = type;
      this.dosage = dosage;
      this.frequency = frequency;
    }
    public Patient getPatient() {
      return patient;
    }

    public void setPatient(Patient patient) {
      this.patient = patient;
    }
```

Create and add an `AbstractFacade` class to the `packt` package as detailed in the previous chapter. Also add a `PatientFacade` and a `MedicationFacade` class to persist the entities as discussed in *Chapter 4, Creating an entity facade* recipe. We will later add methods to these classes to illustrate the use of JPQL and the Criteria API.

The last class we need to create is the `PatientServlet` which we will add to the `servlet` package. Here, only the first part of the servlet is shown. The basic servlet class is discussed in *Chapter 1, Accessing a session bean using dependency injection* recipe. Note the declaration and injection of the entity class and their facade class variables. These will be used later to illustrate the use of JPQL.

```java
public class PatientServlet extends HttpServlet {

  private Patient patient;
  @EJB
  private PatientFacade patientFacade;

  private Medication medication;
  @EJB
  private MedicationFacade medicationFacade;

    // Helper methods

  protected void processRequest(HttpServletRequest request,
    HttpServletResponse response)
    throws ServletException, IOException {
      response.setContentType("text/html;charset=UTF-8");
      PrintWriter out = response.getWriter();
      try {
        // Populate the tables
        populateTables();
        ...
      } finally {
          out.close();
      }
  }
  ...
}
```

Our main task here is to populate the PATIENT and MEDICATION tables. To assist in this process create two methods: `createPatient` and `createMedication`, and add them after the helper methods comment. Also, add a method called `populateTables` to actually add entries to these tables.

```java
// Helper methods
  private Patient createPatient(String firstName, String lastName,
    char sex, int year, int month, int day) {
      Calendar calendar = Calendar.getInstance();
      calendar.set(year, month, day);
```

```
            patient = new Patient(firstName, lastName, sex,
               calendar.getTime());
            patientFacade.create(patient);
            return patient;
        }

    private Medication createMedication(String name, String type,
        int dosage, int frequency) {
            Medication medication;
            medication = new Medication(name, type, dosage, frequency);
            medicationFacade.create(medication);
            return medication;
        }

    private void populateTables() {
        patient = createPatient("Donald", "Baker", 'M', 1976, 3, 13);
        patient.addMedication(createMedication("Accupril", "ACE",
            10, 1));
        patient.addMedication(createMedication("Cleocin",
            "Anti-Bacterial", 2, 2));

        patient = createPatient("Jennifer", "Campbell", 'F', 1982,
            5, 23);
        patient.addMedication(createMedication("Urex", "Anti-Bacterial",
            5, 2));
        patient.addMedication(createMedication("Lasix", "Diuretic",
            12, 1));

        patient = createPatient("Steven", "Young", 'M', 1965, 6, 12);
        patient.addMedication(createMedication("Vasitec", "ACE",
            10, 2));

        patient = createPatient("George", "Thompson", 'M', 1957, 12, 2);
        patient.addMedication(createMedication("Altace", "ACE", 25, 1));
        patient.addMedication(createMedication("Amoxil",
            "Anti-Bacterial", 10, 4));
        patient.addMedication(createMedication("Mycelex", "Anti-Fungal",
            12, 2));

        patient = createPatient("Sandra", "Taylor", 'F', 1998, 1, 23);
        patient.addMedication(createMedication("Accupril", "ACE",
            10, 1));

        patient = createPatient("Maria", "Green", 'F', 1978, 7, 21);
        patient.addMedication(createMedication("Altace", "ACE", 25, 1));

        patient = createPatient("Sarah", "Walker", 'F', 1980, 10, 10);
        patient.addMedication(createMedication("Accupril", "ACE",
            10, 1));
```

```
patient.addMedication(createMedication("Ilosone",
   "Anti-Bacterial", 5, 2));
patient.addMedication(createMedication("Terazol", "Anti-Fungal",
   20, 1));
patient.addMedication(createMedication("Aldactone", "Diuretic",
   5, 3));

patient = createPatient("Kevin", "Hall", 'M', 2005, 4, 2);

patient = createPatient("Carol", "Harris", 'F', 1958, 8, 11);
patient.addMedication(createMedication("Zyvox", "Anti-Bacterial",
   10, 3));

}
```

When the servlet is executed the tables should be created and populated.

In this recipe we set up the foundation for the other recipes in this chapter. While we now have populated these tables, it would be nice if we could examine and verify that our code works as expected. We will delay this activity until the *Using the Select query* recipe.

How it works...

Let's examine the `Patient` class first. Notice the use of the **@OneToMany** annotation. One patient entity may possess zero or more medications. The `mappedBy` attribute indicates a bi-directional relationship. This means we can use JPQL or the Criteria API to navigate in either direction.

Getter and setter methods are easy to add to a class. Most IDEs provide some mechanism to quickly generate and insert these methods based on the existing class fields. For example, from NetBeans right-clicking on the source code and selecting the insert code menu allows you to use a Getter option that presents a set of options for generating these types of methods.

The `dateOfBirth` field was declared as a `Date`. Either the `java.util.Date` or the `java.sql.Date` class could have been used. The `java.util.Date` stores a date as a long value representing the time elapsed since January 1, 1970 00:00:00.000 Greenwich Mean Time. The `java.sql.Date` class extends the `java.util.Date` class and is used where a JDBC SQL DATE value is used. The use of time is covered in more detail in *Chapter 12, Using time within an EJB* recipe.

In the `Medication` entity notice the use of the **@ManyToOne** annotation. It was used to create a bi-directional connection between the `Patient` and `Medication` entities. It allowed us to determine which patient uses which medication.

In the servlet, the `createPatient` and `createMedication` methods used their arguments as parameters to their respective constructors. The `createPatient` method also used a `Calendar` instance to convert the date information into a form assignable to the `Patient`'s `dateOfBirth` field.

The `populateTables` method used these helper methods to populate the database. This simple, but lengthy method added a series of patients each with zero or more medications.

There's more...

Throughout this chapter we will create and use queries to illustrate the various techniques available. Some of these queries will retrieve information from a table while others may delete and modify the contents of a table. In order to insure consistent and predictable behavior, it is best if the tables always start with the same initial contents. We can insure this by removing and then restoring the contents of the tables each time the `PatientServlet` executes. By using the following code we can make this possible. The `findAll` method is part of the facade classes and returns a list of all of the entities in that table. Add the following code sequence before the call to the `populateTables` method.

```
// Remove all medications from the database
List<Patient> patientList = patientFacade.findAll();
for (Patient patient : patientList) {
  patientFacade.remove(patient);
}

// Remove all medications from the database
List<Medication> medicationList = medicationFacade.findAll();
for (Medication medication : medicationList) {
  medicationFacade.remove(medication);
}

// Populate the tables
populateTables();
```

See also

The remainder of the recipes in this chapter builds upon this recipe. The next recipe develops a JPQL query to display the contents of our tables.

Using the Select query

The Select query is a very useful query as it returns a subset of one or more tables of a database. The query can be used to select which rows of a table should be returned and which fields of each row. When the query is executed a list of results is returned and can be processed and/or displayed by the application.

Getting ready

The steps used to create and use a JPQL Select query include:

1. Obtaining an instance of an `EntityManager`

2. Using the `createQuery` method to create an instance of a `Query` based on a Select JPQL string argument

3. Using a method such as the `getResultList` to execute and return the results of the query

The easiest place to find an instance of the `EntityManager` is in a facade class. This is where we will place our JPQL-based methods.

How to do it...

The `findAll` method is provided as part of the `AbstractFacade` base class. However, it uses the Criteria API to return a list of every entity in the underlying database. In this recipe, we will focus on how to use JPQL to accomplish the same task.

Add a `findAll` method to the `PatientFacade`. Use the **@Override** annotation to explicitly override the base class method.

```
@Stateless
public class PatientFacade extends AbstractFacade<Patient> {

  @PersistenceContext(unitName = "PatientApplication-ejbPU")
  private EntityManager entityManager;
  ...
  @Override
  public List<Patient> findAll() {
  Query query = entityManager.createQuery("select p FROM Patient p");
  List<Patient> list = query.getResultList();
  return list;
  }
  ...
}
```

Add a call to the method in the `PatientServlet` after the body tag is displayed.

```
...
out.println("<body>");
List<Patient> firstNameList = patientFacade.findAll();
for (Patient patient : firstNameList) {
  out.println("<h5>" + patient.getLastName() +
    ", " + patient.getFirstName() + "</h5>");
}
```

Execute the servlet. The result is shown in the following screenshot:

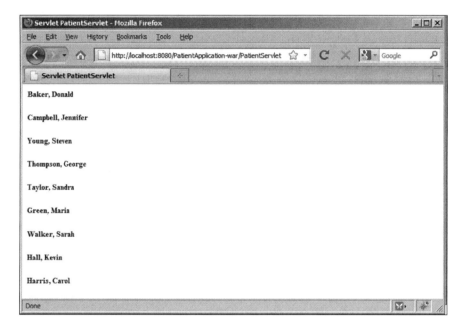

How it works...

The first step created the `Query` instance using the `createQuery` method. This required the use of the `EntityManager` class and a JPQL string. Since this method is a member of the `PatientFacade`, we used the `entityManager` variable and the `createQuery` method to create a `Query` object.

A JPQL query statement string was used as the argument to the `createQuery` method. What we would like the query to do is to make a request such as: "Return a list of all patients from the PATIENT table". The Select JPQL statement is designed to return this type of result. The statement consists of two parts: a `Select` clause and a `From` clause. The `Select` clause indicates what we want to retrieve and the `From` clause determines the origin of this information.

SELECT and **FROM** are keywords and are not case-sensitive. In these examples, they will be written in upper case to clarify the queries. A JPQL statement meeting our needs looks like this: `SELECT p FROM Patient p`. We can add this string to complete the process of creating the query.

Notice the use of the entity name, `Patient`, as opposed to the name of the table, `PATIENT`. The variable, `p`, is called an identification variable. All identification variables are declared in a `From` clause. They can be referenced from a `Select` clause, or as we will see later, from a `Where` clause. Optionally, we can use the **AS** keyword to be more explicit.

```
SELECT p FROM Patient AS p
```

For those familiar with SQL, we would use an * to identify all of the fields of the table row. In JPQL, we simply use the identification variable.

Since we are dealing at the entity level, we need an identifier to specify what we want to select. For example, if we had been interested in only the first name of the entity we would use a dot and the field name. The dot is called a navigation operator.

```
SELECT p.firstName FROM Patient p
```

To complete the process of creating and executing a query we needed to actually execute the query. The `createQuery` method only creates the query, it does not execute it. There are several methods we can use to execute the query. Since we are using a Select query and we need multiple entities returned, we used the `getResultList` method which returns a `java.util.List` object.

There's more...

A more condensed way of writing the method is to use Java's invocation chaining. This process simply eliminates the middleman and avoids intermediate variables.

```
public List<Patient> findAll() {
    return em.createQuery("SELECT e FROM Patient e").getResultList();
}
```

There is more to the Select query than we can present here. However, there are several issues we should address including:

- Eliminating duplicate entities
- Using the `Order By` clause

Eliminating duplicate entities

For some tables, certain Select queries may return multiple entities which are identical. For example, add the following method to the `Medication` class that will return all medications of type ACE (Angiotensin Converting Enzyme Inhibitors):

```java
public List<String> findByType() {
  Query query = entityManager.createQuery("SELECT m.name FROM
    Medication m WHERE m.type = 'ACE'");
  List<String> list = query.getResultList();
  return list;
}
```

Add the following code sequence to the `PatientServlet` after the body tag is displayed.

```java
...
out.println("<body>");
List<String> medications = medicationFacade.findByType();
out.println("<h3>Medications of type ACE</h3>");
for (String m : medications) {
  out.println("<h3>Medication: " + m + "</h3>");
}
```

Execute the `PatientServlet`. Altace is returned twice as illustrated in the following screenshot:

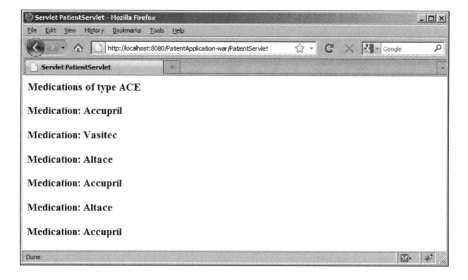

To avoid this duplication of medication names we can use the **DISTINCT** keyword. Only those entities with a distinct set of values will be returned. Replace the query in the `findByType` method with this query:

```
SELECT DISTINCT m.name FROM Medication m WHERE m.type = 'ACE'
```

Re-execute the `PatientServlet`. Duplicate names are now removed as shown here:

Using the Order By clause

The `Order By` clause is useful in controlling the order of entities returned by a `Select` statement. The clause follows the `Where` clause and can consist of a comma delimited list of entity fields. Modify the `findAll` method to use the query:

```
SELECT DISTINCT m.name FROM Medication m ORDER BY m.name
```

Re-execute the `PatientServlet`. The list returned is sorted in ascending order by the medication's name as shown here:

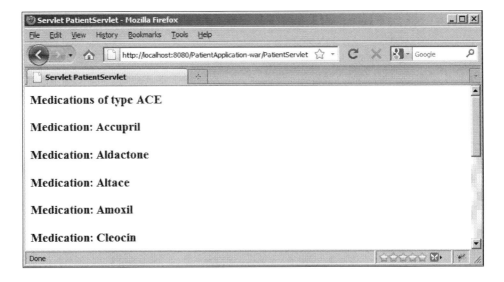

If we need to sort the elements in descending order the **DESC** keyword is used.

```
SELECT DISTINCT m.name FROM Medication m ORDER BY m.name DESC
```

While the keyword **ASC** can be used explicitly to indicate an ascending sort, the `Order By` clause defaults to ascending. If multiple elements are included in the clause, the left-most elements have higher precedence.

See also

The *Using the Where clause* recipe that follows illustrates how to limit the number of rows of a table returned.

Using the Where clause

The `Where` clause is used to narrow down the number of entities handled by a query. In the case of the `Select` statement, it determines the number of entities returned. With a `Delete` statement it determines which entities will be removed from a table.

The `Where` clause uses a number of operators to control which entities will be affected. In this recipe we will illustrate how many of them are used.

Getting ready

The `Where` clause consists of the **WHERE** keyword followed by a conditional expression. The conditional expression determines which entities are affected by the query. The `Where` clause is optional and if omitted will identify all of the entities in a table. If it is present, only those entities matching the conditional expression will be affected.

The process of using a `Where` clause consists of:

1. Adding the **WHERE** keyword to the query
2. Adding a condition expression
3. Executing the query

The condition expression possesses a number of operators that can be used to select a set of entities. The expression will evaluate to either true or false. If the expression is true, then the row will be returned otherwise it will not be returned.

How to do it...

To illustrate these operators we will use a `Select` query. This query, in its initial form, simply returns all entities in the Medication table. The `displayAll` method implements this query and is passed a `PrintWriter` object. The query is created and executed with the resulting list being displayed.

```
public void displayAll(PrintWriter out) {
    Query query = entityManager.createQuery("SELECT m FROM Medication
      m WHERE m.dosage = 10");
    List<Medication> list = query.getResultList();
    for (Medication medication : list) {
      out.println(
        "<h5>Medication ID: " + medication.getId() +
        " Name: " + medication.getName() +
        " Type: " + medication.getType() +
        " Dosage: " + medication.getDosage() +
        " Frequency: " + medication.getFrequency()+ "</h5>");
    }
}
```

Add a call to `displayAll` in the `PatientFacade` class after the body tag is displayed:

```
...
out.println("<body>");
medicationFacade.displayAll(out);
```

Execute the servlet using the URL displayed in the following screenshot:

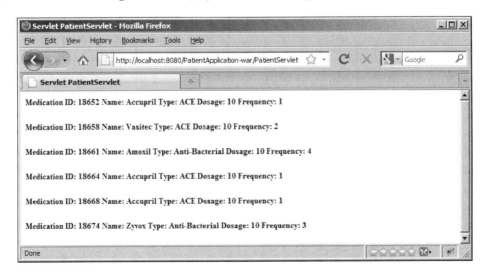

How it works...

In the `Select` query, only those medications whose dosage level is 10 will be returned. It used the navigation operator to select the `dosage` field and used the equality operator to compare it to 10. The `getResultList` method was executed returning a list of medications. Each element of the list was then displayed using the `PrintWriter` object.

There's more...

There are numerous operators available for use with a conditional expression. Specialized comparison operators include:

- **[NOT] BETWEEN** – Used to define a range of values
- **[NOT] LIKE** – Useful when used with wild card characters
- **[NOT] IN** – Used with lists
- **IS [NOT] NULL** – Whether the field is **NULL** or not
- **IS [NOT] EMPTY** – Whether the field is **EMPTY** or not
- **[NOT] MEMBER OF** – Used with collections

There are also three logical operators: **NOT**, **AND,** and **OR** and they perform as you would expect. The `Where` clause also supports these literals:

- String – Enclosed in single quotes (Use two single quotes back-to-back to represent a single quote)
- Numeric – Such as 12, 3.407, and +45
- Boolean – Use either **TRUE** or **FALSE**
- Enum – Any enum used as a field of an entity can also be used as part of the `Where` clause

Here we will examine several different types:

- Comparison operators
- Between operator
- Like operator
- **IN** and **IS** operators

Comparison operators

The comparison operators are similar to those used in Java. They include:

Operator	Symbol
Equal	=
Greater than	>
Less than	<
Greater than or equal	>=
Less than or equal	<=
Not equal	<>

For example, the following query will select those medications whose dosage level exceeds 5.

```
SELECT m FROM Medication m WHERE m.dosage > 5
```

Arithmetic operators are also available and perform simple arithmetic operations including: unary + and -, *, /, + and -. These operators work in the same way as they do in Java.

Between operator

The Between operator is used to determine whether a number falls between a range of values. We can also use arithmetic operators in conjunction with logical operators to make the same determination. For example, these two expressions are equivalent:

```
SELECT m FROM Medication m WHERE m.dosage >= 5 AND m.dosage <= 10
SELECT m FROM Medication m WHERE m.dosage BETWEEN 5 AND 10
```

Notice the entity and field name had to be used twice in the first expression. One of the advantages of the Between operator is the entity and field name is used only once. The Not operator is not inclusive, that is, in this case the dosage is not 5 or 10 or any number in between.

```
SELECT m FROM Medication m WHERE m.dosage <5 OR m.dosage > 10
SELECT m FROM Medication m WHERE m.dosage NOT BETWEEN 5 AND 10
```

Replace the query used in the `MedicationFacde` class's `displayAll` method with the following query:

```
SELECT m FROM Medication m WHERE m.dosage BETWEEN 5 AND 10
```

Execute the `PatientServlet` and you should get the results as shown in the following screenshot:

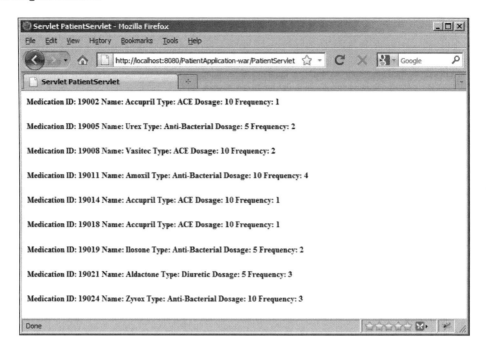

Like operator

The Like expression allows us to use wild cards to specify a match using either strings or numbers. Two wild card characters are supported:

- ▸ % – Percent which matches 0 or more characters
- ▸ _ – Underscore character which matches any single character

For example, the % character can be used to match any medication name starting with a capital A.

```
SELECT m FROM Medication m WHERE m. name LIKE 'A%'
```

Replace the query used in the `MedicationFacde` class's `displayAll` method with this
query and you should get the same values as shown in the following screenshot:

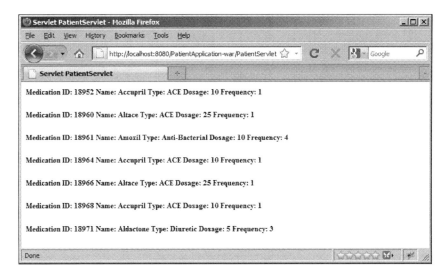

The underscore is used here to match any six character last name starting with 'B' and ending
with 'nson' such as 'Benson' or 'Binson'.

```
WHERE patient.lastName LIKE 'B_nson'
```

If either of these wild card characters needs to be used as part of an expression, then
they can be escaped using the back slash character. Here, the name must start with
an underscore.

```
WHERE patient.lastName LIKE '\_%'
```

IN and IS Operators

The **IN** operator can be used with strings or numbers to determine whether a value is in a
set of values. The values representing the set are enclosed in parentheses. For example, the
following illustrates using the **IN** operator to select from a set of frequencies.

```
SELECT m FROM Medication m WHERE m.frequency IN (1, 2)
SELECT m FROM Medication m WHERE m.frequency NOT IN (1, 2)
```

Strings can also be used in a list.

```
SELECT m FROM Medication m WHERE m.type IN ('Anti-Fungal',
   'Diuretic')
SELECT m FROM Medication m WHERE m.type NOT IN ('Anti-Fungal',
   'Diuretic')
```

Replace the query used in the `MedicationFacde` class's `displayAll` method with the second to last query and you should get the same values as shown in the following screenshot:

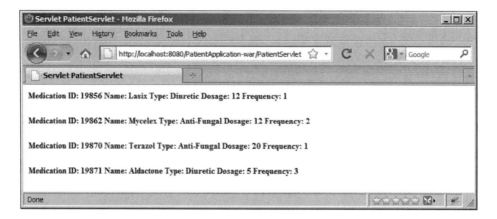

The **IS NULL** operator determines whether a field is **NULL**. The following queries illustrate how this operator can be used.

```
SELECT m FROM Medication m WHERE m.type IS NULL
SELECT m FROM Medication m WHERE m.type IS NOT NULL
```

See also

The next recipe illustrates a different way of limiting the number of entities returned at one time.

Controlling the number of entities returned by a Select query

In addition to using a `Where` clause to limit the number of entities returned, there are a couple of other approaches possible. This recipe addresses the use of methods to control the number of entities returned and to specify the first entity of the set to return. This permits us to retrieve the results of a query as a series of subsets.

This technique is useful when we want to display only a subset of entities at a time. By displaying a partial set, the user is not overwhelmed with a long list and a partial list will be returned faster than a complete list.

Getting ready

We will execute a query in the same way as before, but limit the number returned using a combination of `Query` methods. If only one entity is needed then the `getSingleResult` method can be used.

If subsets are needed, then the `getResultList` method can be used in conjunction with the `setMaxResults` and `setFirstResult` methods. The steps used for this approach include:

1. Creating the query
2. Setting the number of entities to return and a beginning index
3. Executing the query
4. Processing the entities returned

How to do it...

To illustrate this technique, add a method called `processAllPatients` to the `PatientFacade` class. In this method we will create a query to return all of the entities in the corresponding table. We will then use the `setMaxResults` method to restrict the number of entities returned and the `setFirstResult` to specify the first entity to be returned. The resulting list is then used to display the patient's name.

```java
public void processAllPatients(PrintWriter out) {
  int querySize = 5;
  int beginIndex = 0;
  while(true) {
  Query query = entityManager.createQuery("SELECT p FROM
    Patient p");
  query.setMaxResults(querySize);
  query.setFirstResult(beginIndex);
  List<Patient> list = query.getResultList();
  // Process list
  if (list.isEmpty()) {
    break;
  } else {
      // Process
      for (Patient patient : list) {
      out.println("<h5>"+patient.getFirstName()+"</h5>");
      }
      entityManager.clear();
      beginIndex = beginIndex + list.size();
    }
  }
}
```

Add a call to the method in the `PatientServlet` after the body tag is displayed.

```
. . .
out.println("<body>");
patientFacade.processAllPatients(out);
```

Execute the `PatientServlet` and you should get the output as illustrated in the following screenshot:

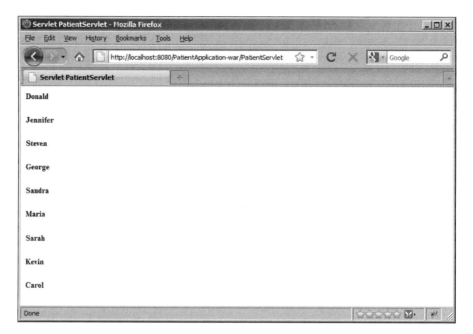

How it works...

The query used will normally return all of the elements from the patient table. However, the `setMaxResults` was set to `querySize` restricting the number of entities actually returned. In this example it was set to 5. The `setFirstResult` method determined the index of the first entity of the larger result set to return. The query was then executed using the `getResultList` method.

If the list is empty then the loop is terminated with the `break` statement. This will happen when all of the entities have been returned.

The processing simply displayed the first name of each entity returned. After the processing was complete, the `clear` method was executed to detach the objects processed so far. This resulted in a more efficient retrieval of the entities. Next, the `beginIndex` was incremented by the size of the list. During subsequent iterations of the loop, different sets of entities will be retrieved.

There's more...

Instead of retrieving several entities at a time, it is possible to return a single entity at a time. If you know the query will return a single entity, it is more efficient to use the `getSingleResult` method.

```
Query query = entityManager.createQuery("...");
Patient patient = query.getSingleResult();
```

The `getSingleResult` method will throw an `EntityNotFoundException` if it is unsuccessful.

We can also limit the number of entities returned to one using the `setMaxResults` method. We can achieve the same result using a value of one.

```
query.setMaxResults(1);
```

See also

The previous recipe illustrates how to control which entities are returned using a `Where` clause.

Using the Delete query

Deleting records from a database is a common activity. We can use JPQL to delete individual records or multiple records. JPQL query deals with entities as opposed to database records. In this recipe we will explore the process of deleting entities.

Getting ready

The basic form of the Delete query consists of:

```
DELETE FROM entity entityIdentificationVariable WHERE condition
```

For example, to delete the entity whose name is "Donald Baker" we would use the query.

```
DELETE FROM Patient p WHERE p.firstName = 'Donald' AND p.lastName =
    'Baker'
```

The steps used to create and use a JPQL Delete query include:

1. Obtaining an instance of an `EntityManager`
2. Using the `createQuery` method to create an instance of a `Query` based on a Delete JPQL string argument
3. Using the `executeUpdate` method to execute and return the result of the query

The easiest place to find an instance of the `EntityManager` is in a facade class. This is where we will place our JPQL-based methods.

How to do it...

To illustrate the process add a `delete` method to the `PatientFacade`. The method should have first and last name parameters and should return an integer. The return value will indicate whether any entities have actually been deleted.

```
@Stateless
public class PatientFacade extends AbstractFacade<Patient> {

    @PersistenceContext(unitName = "PatientApplication-ejbPU")
    private EntityManager entityManager;
    ...
    public int delete(String firstName, String lastName) {
      Query query = entityManager.createQuery("DELETE FROM Patient p
        WHERE p.firstName = '" + firstName + "' AND p.lastName = '" +
        lastName + "'");
      int numberDeleted = query.executeUpdate();
      return numberDeleted;
    }
    ...
}
```

Next, modify the `PatientServlet` to use this method after the body tag is written.

```
    ...
    out.println("<body>");
    int numberDeleted = patientFacade.delete("Donald", "Baker");
    out.println("<h3>" + numberDeleted + " Entities deleted</h3>");
```

Execute the `PatientServlet` and you should see a message indicating the deletion of the entity as illustrated next:

How it works...

The `EntityManager` was inserted using the **@PersistenceContext** annotation. In the `delete` method, string concatenation was used to integrate the two method parameters into the query string.

To execute the query, we used the `executeUpdate` method. This method can be used for both a `Delete` query and an `Update` query as discussed in the next recipe. The method returned the number of entities affected, in this case, the number of entities deleted. We used this number as the method's return value.

There's more...

The `AbstractFacade` class provides a `remove` method to delete an entity. This method is passed a reference to the entity and uses the Criteria API to delete the entity from the database. The `delete` method we used provides the foundation for more powerful queries where we can select one or more entities to delete based on an arbitrarily complex `Where` clause. The Criteria API can be used to achieve similar results.

See also

The *Using the Criteria API* recipe examines the use of the Criteria API.

Using the Update query

The Update query will modify one or more stored entities. This query is used to modify the content of a data store. It specifies the fields of the entity to be modified, their new values and which entities to be affected.

Getting ready

The Update query normally will include the `Update` clause, a `Set` clause and a `Where` clause. The `Update` clause is similar in structure to a `Select` clause, but uses the **UPDATE** keyword instead. The `Set` clause follows and starts with the **SET** keyword and has an assignment looking expression. The `Where` clause follows the `Set` clause.

For example, to update the dosage for a specific type of mediation we can use this query:

```
UPDATE Medication m SET m.dosage = 6 WHERE m.type = 'ACE'
```

The `Update` clause specifies the name of the entity and declares an identification variable. The `Set` clause assigns 6 to the dosage field and the `While` clause selects only those medications whose type is ACE.

The steps used to create and use a JPQL Update query include:

1. Obtaining an instance of an `EntityManager`
2. Using the `createQuery` method to create an instance of a `Query` based on an Update query JPQL string argument
3. Using the `executeUpdate` method to execute and return the result of the query

The easiest place to find an instance of the `EntityManager` is in a facade class. This is where we will place our JPQL-based methods.

How to do it...

We will modify the `MedicationFacade` class to illustrate the UPDATE query. Add an `updateDosage` method to the `MedicationFacade` class and pass two string arguments representing a type and a dosage. The method will invoke the `executeUpdate` method and return the number of entities affected.

```
@Stateless
public class MedicationFacade extends AbstractFacade<Medication> {

    @PersistenceContext(unitName="PatientApplication-ejbPU")
    private EntityManager entityManager;
    . . .
    public int updateDosage(String type, int dosage) {
      Query query = entityManager.createQuery("UPDATE Medication m " +
        "SET m.dosage = " + dosage + " WHERE m.type = '" + type + "'");
      int numberUpdated = query.executeUpdate();
      return numberUpdated;
    }
    . . .
}
```

Next, modify the `PatientServlet` by adding code to call `updateDosage` and display the results. Add this code after the body tag is written.

```
. . .
out.println("<body>");
int numberUpdated = medicationFacade.updateDosage("ACE", 6);
out.println("<h3>" + numberUpdated + " Entities updated</h3>");
```

Execute the `PatientServlet` and you should get a message similar to the following indicating that 6 entities have been updated.

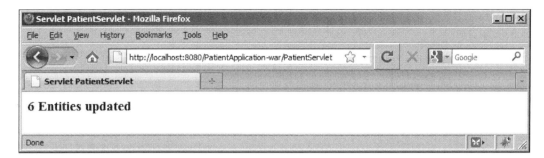

How it works...

We used the `entityManager` variable to create a new query. Notice, the query used string concatenation to create a query with the two method parameters.

The `executeUpdate` method was used to execute the query. The actual number of entities affected by the query was returned. If necessary, we can use this number to verify the correctness of the operation. The number of entities affected was then returned by the method.

See also

The *Using the Delete query* recipe to learn how to delete an entity from a database.

Using parameters in a query

If a query could not use parameters in the same manner as methods, they would have limited utility. JPQL supports two types of query parameters: named and positional. This recipe illustrates their use and how they can enhance the utility of a query. The use of this technique will improve your ability to use JPQL in an efficient and reusable manner.

Getting ready

Named and positional parameters are used as part of the query string and are assigned values using the `setParameter` method. We use parameters in a query by:

1. Creating a query using either a named or positional parameter
2. Using the `setParameter` method to assign a value to the parameter
3. Executing the query

Named parameters are prefixed with a : and are embedded as part of a query statement.

```
SELECT p FROM Patient p WHERE p.lastName = :lastName
```

Positional parameters are prefaced with a ? and are also embedded in the query.

```
SELECT p FROM Patient p WHERE p.lastName = ?1
```

The setParameter method assigns a value to the parameter before it is executed. Otherwise, queries using parameters are created and executed in the same way as non-parameterized queries.

How to do it...

Let's examine named parameters first. Add a method to the PatientFacade called findByLastname. Pass it a single string argument and have it return a list of patients.

```
@Stateless
public class MedicationFacade extends AbstractFacade<Medication> {

    @PersistenceContext(unitName="PatientApplication-ejbPU")
    private EntityManager entityManager;
    . . .
    public List<Patient> findByLastName(String lastName) {
        Query query = em.createQuery("SELECT p FROM Patient p WHERE
            p.lastName = :lastName");
        query.setParameter("lastName", lastName);
        List<Patient> list = query.getResultList();
        return list;
    }
    . . .
}
```

Next, add code to call this method and display the results in the PatientServlet after the statement that writes out the body tag.

```
. . .
out.println("<body>");
List<Patient> patients = patientFacade.findByLastName("Walker");
out.println("<h3>Patient with a last name of Walker</h3>");
for(Patient patient : patients) {
    out.println("<h3>Patient: " + patient.getLastName() + ", " +
        patient.getFirstName() + "</h3>");
}
```

Execute the `PatientServlet`. Since there is only one person with a last name of "Walker", only one entity is returned as shown in the following screenshot:

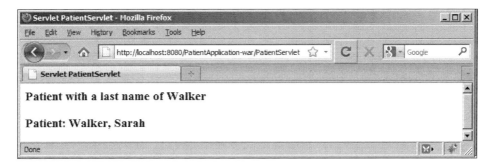

Positional parameters use a question mark and a number to denote parameters. We will rewrite the `findByLastName` method to use positional parameters. The only difference between the first version of the `findByLastName` method and this version is the query. The `setParameter` method uses an integer as its first argument which corresponds to the parameter `?1`. Input parameters are numbered starting with 1.

```
public List<Patient> findByLastName(String lastName) {
    Query query = em.createQuery("SELECT p FROM Patient p WHERE
        p.lastName = ?1");
    query.setParameter(1, lastName);
    List<Patient> list = query.getResultList();
    return list;
}
```

Re-execute the `PatientServlet`. You should get the same results as before.

How it works...

We used the `entityManager` variable to create a new query. Notice, the query did not use string concatenation to create a query.

A value was assigned to the parameter using the `setParameter` method. Notice with the named parameter, the first parameter contained the name of the parameter and did not include the colon. Named parameters are case-sensitive. With a positional parameter, the question mark is not used in the `setParameter` method. Only its ordinal position is used.

Instead of using a named parameter, we could have used string concatenation to build the query.

```
Query query = em.createQuery("SELECT p FROM Patient p WHERE
    p.lastName = " + lastName);
```

However, the use of the named parameter offers more flexibility in the construction of the query.

There's more...

We can make the `findByLastName` method more flexible by using the `LIKE` operator instead of the = operator.

```
public List<Patient> findByLastName(String lastName) {
    Query query = em.createQuery("SELECT p FROM Patient p WHERE
        p.lastName LIKE :lastName");
    query.setParameter("lastName", lastName);
    List<Patient> list = query.getResultList();
    return list;
}
```

We can use either the original query or use the wildcard characters _ or % as explained in the *Using the Where clause* recipe. Here we use the % to select those patients whose last name starts with a "T".

```
List<Patient> patients = patientFacade.findByLastName("T%");
```

See also

The *Using the Where clause* recipe discusses the use of wildcard characters.

Using a Named query

A named query, also called a static query, is defined with the entity class. When the query is deployed, JPA can translate the query into native SQL resulting in an improvement in the query's performance.

Getting ready

The process of creating and using a named query has three steps:

1. Declaring the named query using the **@NamedQuery** annotation as part of an entity class
2. Using the `createNamedQuery` method to create the query
3. Executing the query

A named query is declared as part of the entity class. In its simplest form, the **@NamedQuery** annotation precedes the class declaration and uses two attributes. The first attribute, name, sets the name of the query and the second attribute, query, contains the query. The query itself can be any valid JPQL statement.

Once we have defined the named query, we can use it in the same manner as for other queries. However, instead of creating the query using the createQuery method we will use the createNamedQuery method.

How to do it...

We will use the Medication entity to illustrate the use of named queries. Add a named query to the Medication class called findByType. As with all annotations, attribute names are enclosed within the annotation's parentheses and are followed by an equal sign and then its value enclosed in parentheses.

```
@Entity
@Table(name="MEDICATIONS")
@NamedQuery(name="findByType",
   query="SELECT m FROM Medication m WHERE m.type = ?1")
public class Medication implements Serializable {
```

As the name of the query implies, we will return a list of entities based on their type. For this query, we used positional notation to pass the type of medication as discussed in the previous recipe.

To demonstrate the use of the named query, add a method called findByType to the MedicationFacade class. The method is passed a string representing the medication type. The method will use the named query and return a list of Medication entities.

```
@Stateless
public class MedicationFacade extends AbstractFacade<Medication> {

    @PersistenceContext(unitName="PatientApplication-ejbPU")
    private EntityManager entityManager;
    . . .
    public List<Medication> findByType(String type) {
      Query query = entityManager.createNamedQuery("findByType");
      query.setParameter(1,type);
      return query.getResultList();
    }
    . . .
}
```

Next, add code to use the `findByType` method and display the results to the `PatientServlet` after the statement that writes out the body tag.

```
...
out.println("<body>");
List<Medication> medications = medicationFacade.findByType("ACE");
out.println("<h3>Medications of type ACE</h3>");
for (Medication m : medications) {
  out.println("<h3>Medication: " + m.getName() + "</h3>");
}
```

Execute the `PatientServlet` and you should get a list of medications as shown in the following screenshot:

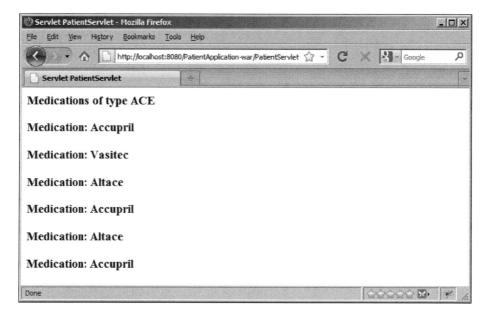

How it works...

The `EntityManager` was inserted using the **@PersistenceContext** annotation. We used the `entityManager` variable to create a new query. Notice that the `createNamedQuery` method was passed a string containing the name of the query. The `setParameter` method assigned the method parameter, `type`, to the first and only argument of the named query. The query was then executed with the list of entities of that type being returned.

For many entities, more than one named query may be needed. To add additional named queries, use the **@NamedQueries** annotation. This annotation groups named queries together.

The **@NamedQueries** annotation's **value** attribute consists of an array of NamedQuery objects. The default property for **@NamedQueries** annotation is **value** so there is no need to explicitly use it. An easy way to create this array is to use a set of curly braces to group the named queries. Curly braces can be used in Java to initialize an array. Here, a second named query called deleteByType has been added to the Medication class.

```
@NamedQueries({
  @NamedQuery(name = "findByType", query = "SELECT m FROM Medication
    m WHERE m.type = ?1"),
  @NamedQuery(name = "deleteByType", query = "DELETE m FROM
    Medication m WHERE m.type = ?1")
})
public class Medication implements Serializable {
```

See also

The *Using parameters in a query* recipe shows how to build queries using parameters.

Using the Criteria API

The Criteria API provides a way of creating type-safe queries. Its type-safe quality is the result of the Java compiler's ability to perform syntax checking at compile-time and the run-time environment's ability to catch and handle exceptions. Using this API can result in more robust and stable applications.

The Criteria API is a complex API. Complete coverage is not possible here. The intent is to provide an introduction to its use.

Getting ready

The essential steps in creating and using a Criteria API-based query are:

1. Creating an instance of the CriteriaBuilder class
2. Using this instance to create an instance of a CriteriaQuery class containing a query
3. Executing the query

How to do it...

There are two basic approaches for using the Criteria API. The first is through the use of strongly-typed queries based on the use of `java.persistence.metamodel` interfaces. This is a more complex approach requiring the use of metamodel objects for the management of the queries. A second approach uses strings but is not as type safe. It is this latter approach that we will demonstrate here.

Add a method called `findAllMales` to the `PatientFacade` class. The method is passed a `PrintWriter` object and returns void. Within the method, Criteria API classes are used to return a list of male patients and then the list is displayed.

```
public void findAllMales(PrintWriter out) {
  CriteriaBuilder criteriaBuilder;
  criteriaBuilder = getEntityManager().getCriteriaBuilder();

  CriteriaQuery<Patient> criteriaQuery =
    criteriaBuilder.createQuery(Patient.class);
  Root<Patient> patientRoot = criteriaQuery.from(Patient.class);

  criteriaQuery.where(criteriaBuilder.equal(
  patientRoot.get("sex"),"M"));
  List<Patient> patients =
    getEntityManager().createQuery(criteriaQuery).getResultList();
  for (Patient p : patients) {
    out.println("<h5>" + p.getFirstName() + "</h5>");
  }
}
```

Modify the `Patient` Servlet and add a call to the `findAllMales` method after the display of the body tag.

```
. . .
out.println("<body>");
patientFacade.findAllMales(out);
```

Execute the `PatientServlet` and you should get a list of male patients as shown in the following screenshot:

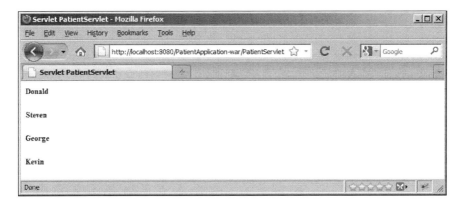

How it works...

An instance of the `CriteriaBuilder` was created using the `EntityManager` class's `getCriteriaBuilder` method. Next, an instance of a `CriteriaQuery` was created based on the `Patient` class. This instance represents a query. A `Root` instance was created using the `from` method. This root referenced the `Patient` entity.

The `where` method was executed against the `CriteriaQuery` object to restrict the query results to those specified by its argument. This argument was a `Predicate` object returned by the `equal` method. The argument of this method restricted matches to those where the patient was a male. The get method used an argument of `sex` which was compared to the `"M"` string to determine if the patient was male.

A `List` of patients was then returned using the `getResultList` method executed against the `CriteriaQuery` object. The list was then displayed.

6
Transaction Processing

In this chapter, we will cover:

▸ Creating the Demonstration classes

▸ Handling transactions the easy way

▸ Using the `SessionSynchronization` interface with session beans

▸ Understanding how the `TransactionAttributeType` affects transactions

▸ Handling transactions manually

▸ Rolling back a transaction

▸ Handling errors in a transaction

▸ Using timeouts with transactions

Introduction

Transactions are concerned with the execution of a sequence of database operations which execute to completion or, if there is a problem, any changes made are reversed and the database is restored to its initial state. The process of restoring the database to its initial state is called rolling back the transaction. A transaction is considered to be an indivisible unit used to ensure the integrity of data.

EJB support transactions using the **Java Transaction API (JTA)**. Many of the details of this API are hidden from the developer through the use of annotations. This API uses a transaction manager to control the process. While transactions are not restricted to database operations, most transactions execute against a database.

Transactions can be incorporated in session beans, message-driven beans, and entities. These transactions can be JTA transactions or local resource-based transactions. Local resources include database connections which avoid the overhead of distributed transaction support as provided by JTA. The type of transaction support used is determined when the `EntityManager` is specified for an application.

In many applications a decision is made as to whether the database operations require a transaction or not. If transactions are required, the next decision is to determine whether the container should manage the transaction or if the transaction should be managed by the developer. Transactions managed by the EE container are called **Container Managed Transactions (CMT)** and those managed by the developer are called **Bean Managed Transactions (BMT)**. The *Handling transactions the easy way* recipe details CMT while the *Handling transactions manually* recipe explains BMT.

In most situations BMTs should be used with care. They are more complex and verbose. In addition, this approach results in transactional code being intermixed with the business logic of your application. If your transaction is part of a session bean which spans multiple methods then it is necessary to use BMTs. BMT is useful for complex transactions and rollback situations. *Chapter 8, Using interceptors to handle transactions* recipe, illustrates how to separate an EJB's BMT transaction code from the business logic.

As little time as possible should be spent in transactions since normally they will lock any resources being used. This lock results in the inability of other processes to access the resource and thus slows them down.

The management of a transaction involves starting the transaction, specifying the database operations to perform and then either committing or rolling back the transaction. Beginning a transaction and committing a transaction form the boundaries of the transaction. With CMT, the boundaries normally begin when a method starts and commits just before the method terminates. With BMT, the developer explicitly sets the boundaries using a `begin` and a `commit` method.

CMTs can be used with session beans, message-driven beans, and entities. However, BMTs can only be used with session- and message-driven beans.

Transactions are designated using the **@TransactionManagement** annotation. This annotation has a **TransactionManagementType** attribute which can be set to either: **TransactionManagementType.CONTAINER** or **TransactionManagementType.BEAN**. If the **TransactionManagementType** attribute is not used, then it defaults to **TransactionManagementType.CONTAINER**.

In this chapter, we will demonstrate transaction processing using a series of classes built around a city. The `City` class holds the name of a city, its country and population. Transactions will be executed against these and supporting classes to facilitate the understanding of transactions as used in EJBs.

The first recipe, *Creating the Demonstration classes*, explains how these and their supporting classes work together. An `updatePopulation` method is used to modify the populations of the entity. We will use the `updatePopulation` method to demonstrate transactions.

A `SessionSynchronization` interface provides insight into the progress of a CMT. This interface is examined in the *Using the SessionSynchronization interface with session beans* recipe. Later, in the *Understanding how the TransactionAttributeType affects transactions* recipe, it is used to explain transaction attribute types.

The *Rolling back a transaction* recipe explains the mechanics of this important process. EJB support for exception handling is explained in the *Handling errors in a transaction* recipe. Another important aspect of a transaction is the duration of a transaction. The control of a transaction's duration is detailed in the *Using timeouts with transactions* recipe.

Creating the Demonstration classes

The `City` entity and its supporting classes will provide methods which will illustrate the use of transactions. A session facade is created for the class along with a servlet and a `PopulationManager` class. This class along with the session facade is where we will find most of the transactions used in this chapter.

Getting ready

In this recipe, we will create a series of classes to support the illustration of transaction processing. These classes include:

- `City` – An entity class representing a city
- `CityFacade` – A facade class supporting the `City` entity
- `AbstractFacade` – The base class for `CityFacade`
- `PopulationServlet` – A servlet to drive the application

Subsequent recipes will build upon these classes.

How to do it...

Create a new Java EE application called `PopulationApplication` with an EJB and a WAR module. Add a `packt` package to the EJB module and a `servlet` package to the WAR module. Create the `City` entity in the `packt` package and add instance variables for its ID, name, country, and population. While not shown below, add getter and setter methods for the instance variables. Add a default and a three argument constructor.

```
@Entity
public class City implements Serializable {
  private String name;
```

```
        private String country;
        private long population;
        @Id
        @GeneratedValue(strategy = GenerationType.AUTO)
        private Long id;

        public City() {
        }

        public City(String name, String country, long population) {
          this.name = name;
          this.country = country;
          this.population = population;
        }
```

Next, create a `CityFacade` class based on the `AbstractFacade` class developed in *Chapter 4, Creating an entity facade* recipe.

```
    @Stateful
    @TransactionManagement(TransactionManagementType.CONTAINER)
    public class CityFacade extends AbstractFacade<City> {

      @PersistenceContext(unitName = "PopulationApplication-ejbPU")
      private EntityManager em;

      protected EntityManager getEntityManager() {
        return em;
      }

      public void create(City entity) {

        getEntityManager().persist(entity);

      }

      public CityFacade() {
        super(City.class);
      }

    }
```

Add a `changePopulation` method to this class. The method is passed the name of a city and a population. Within the method, add a `println` statement to reflect the progress through the method and a query to modify the population. The use of the `Query` object and the **Java Persistence Query Language (JPQL)** is covered in *Chapter 5, Using the Update query* recipe:.

```java
public void changePopulation(String cityName, long count) throws
  IllegalPopulationException {
  System.out.println("Executing changePopulation");
  Query query = em.createQuery( "UPDATE City c " +
    "SET c.population = c.population+:count " +
    "WHERE c.name = :cityName");
  query.setParameter("count", count);
  query.setParameter("cityName", cityName);
  int result = query.executeUpdate();
  System.out.println("result: " + result);
  System.out.println("--- end changePopulation");
}
```

Next, add a `PopulationServlet` to a servlet package in the WAR module. It should appear similar to the following:

```java
public class PopulationServlet extends HttpServlet {

  protected void processRequest(HttpServletRequest request,
    HttpServletResponse response)
    throws ServletException, IOException {
      response.setContentType("text/html;charset=UTF-8");
      PrintWriter out = response.getWriter();
      try {
        out.println("<html>");
        out.println("<head>");
        out.println("<title>Servlet PopulationServlet</title>");
        out.println("</head>");
        out.println("<body>");
        out.println("</body>");
        out.println("</html>");

      } finally {
        out.close();
      }
  }

  @Override
  protected void doGet(HttpServletRequest request,
    HttpServletResponse response)
```

```
      throws ServletException, IOException {
        processRequest(request, response);
    }

    @Override
    protected void doPost(HttpServletRequest request,
      HttpServletResponse response)
        throws ServletException, IOException {
          processRequest(request, response);
    }

}
```

Execute the servlet as illustrated in the following screenshot. Notice, there is no output for the current servlet. Subsequent recipes will provide output.

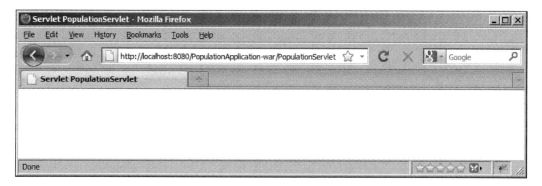

That's it for the moment. In the next recipe, we will augment these classes to support transactions.

How it works...

The `City` entity was used to hold information about a city. The `CityFacade` used the `changePopulation` method to update the population for a city. It was passed the name of the city and a count value. A new query was created using the `createQuery` method that contained a JPQL **UPDATE** query command. Named parameters, as detailed in *Chapter 5, Using parameters in a query* recipe, was used to specify the city to be changed. In this query, `count` was simply added to the city's population.

The `PopulationServlet` does not display anything at this point. In later recipes, we will modify the servlet display population information.

Handling transactions the easy way

The easiest way of handling transactions is to let the EJB container manage transactions. This is facilitated through the use of the **@TransactionManagement** annotation. When **Container Managed Transactions (CMT)** are used, the developer can select the appropriate transaction attributes for the class and/or methods.

Getting ready

The use of CMT is effected by:

1. Using the **@TransactionManagement** annotation for the class

2. Using the **TransactionManagementType.CONTAINER** element, as part of the previous annotation, to specify that CMT is being used

3. Using the **@TransactionAttribute** annotation at the class or method level to specify the scope of the transaction

By default, classes and methods use CMT. This means that the above annotations are not strictly needed but it is a good practice to include them so as to convey explicitly the intent of the code.

Next, the class and/or its methods should be annotated with a **@TransactionAttribute** annotation along with a **TransactionAttributeType** element. The **TransactionAttributeType** element is assigned one of six possible values as detailed in the There's more section.

The default **TransactionAttributeType** element is **REQUIRED**. The transaction type can be applied to the entire class and/or overridden at the method level. The transaction type effectively determines the scope of the transaction and how a method of another class invoked from a transaction sequence is handled. In some situations, it may be necessary to explicitly rollback the transaction.

How to do it...

We will use a `PopulationManager` session bean to demonstrate the use of CMTs. If the EJB using transactions is a stateful bean, then it is possible for the bean to receive messages relating to the state of the transaction. We will make this EJB a stateful bean to explore the usefulness of accessing state information in the *Using the SessionSynchronization interface with session beans* recipe.

Add a stateful session bean called `PopulationManager` to the `packt` package and add the **@TransactionManagement** annotation specifying CMT. Use dependency injection to add references to the `CityFacade`. Also, add a default constructor to the class along with utility methods `addCity` and `updatePopulation`.

```
@Stateful
@TransactionManagement(TransactionManagementType.CONTAINER)
public class PopulationManager {

  @EJB
  CityFacade cityFacade;

  public PopulationManager() {
  }


  public void addCity(String cityName, String county,
    long population) {
    City city = new City(cityName, county, population);
    cityFacade.create(city);
  }

  public void updatePopulation(String cityName, long count) {
    cityFacade.changePopulation(cityName, count);
  }
```

To test these methods, we need to modify the `PopulationServlet`. Use the **@EJB** annotation to inject the following references to the `CityFacade` and `PopulationManager` classes.

```
@EJB
CityFacade cityFacade;
@EJB
PopulationManager populationManager;
```

In order to simplify the demonstrations of transactions, it is convenient if the tables are always in the same initial state. This can be achieved by removing all of their contents and then add just those entities we want to affect. To remove all of the records in the tables, add the `clearTables` method to the `PopulationServlet`.

```
private void clearTables() {
  List<City> cities = cityFacade.findAll();
  for (City c : cities) {
    cityFacade.remove(c);
  }
}
```

We can demonstrate an initial use of transactions using the `addCity` method and then update the city's population. Replace the body of the `processRequest` method's try block with the following code sequence:

```
clearTables();
populationManager.addCity("Tokyo", "Japan", 32450000);
populationManager.updatePopulation("Tokyo", 1000);

cities = cityFacade.findAll();

out.println("<html>");
out.println("<head>");
out.println("<title>Servlet PopulationServlet</title>");
out.println("</head>");
out.println("<body>");
for(City c : cities) {
   out.println("<h5>" + c.getName() + " - " + c.getPopulation() +
      "</h5>");
}

out.println("</body>");
out.println("</html>");
```

Execute the `PopulationServlet` and you should get output as shown in the following screenshot:

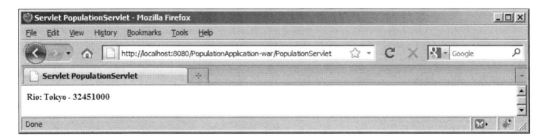

How it works...

When the servlet was executed, the `clearTables` method removed the entries in the `City` table. A new city was added using the `addCity` method and then its population was updated using the `updatePopulation` method. A list of all of the cities was then displayed. In this case, only one city was added.

Notice while CMT has been explicitly specified, there is no visible indication that a transaction has been performed. We will use the `SessionSynchronization` interface in the next recipe to show the execution of a transaction. Also notice we did not explicitly use the **@TransactionAttribute** annotation for any method. This is automatically added as explained in the next section.

There's more...

The **TransactionAttributeType** element is used with the **@TransactionAttribute** annotation. It can be assigned one of six possible values:

- ▸ **REQUIRED** – Must always be part of a transaction
- ▸ **REQUIRES_NEW** – Requires the creation of a new transaction
- ▸ **SUPPORTS** – Becomes part of another transaction if present
- ▸ **MANDATORY** – Must be used as part of another transaction
- ▸ **NOT_SUPPORTED** – May not be used as part of a transaction
- ▸ **NEVER** – Similar to **NOT_SUPPORTED** but will result in an `EJBException` being thrown

A **Message Driven Bean (MDB)** only supports the **REQUIRED** and **NOT_SUPPORTED** values. These attributes determine whether and which transactions should be used with a specific method. The **@TransactionAttribute** annotation is used with a method or at the class level. Here, a **changePopulation** method uses the **REQUIRES_NEW** attribute.

```
@TransactionAttribute(TransactionAttributeType.REQUIRES_NEW)
    public void changePopulation(String cityName, long count)
```

These attributes require further explanation. However, instead of providing the explanation here, we will postpone discussion of their exact meanings to the *Understanding how the TransactionAttributeType affects transactions* recipe.

See also

See the next recipe: *Using the SessionSynchronization interface with session beans* for more details regarding the `SessionSynchronization` interface.

Using the SessionSynchronization interface with session beans

When a transaction executes as part of a stateful session bean, the bean can receive synchronous notifications of the progress of the transaction using the `SessionSynchronization` interface. While there is not a specific field or variable which indicates the state of a transaction when using CMT, the invocation of one of its interface methods implies the transaction's state.

One possible use of this technique is to synchronize the instance variables of the bean to their corresponding values in a database. In this recipe, we will examine how the interface works. In the next recipe, *Understanding how the TransactionAttributeType affects transactions*, we will demonstrate how CMT work with different transaction attribute type settings.

Getting ready

The steps for using the `SessionSynchronization` interface include:

1. Declaring that the class implements the interface
2. Implementing the methods of the interface

In order for a stateful session bean to become aware of the state of a transaction, it must implement the `SessionSynchronization` interface. The methods of this interface include:

- `afterBegin` – Indicates when a transaction begins
- `beforeCompletion` – Occurs after the method is complete but before the transaction commits.
- `afterCompletion` – Occurs after the transaction has completed

The `afterBegin` method is invoked before the business method is invoked. Any special processing needed by the session bean may be performed at this time.

The `beforeCompletion` method provides an opportunity for the session bean to rollback the transaction using the `setRollbackOnly` method. The transaction is not rolled back at this time but the use of the method will eventually result in rolling back of the transaction.

The `afterCompletion` method receives a **Boolean** value. A value of true is received when the transaction is committed. A value of false is received when the transaction is rolled back.

How to do it...

Modify the `CityFacade` class to implement the `SessionSynchronization` interface. Add `println` statements to reflect the execution of the methods.

```
@Stateful
@TransactionManagement(TransactionManagementType.CONTAINER)
public class CityFacade extends AbstractFacade<City>
  implements SessionSynchronization {
  ...

  @Override
  public void afterBegin() throws EJBException, RemoteException {
    System.out.println("\nCityFacade afterBegin");
  }

  @Override
  public void beforeCompletion() throws EJBException,
    RemoteException {
    System.out.println("CityFacade beforeCompletion");
  }

  @Override
  public void afterCompletion(boolean committed) throws EJBException,
    RemoteException {
    System.out.println("CityFacade afterCompletion\n");
  }
}
```

By default, each method of the `CityFacade` requires a transaction. To illustrate the execution of the transaction, we will modify the `remove` and `findAll` methods of the `AbstractFacade` class by adding `println` methods showing when the methods are executed.

```
public void remove(T entity) {
  System.out.println("--- AbstractFacade remove - " +
    this.getClass().getSimpleName());
  getEntityManager().remove(getEntityManager().merge(entity));
}


public List<T> findAll() {
  System.out.println("--- AbstractFacade findAll - " +
    this.getClass().getSimpleName());
  javax.persistence.criteria.CriteriaQuery cq =
    getEntityManager().getCriteriaBuilder().createQuery();
  cq.select(cq.from(entityClass));
  return getEntityManager().createQuery(cq).getResultList();
}
```

In the `PopulationServlet`, modify the `processRequest` method and use the following code sequence for the body of the try block:

```
clearTables();

out.println("<html>");
out.println("<head>");
out.println("<title>Servlet PopulationServlet</title>");
out.println("</head>");
out.println("<body>");
```

Execute the `PopulationServlet`. The browser output should be empty; however, the console window for the server should appear as follows. Notice the start and end of the transactions when the `CityFacade`'s `findAll` and `remove` methods are invoked from within the `clearTables` methods. Using the methods of the `SessionSynchronization` interface clearly illustrates the use of transactions.

INFO: CityFacade afterBegin

INFO: --- AbstractFacade findAll - _CityFacade_Serializable

INFO: CityFacade beforeCompletion

INFO: CityFacade afterCompletion

INFO: CityFacade afterBegin

INFO: --- AbstractFacade remove - _CityFacade_Serializable

INFO: CityFacade beforeCompletion

INFO: CityFacade afterCompletion

How it works...

When the servlet was executed, the `clearTables` method was called. This method called the `findAll` and `remove` methods. As these two methods executed, the `SessionSynchronization` interface methods were executed.

Within the `findAll` and `remove` methods, the `getClass` method was executed against the Java keyword: `this`. It returns a reference to a `java.lang.Class` object for the current object. The `getSimpleName` method returned a simple name which was then displayed.

The next recipe, *Understanding how the TransactionAttributeType affects transactions*, uses this interface to illustrate transaction type attribute settings.

Understanding how the TransactionAttributeType affects transactions

The **TransactionAttributeType** attribute is used with the **@TransactionAttribute** annotation. It can be assigned one of six possible values which controls the creation and use of transactions. In this recipe, we will use the `SessionSynchronization` interface to illustrate how the **TransactionAttributeType** element works.

Getting ready

The use of CMT is effected by:

1. Using the **@TransactionManagement** annotation for the class
2. Using the **TransactionManagementType.CONTAINER** element, as part of the above annotation, to specify that CMT is being used
3. Using the **@TransactionAttribute** annotation at the class or method level to specify the scope of the transaction

The **@TransactionAttribute** annotation, along with a **TransactionAttributeType** attribute, is often used at the method level. While the annotation can be applied to a class, it is more frequently applied to individual methods. When the method is invoked, a transaction may or may not be present. The meaning of these attributes is dependent upon whether a transaction is present or not. The table below details the meaning of these attributes.

Attribute Value	Transaction Present	Meaning
REQUIRED	Yes	Join the existing transaction
	No	Create a new transaction
REQUIRES_NEW	Yes	Suspend the current transaction and start a new one. The success or failure of this new transaction has no effect on the suspended transaction
	No	Create a new transaction
SUPPORTS	Yes	Join the existing transaction
	No	No transaction is created or used

Attribute Value	Transaction Present	Meaning
MANDATORY	Yes	Join the existing transaction
	No	Throws an `EJBTransactionRequiredException`
NOT_SUPPORTED	Yes	Suspend the current exception but does not create a new one
	No	No transaction is created or used
NEVER	Yes	Throws an `EJBException`
	No	No transaction is created or used

The transaction type can be applied to the entire class and/or overridden at the method level. To use this annotation, use the annotation immediately before the method.

```
@TransactionAttribute(TransactionAttributeType.REQUIRES_NEW)
   public void changePopulation(String cityName, long count)
```

The **REQUIRED** attribute is the default attribute making the following annotations equivalent:

```
@TransactionAttribute(TransactionAttributeType.REQUIRED)
@TransactionAttribute()
```

How to do it...

Here we will use the `SessionSynchronization` interface to demonstrate the use of the transaction attributes. Modify the `PopulationManager` class to implement the `SessionSynchronization` interface and display messages indicating when the call back methods are invoked.

```
@Stateful
@TransactionManagement(TransactionManagementType.CONTAINER)
public class PopulationManager
   implements SessionSynchronization {
   ...

   @Override
   public void afterBegin() throws EJBException, RemoteException {
     System.out.println("\nPopulationManager afterBegin");
   }

   @Override
   public void beforeCompletion() throws EJBException,
     RemoteException {
     System.out.println("PopulationManager beforeCompletion");
```

```
    }

    @Override
    public void afterCompletion(boolean committed) throws EJBException,
      RemoteException {
      System.out.println("PopulationManager afterCompletion\n");
    }
  }
```

Modify the updatePopulation method to use the **REQUIRED** transaction attribute.

```
@TransactionAttribute(TransactionAttributeType.REQUIRED)
public void updatePopulation(String cityName, long count) {
  cityFacade.changePopulation(cityName, count);
}
```

Modify the CityFacade's changePopulation method to use the REQUIRED attribute.

```
@TransactionAttribute(TransactionAttributeType.REQUIRED)
public void changePopulation(String cityName, long count) {
  System.out.println("--- start changePopulation");
  Query query = em.createQuery(
    "UPDATE City c " + "SET c.population = c.population+:count " +
    "WHERE c.name = :cityName");
  query.setParameter("count", count);
  query.setParameter("cityName", cityName);
  int result = query.executeUpdate();
  System.out.println("result: " + result);
  System.out.println("--- end changePopulation");
}
```

Next, in the PopulationServlet's processRequest method, replace the body of the try block with the following code:

```
clearTables();

populationManager.addCity("Tokyo", "Japan", 32450000);
populationManager.updatePopulation("Tokyo", 1000);

List<City> cities = cityFacade.findAll();

out.println("<html>");
out.println("<head>");
out.println("<title>Servlet PopulationServlet</title>");
out.println("</head>");
out.println("<body>");
for (City c : cities) {
```

```
    out.println("<h5>Rio: " + c.getName() + " - " +
        c.getPopulation() + "</h5>");
}

out.println("</body>");
out.println("</html>");
```

Execute the code and examine the output. Ignore the output generated from the `clearTables` method. What remains illustrates the start of a transaction in the `updatePopulation`, its continued use in the `changePopulation` method and eventually the completion of the transaction.

...

INFO: PopulationManager afterBegin

INFO: CityFacade afterBegin

INFO: --- start changePopulation

INFO: result: 1

INFO: --- end changePopulation

INFO: PopulationManager beforeCompletion

INFO: CityFacade beforeCompletion

INFO: PopulationManager afterCompletion

INFO: CityFacade afterCompletion

The combination of using the **REQUIRED** attribute for both methods illustrates the execution sequence of the methods. Next, we will look at various combinations of the **TransactionAttributeType** attribute.

First, we will look at a combination of **REQUIRED** and **REQUIRES_NEW** attributes. Change the attribute setting for the `changePopulation` method to **REQUIRES_NEW**. When the servlet is executed, the output, in part, appears as follows:

INFO: PopulationManager afterBegin

INFO: CityFacade afterBegin

INFO: Executing changePopulation

INFO: CityFacade beforeCompletion

INFO: CityFacade afterCompletion

INFO: PopulationManager beforeCompletion

INFO: PopulationManager afterCompletion

Notice that the `CityFacade` methods are executed between the `afterBegin` and `beforeCompletion` methods of the `PopulationManager` class. This illustrates the start of a new transaction.

Next, let's look at a combination of **REQUIRED** and **SUPPORTS**. Change the attribute setting for `changePopulation` method to **SUPPORTS**. When the servlet is executed, the output appears as follows:

INFO: PopulationManager afterBegin

INFO: CityFacade afterBegin

INFO: Executing changePopulation

INFO: PopulationManager beforeCompletion

INFO: CityFacade beforeCompletion

INFO: PopulationManager afterCompletion

INFO: CityFacade afterCompletion

The `SessionSynchronization` interface methods are grouped together. This illustrates the joining of the `CityFacade` transaction with the `PopulationManager` transaction. There is only a single transaction used here.

Next, let's use a combination of **MANDATORY** and **SUPPORTS**. Change the attribute setting for the `updatePopulation` method to **MANDATORY**. When the servlet is executed, the output appears as follows:

INFO: PopulationManager afterBegin

INFO: CityFacade afterBegin

INFO: Executing changePopulation

INFO: PopulationManager beforeCompletion

INFO: CityFacade beforeCompletion

INFO: PopulationManager afterCompletion

The `SessionSynchronization` interface methods are again grouped together. There is only a single transaction used with this combination of attribute types.

Next, use a combination of **MANDATORY** and **NOT_SUPPORTED**. Change the attribute setting for the `changePopulation` method to **NOT_SUPPORTED**. When the servlet is executed, the output appears as follows:

...

javax.persistence.TransactionRequiredException: executeUpdate is not supported for a Query object obtained through non-transactional access of a container-managed transactional EntityManager

...

The normal result of this combination of attribute type values is a suspension of the current transaction without creating a new one. However, the `executeUpdate` method must execute within a transaction and thus an exception is thrown. If the `changePopulation` method did not use a method such as `executeUpdate`, the exception would not have been thrown and the overall process would execute to completion successfully.

Next, use a combination of **MANDATORY** and **NEVER**. Change the attribute setting for the `changePopulation` method to **NEVER**. When the servlet is executed, the output appears as follows:

...

javax.ejb.EJBException: EJB cannot be invoked in global transaction

...

This executes as it should. **NEVER** means never and the `EJBException` is thrown when the `changePopulation` method is executed as part of a transaction.

So far we have looked at those situations where the first method uses a transaction. The effect of not using a transaction is not as clearly illustrated using the `SessionSynchronization` interface as long as we are using a method requiring a transaction, as we do in the `changePopulation` method. This is because most of the attribute types will not create or use a transaction. Since the `executeUpdate` method requires one, these combinations will throw exceptions.

When a transaction is not present, the effect of an invocation of a method possessing a transaction type attribute of either **REQUIRED** or **REQUIRES_NEW** results in a new transaction being created. If the attribute is **MANDATORY** then an `EJBTransactionRequiredException` exception is thrown. Otherwise, no transaction is either created or used.

How it works...

In these examples, we set the **TransactionAttributeType** attribute to one of several values. The effects of these assignments were dependent on the nature of the transaction in place. These effects were summarized in the table presented earlier in this recipe.

When the application was executed, the creation and use of transactions was controlled by the attribute settings. The use of the **TransactionAttributeType** attribute provided us with considerable flexibility in how our application behaved. We can use this control to create more reliable and robust applications.

There's more...

There are a few restrictions on the use of transaction attributes. First, the **REQUIRED** attribute cannot be used for methods of web service endpoints. This is because the caller of the endpoint has not started a transaction and since the **REQUIRED** attribute requires one, it will fail.

While all transaction attributes are available for session beans, some of the attributes are not available for a timeout call back method. In addition, MDB only supports the **REQUIRED** and **NOT_SUPPORTED** attributes.

See also

The `SessionSynchronization` interface is explained in the *Using the SessionSynchronization interface with session beans* recipe.

Handling transactions manually

Handling a transaction manually provides the developer with more control over the transaction, but requires more work. This type of transaction control is called a BMT.

It is possible to begin and start a transaction anywhere within a method. The boundaries of a transaction are explicitly set using the `begin` and `commit` transaction methods. For CMT the boundaries of a transaction are effectively the method. BMTs are only possible for session- and message-driven beans. They cannot be used for entities.

Getting ready

The steps used to handle transactions manually include:

1. Using the **@TransactionManagement** annotation to specify bean-managed transactions
2. Injecting an instance of the `UserTransaction` object
3. Enclosing the transaction code using the `begin` and `commit` methods

We specify that an EJB uses BMT by using the **@TransactionManagement** annotation and setting its **TransactionManagementType** element to **BEAN**.

```
@TransactionManagement(TransactionManagementType.BEAN)
```

Within methods using BMT, an instance of a `UserTransaction` object is needed. This class possesses the methods used to control a transaction. The class can be injected as an instance variable of the class.

```
// Injects UserTransaction
  @Resource
  private UserTransaction userTransaction;
```

Next, the transaction operations are enclosed in a code sequence starting with the `UserTransaction`'s `begin` method and ending with the `commit` method. Since any transaction may encounter problems requiring the transaction to be rolled backed, the `setRollbackOnly` method can be used in one or more places to affect the rollback. This method is frequently found in catch blocks. The basic structure of the process is illustrated below.

```
try {
  // Starts the transaction
  userTransaction.begin;
  ...
  // Commits the transaction
  userTransaction.commit();
} catch (FirstException fe ) {
    userTransaction.setRollbackOnly();
} catch (SecondException se ) {
      userTransaction.setRollbackOnly();
}
```

How to do it...

It is not possible for one EJB to support both CMT and BMT. If the **@TransactionManagement** annotation is not used, the EJB will default to CMT.

To illustrate BMT using the `PopulationApplication`, we will add another class to the `packt` package called `BeanManagedPopulationManager`. This class will use essentially the same `changePopulation` methods as used in the `CityFacade` class.

Once you have created the `BeanManagedPopulationManager` stateful session bean, add the **@TransactionManagement** annotation for BMT. Use dependency injection to provide access to a `UserTransaction` object and an `EntityManager` object.

```
@Stateful
@TransactionManagement(TransactionManagementType.BEAN)
public class BeanManagedPopulationManager {

  @Resource
  private UserTransaction userTransaction;

  @PersistenceContext(unitName = "PopulationApplication-ejbPU")
  private EntityManager em;
```

The persistence unit name, PopulationApplication-ejbPU, was created when the entity was defined. Next, add a `changePopulation` method which is passed the name of the city and a population count to add to its current population. In a try block, add code for beginning and committing a transaction where a JPQL **UPDATE** command is used to change the population of a city. Use `println` methods to show the execution of the method.

```
public void changePopulation(String cityName, long count) {
  try {
    System.out.println("Executing changePopulation");
    userTransaction.begin();
    Query query = em.createQuery(
      "UPDATE City c " + "SET c.population = c.population+:count "
      + "WHERE c.name = :cityName");
    query.setParameter("count", count);
    query.setParameter("cityName", cityName);
    int result = query.executeUpdate();
    userTransaction.commit();
  } catch (Exception e) {
    e.printStackTrace();
  }
}
}
```

In this example, we don't use the return value from the `executeUpdate` method. Other `println` statements can be used to clarify the operation of the method.

To illustrate the use of this method, we will modify the `PopulationServlet`. First, inject an instance of the `BeanManagedPopulationManager`. Failure to use injection will result in errors when trying to inject resources in the `changePopulation` method.

```
@EJB
BeanManagedPopulationManager bean;
```

Replace the body of the try block in the `processRequest` method with the following statements:

```
clearTables();
bean.changePopulation("Tokyo", 1000);
List<City> cities = cityFacade.findAll();

out.println("<html>");
out.println("<head>");
out.println("<title>Servlet PopulationServlet</title>");
out.println("</head>");
out.println("<body>");
for (City c : cities) {
  out.println("<h5>Rio: " + c.getName() + " - " + c.getPopulation()
    + "</h5>");
}
out.println("</body>");
out.println("</html>");
```

Execute the servlet. Notice the population has increased and the output of the `println` method does not show the use of CMT for the query execution.

...

INFO: Executing changePopulation

INFO: CityFacade afterBegin

INFO: --- AbstractFacade findAll - _CityFacade_Serializable

INFO: CityFacade beforeCompletion

INFO: CityFacade afterCompletion

How it works...

The `begin` method specified the start of a transaction. All operations that constituted the transaction were included between this method and the `commit` method. The `CityFacade` output lines reflect the use of the `SessionSynchronization` methods that are discussed in the *Using the SessionSynchronization interface with session beans* recipe. They reflected the execution sequence of the transaction. The JPQL `UPDATE` command used a named query as discussed in *Chapter 5, Using a Named query* recipe.

There's more...

There are two other issues that need to be addressed:

▶ General transaction restrictions

▶ Using the `getStatus` method

General transaction restrictions

Transactions are supported for either JDBC or JTA transactions. JTA transactions can work with multiple databases whereas a particular JDBC transaction manager may not work with multiple databases. JTA does not support nested transactions.

A transaction can be maintained across multiple client calls using session beans. When using a transaction with message-driven beans, the transaction must commit or rollback before the method returns.

Do not use the EJBContext methods, `getRollbackOnly` and `setRollbackOnly` from BMTs. These methods are only valid for CMTs. Instead, use the `getStatus` and rollback methods of the `UserTransaction` class.

Using the getStatus Method

The `UserTransaction` class possesses a `getStatus` method which returns the status of a transaction. To demonstrate the use of this method, create a `getTransactionStateString` method. This method returns a string based on an integer value passed to it. This value corresponds to the values found in the `javax.transaction.Status` interface and explains the meaning of the status values.

```
private String getTransactionStateString (int state) {
  switch (state) {
    case Status.STATUS_ACTIVE:
    return "STATUS_ACTIVE: The transaction is active";

    case Status.STATUS_COMMITTED:
    return "STATUS_COMMITTED: The transaction has been committed";
```

```
        case Status.STATUS_COMMITTING:
        return "STATUS_COMMITTING: The transaction is being committed";

        case Status.STATUS_MARKED_ROLLBACK:
        return "STATUS_MARKED_ROLLBACK: The transaction is marked for
          rollback";

        case Status.STATUS_NO_TRANSACTION:
        return "STATUS_NO_TRANSACTION: There is not transaction";

        case Status.STATUS_PREPARED:
        return "STATUS_PREPARED: The transaction is in a prepared
          state, ready to commit";

        case Status.STATUS_PREPARING:
        return "STATUS_PREPARING: The transaction is preparing to
          commit";

        case Status.STATUS_ROLLEDBACK:
        return "STATUS_ROLLEDBACK: The transaction has been
          rollbacked";

        case Status.STATUS_ROLLING_BACK:
        return "STATUS_ROLLING_BACK: The transaction is being
          rollbacked";

        case Status.STATUS_UNKNOWN:
        return "STATUS_UNKNOWN: The transaction is in a unknown state";

        default:
        return "Status is not available";
    }
  }
```

Next, augment the changePopulation method to use the getTransactionStateString to display the status of the transaction at various points in the method.

```
  public void changePopulation(String cityName, long count) {
    try {
      System.out.println("Executing changePopulation");
      System.out.println("Transaction State: " +
        getTransactionStateString (userTransaction.getStatus()));
      userTransaction.begin();
      System.out.println("Transaction State: " +
        getTransactionStateString (userTransaction.getStatus()));
      Query query = em.createQuery(
```

```
             "UPDATE City c " + "SET c.population = c.population+:count "
             + "WHERE c.name = :cityName");
        query.setParameter("count", count);
        query.setParameter("cityName", cityName);
        int result = query.executeUpdate();
        userTransaction.commit();
        System.out.println("Transaction State: " +
          getTransactionStateString (userTransaction.getStatus()));
        System.out.println("result: " + result);
        System.out.println("--- end changePopulation");
    } catch (Exception e) {
        e.printStackTrace();
    }
}
```

Execute the `PopulationServlet`. Its output should contain:

...

INFO: Executing changePopulation

INFO: Transaction State: STATUS_NO_TRANSACTION: There is no transaction

INFO: Transaction State: STATUS_ACTIVE: The transaction is active

INFO: Transaction State: STATUS_NO_TRANSACTION: There is no transaction

See also

The *Handling transactions the easy way* recipe explains how to use CMTs.

Rolling back a transaction

Transaction errors will frequently result in the transaction being roll backed. That is, any and all operations performed would be reversed and the database will be restored to its previous state. Rollback will automatically occur when a Java unchecked exception is thrown. A rollback may also be performed explicitly by the EJB when conditions warrant a rollback. In a BMT either the `UserTransaction`'s `rollback` or `setRollbackOnly` methods are used to explicitly rollback the transaction. In a CMT, the `setRollbackOnly` method is used. The `setRollbackOnly` method is designed to be used with a two-phase commit protocol. The invocation of the method is a way to vote for a rollback.

Getting ready

The general approach to rolling back a transaction involves:

1. Structuring the code to determine points of failure
2. Using the appropriate rollback method to actually roll back the transaction

Most rollbacks will normally occur in a catch block. This is where you should use the `UserTransaction`'s `rollback` method or the `SessionContext`'s `setRollbackOnly` method. There is nothing magical about catch blocks and rollbacks. They are simply a good place to perform a rollback since an exception has occurred and probably means there is a problem with the transaction.

How to do it...

To illustrate rollbacks, we will augment the `BeanManagedPopulationManager` class's `changePopulation` method developed in the *Handling transactions manually* recipe. In this method, use the `rollback` method to roll back the transaction when an exception occurs.

```
public void changePopulation(String cityName, long count) throws
  SystemException {
  try {
    System.out.println("BeanManagedPopulationManager -Executing
      changePopulation");
    userTransaction.begin();
    Query query = em.createQuery(
      "UPDATE City c " + "SET c.population = c.population+:count "
      + "WHERE c.name = :cityName");
    query.setParameter("count", count);
    query.setParameter("cityName", cityName);
    int result = query.executeUpdate();
    userTransaction.commit();
  } catch (Exception e) {
    userTransaction.rollback();
  }
}
}
```

The use of the `rollback` method results in the immediate rollback of the transaction. However, using the `setRollbackOnly` method only marks the transaction for rollback. It will not be rolled back until the transaction actually ends. Delaying the rollback can be advantageous since it permits other activities to be performed, such as logging the error conditions.

Create a new version of the `CityFacade`'s `changePopulation` method to illustrate the use of the `setRollbackOnly` method in a CMT EJB. First, inject the `SessionContext` variable.

```
@Resource
private SessionContext context;
```

Next, have the `changePopulation` method check the return value of the `executeUpdate` method and, if it is greater than 1, assume an error condition and issue the `setRollbackOnly` method.

```
@TransactionAttribute(TransactionAttributeType.REQUIRED)
public void changePopulation(String cityName, long count) {
  System.out.println("Executing changePopulation");
  Query query = em.createQuery(
    "UPDATE City c " + "SET c.population = c.population+:count " +
    "WHERE c.name = :cityName");
  query.setParameter("count", count);
  query.setParameter("cityName", cityName);
  int result = query.executeUpdate();
  if(result>1) {
    context.setRollbackOnly();
  }
  System.out.println("result: " + result);
  System.out.println("--- end changePopulation");
}
```

Modify the `PopulationServlet` to add the following code sequence after the `updatePopulationManager` method is called:

```
try {
  bean.changePopulation("Tokyo", 1000);
} catch (SystemException ex) {
    System.out.println("SystemException");
    Logger.getLogger(PopulationServlet.class.getName())
      .log(Level.SEVERE, null, ex);
  }
```

Execute the `PopulationServlet`. The server console should reflect the following output illustrating the execution of the `BeanManagedPopulationManager` call and the subsequent use of a transaction.

...

INFO: BeanManagedPopulationManager - Executing changePopulation

INFO: CityFacade afterBegin

INFO: --- AbstractFacade findAll - _CityFacade_Serializable

INFO: CityFacade beforeCompletion

INFO: CityFacade afterCompletion

How it works...

Notice the `BeanManagedPopulationManager` class's `changePopulation` method throws a `SystemException`. This was needed because the `UserTransaction`'s `commit` method may throw this exception to indicate that the thread was not permitted to roll back the transaction. This exception was caught in the `PopulationServlet`.

There's more...

A CMT cannot use the `UserTransaction` class. Even the declaration of an instance of the class in a CMT will result in an error. In a CMT, there are only two rollback-related methods available: `getRollbackOnly` and `setRollbackOnly`. Both of them are methods of the `SessionContext` class. As their names imply, the `getRollbackOnly` returns a Boolean value indicating whether the transaction has been rolled back or not. The `setRollbackOnly` method marks the transaction for rollback. In addition, the `getRollbackOnly` method can only be used in a CMT whose transaction attribute is either: **REQUIRED**, **REQUIRES_NEW** or **MANDATORY**.

The `getRollbackOnly` method is not available in a BMT. Instead, use the `getStatus` method as detailed in the *Handling transactions manually* recipe. For example, if the result of a previous operation in a transaction used the `setRollbackOnly` method, the `getStatus` method will return a value of `Status.STATUS_MARKED_ROLLBACK`. This can then be used to explicitly roll back the transaction.

```
if(userTransaction.getStatus() ==
    javax.transaction.Status.STATUS_MARKED_ROLLBACK) {
      userTransaction.rollback();
    }
```

It is possible a BMT will start a transaction and then invoke a method of a CMT. As a result, the CMT will not be aware who started the transaction. In contrast, a BMT can only participate in a transaction that it started. It is not possible to propagate a transaction to another BMT EJB.

When a rollback is affected within an MDB, the message being processed is pushed back on the message queue. It will be redelivered to another MDB. If repeated attempts to use the message fail and it reaches the server's retry limit, it will be placed in a "dead letter" queue. This process can be expensive.

To avoid this expense, the `javax.jms.Message`'s `getJMSRedelivered` method can be invoked to determine if the message is being redelivered. If it is, then the method can decide to discard the message.

Handling errors in a transaction

When an error occurs during the execution of a transaction, the transaction may or may not need to be rolled back. It all depends on the nature of the error. Exceptions are classified as either checked exceptions, a `java.lang.Exception` derived class, or unchecked exceptions, a `java.lang.RuntimeException` derived class.

If an unchecked exception is thrown, a transaction is automatically rolled back. For checked exceptions, the `UserTransaction`'s `rollback` method or the `SessionContext`'s `setRollbackOnly` method are used to explicitly force a rollback.

Checked exceptions are considered to be application exceptions while unchecked exceptions are system exceptions. However, an application can declare its own unique exceptions which can be checked or unchecked.

To assist in the creation and use of application-specific exceptions, the `@ApplicationException` annotation is available. This annotation is used to mark an application-specific exception and specify whether a rollback should occur when this exception occurs. Here we focus on the use of this annotation.

Getting ready

The steps used to create such an application-specific exception involve:

1. Creating the exception class
2. Applying the **@ApplicationException** annotation
3. Creating and throwing the exception where appropriate

The EJB `@ApplicationException` annotation is used to declare a class as an application exception. The annotation has two optional elements: **inherited** and **rollback**. The **inherited** element is used to indicate whether any derived classes should have the annotation applied to them. The **rollback** element indicates whether the exception should force a rollback of a transaction or not. Both of these elements are Boolean. The **inherited** element defaults to true and the **rollback** element defaults to false.

How to do it...

To illustrate the use of this annotation, add a class called `IllegalPopulationException`, which extends the `Exception` class to the `packt` package. Add a default constructor and a single argument constructor that uses a simple error message. The **rollback** element should be set to `true`.

```
@ApplicationException(rollback=true)
public class IllegalPopulationException extends Exception {
```

```
    public IllegalPopulationException() {

    }

    public IllegalPopulationException(String message) {
      super("IllegalPopulationException");
    }
  }
```

To test its use, modify the `CityFacade`'s `changePopulation` method to throw an `IllegalPopulationException` exception if the `count` parameter is a negative value. While a negative value is not necessarily an incorrect value, we will use this test to illustrate the exception handling process.

```
@TransactionAttribute(TransactionAttributeType.REQUIRED)
public void changePopulation(String cityName, long count) throws
   IllegalPopulationException {
   System.out.println("Executing changePopulation");
   if(count<0) {
     throw new IllegalPopulationException();
   }
   ...
}
```

Next, modify the `PopulationManager`'s `updatePopulation` method by catching the `IllegalPopulationException` when the `changePopulation` method is invoked. In the catch block, use the `println` method to display a message that the exception has been caught.

```
@TransactionAttribute(TransactionAttributeType.REQUIRED)
public void updatePopulation(String cityName, long count) {
   try {
     cityFacade.changePopulation(cityName, count);
   } catch(IllegalPopulationException e) {
      System.out.println("IllegalPopulationException caught");
   }
}
```

Modify the `PopulationServlet`'s `processRequest` method. Replace the body of the try block with the following:

```
clearTables();
populationManager.addCity("Tokyo", "Japan", 32450000);
populationManager.updatePopulation("Tokyo", -1000);
List<City> cities = cityFacade.findAll();

out.println("<html>");
```

```
out.println("<head>");
out.println("<title>Servlet PopulationServlet</title>");
out.println("</head>");
out.println("<body>");
for (City c : cities) {
  out.println("<h5>Rio: " + c.getName() + " - " + c.getPopulation()
    + "</h5>");
}

out.println("</body>");
out.println("</html>");
```

This code sequence adds a city and then attempts to update its population with a negative number.

Execute the `PopulationServlet`. The browser output will show that the population has not been updated as shown in the following screenshot:

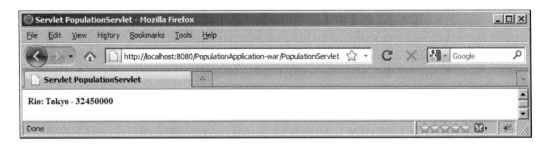

The console output will show the `IllegalPopulationException` exception being caught.

INFO: PopulationManager afterBegin

INFO: CityFacade afterBegin

INFO: Executing changePopulation

INFO: IllegalPopulationException caught

INFO: PopulationManager afterCompletion

INFO: CityFacade afterCompletion

How it works...

The **ApplicationException** annotation marked the `IllegalPopulationException` as one which will result in a rollback if thrown. The exception was created and thrown in the `changePopulation` method and propagated to the `updatePopulation` method where it was caught. Notice that the output from the `changePopulation` method did not reflect the execution of the last two `println` methods:

INFO: result: 1

INFO: --- end changePopulation

These statements were bypassed and the population was not changed.

See also

The *Rolling back a transaction* recipe explains the roll back process in more detail.

Using timeouts with transactions

There are situations where the time used to execute a transaction takes too long. This can result in unresponsive applications or the appearance that the application has locked up. To control this behavioral aspect of transaction we need to limit the amount of time allocated to a transaction. In this recipe, we will address how this is done.

Getting ready

Using timeouts involves:

1. Determining whether a timeout period is needed
2. Determining what that period should be
3. Using the `setTransactionTimeout` method in the case of BMT

Determining whether timeouts should occur or what the timeout period should be is application-specific. As a result we will not address the first two steps here.

If it is a CMT, we can use the container services to set this limit. The process for doing this is container-specific. For example, in GlassFish the **Transaction Timeout** period can be configured using the **Transaction Service** as illustrated in the following screenshot. Notice a **Retry Timeout** value can also be specified.

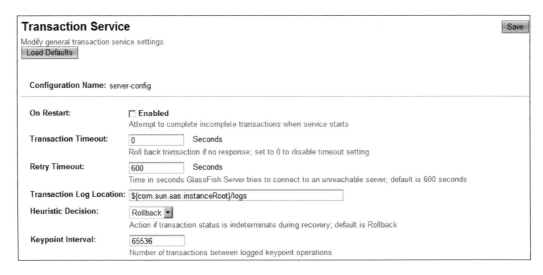

For a BMT transaction, we can use the setTransactionTimeout method. The focus of this recipe is on the use of this method.

How to do it...

Using the setTransactionTimeout method is pretty simple. The method has a single argument which represents the duration of the time out in seconds. To illustrate its use, modify the changePopulation method of the BeanManagedPopulationManager as developed in the *Handling transactions manually* recipe. Add a call to the setTransactionTimeout with an argument of 10. After the begin method, add a sleep method to force the current thread to sleep for 20 seconds.

```
public void changePopulation(String cityName, long count) throws
  SystemException {
  try {
    System.out.println("Executing changePopulation");
    userTransaction.setTransactionTimeout(10);
    userTransaction.begin();
    System.out.println("Transaction State: " +
      getTransactionStateString(userTransaction.getStatus()));
    Thread.sleep(20000);
    Query query = em.createQuery(
```

```
        "UPDATE City c " + "SET c.population = c.population+:count "
        + "WHERE c.name = :cityName");
    query.setParameter("count", count);
    query.setParameter("cityName", cityName);
    int result = query.executeUpdate();
    userTransaction.commit();
    System.out.println("result: " + result);
    System.out.println("--- end changePopulation");
  } catch (Exception e) {
      System.out.println("Transaction State: " +
        getTransactionStateString(userTransaction.getStatus()));
    }
  }
}
```

Modify the `PopulationServlet`'s `processRequest` method. Replace the body of the try block with the following:

```
clearTables();
populationManager.addCity("Tokyo", "Japan", 32450000);
try {
  bean.changePopulation("Tokyo", 1000);
} catch (SystemException ex) {
    System.out.println("SystemException");
    Logger.getLogger(PopulationServlet.class.getName())
      .log(Level.SEVERE, null, ex);
  }

List<City> cities = cityFacade.findAll();

out.println("<html>");
out.println("<head>");
out.println("<title>Servlet PopulationServlet</title>");
out.println("</head>");
out.println("<body>");
for (City c : cities) {
  out.println("<h5>Rio: " + c.getName() + " - " + c.getPopulation()
    + "</h5>");
}

out.println("</body>");
out.println("</html>");
```

Execute the `PopulationServlet`. It will pause and after 20 seconds the output of the servlet will show that the population has not been updated. In the console you will see the following output:

...

INFO: Executing changePopulation

INFO: Transaction State: STATUS_ACTIVE: The transaction is active

INFO: Transaction State: STATUS_NO_TRANSACTION: There is no transaction

...

How it works...

The `setTransactionTimeout` argument is expressed in seconds. The value of 10 meant it should not wait for more than 10 seconds before rolling back the transaction.

To test the method, we used the `sleep` method to suspend the current thread for 20 seconds. This argument is expressed in milliseconds so we used a value of 20000 to direct the method to sleep for 20 seconds.

In the console output, the transaction's status was displayed as explained in the *Handling transactions manually* recipe. It reflected an initial active transaction but when the exception was thrown, the status indicated that a transaction was no longer present.

See also

The *Handling transactions manually* recipe illustrates how to use BMTs and the *Rolling back a transaction* recipe explains the process of rolling back a transaction.

7
EJB Security

In this chapter, we will cover:

- ▸ Creating the `SecurityApplication`
- ▸ Configuring the server to handle security
- ▸ Understanding and declaring roles
- ▸ Controlling security using declarations
- ▸ Propagating identity
- ▸ Controlling security programmatically

Introduction

Security is an important aspect of many applications. Central to EJB security is the control of access to classes and methods. There are two approaches to controlling access to EJBs. The first, and the simplest, is through the use of declarative annotations to specify the types of access permitted. The second approach is to use code to control access to the business methods of an EJB. This second approach should not be used unless the declarative approach does not meet the needs of the application. For example, access to a method may be denied during certain times of the day or during certain maintenance periods. Declarative security is not able to handle these types of situations.

In order to incorporate security into an application, it is necessary to understand the Java EE environment and its terminology. The administration of security for the underlying operating system is different from that provided by the EE server. The EE server is concerned with realms, users and groups. The application is largely concerned with roles. The roles need to be mapped to users and groups of a realm for the application to function properly.

A realm is a domain for a server that incorporates security policies. It possesses a set of users and groups which are considered valid users of an application. A user typically corresponds to an individual while a group is a collection of individuals. Group members frequently share a common set of responsibilities. A Java EE server may manage multiple realms.

An application is concerned with roles. Access to EJBs and their methods is determined by the role of a user. Roles are defined in such a manner as to provide a logical way of deciding which users/groups can access which methods. For example, a management type role may have the capability to approve a travel voucher whereas an employee role should not have that capability. By assigning certain users to a role and then specifying which roles can access which methods, we are able to control access to EJBs.

The use of groups makes the process of assigning roles easier. Instead of having to map each individual to a role, the user is assigned to a group and the group is mapped to a role. The business code does not have to check every individual. The Java EE server manages the assignment of users to groups. The application needs only be concerned with controlling a group's access.

A group is a server level concept. Roles are application level. One group can be associated with multiple applications. For example, a student group may use a student club and student registration application while a faculty group might also use the registration application but with more capability.

A role is simply a name for a set of capabilities. For example, an auditor role may be to review and certify a set of accounts. This role would require read access to many, if not all, of the accounts. However, modification privileges may be restricted. Each application has its own set of roles which have been defined to meet the security needs of the application.

The EE server manages realms consisting of users, groups, and resources. The server will authenticate users using Java's underlying security features. The user is then referred to as a principal and has a credential containing the user's security attributes. During the deployment of an application, users and groups are mapped to roles of the application using a deployment descriptor. The configuration of the deployment descriptor is normally the responsibility of the application deployer. During the execution of the application, the **Java Authentication and Authorization Service (JAAS)** API authenticates a user and creates a principal representing the user. The principal is then passed to an EJB.

Security in a Java EE environment can be viewed from different perspectives. When information is passed between clients and servers, transport level security comes into play. Security at this level can include **Secure HTTP (HTTPS)** and **Secure Sockets Layer (SSL)**. Messages can be sent across a network in the form of **Simple Object Access Protocol (SOAP)** messages. These messages can be encrypted. The EE container for EJBs provides application level security which is the focus of the chapter. Most servers provide unified security support between the web container and the EJB container. For example, calls from a servlet in a web container to an EJB are handled automatically resulting in a flexible security mechanism.

Most of the recipes presented in this chapter are interrelated. If your intention is to try out the code examples, then make sure you cover the first two recipes as they provide the framework for the execution of the other recipes. In the first recipe, _Creating the SecurityApplication_, we create the foundation application for the remaining recipes. In the second recipe, _Configuring the server to handle security_, the basic steps needed to configure security for an application are presented.

The use of declarative security is covered in the _Controlling security using declarations_ recipe while programmatic security is discussed in the _Controlling security programmatically_ recipe. The _Understanding and declaring roles_ recipe examines roles in more detail and the _Propagating identity_ recipe talks about how the identity of a user is managed in an application.

Creating the SecurityApplication

In this chapter we will create a `SecurityApplication` built around a simple **Voucher** entity to persist travel information. This is a simplified version of an application that allows a user to submit a voucher and for a manager to approve or disapprove it. The voucher entity itself will hold only minimal information.

Getting ready

The illustration of security will be based on a series of classes:

- `Voucher` – An entity holding travel-related information
- `VoucherFacade` – A facade class for the entity
- `AbstractFacade` – The base class of the `VoucherFacade` class as described in _Chapter 4, Creating an entity facade_ recipe
- `VoucherManager` – A class used to manage vouchers and where most of the security techniques will be demonstrated
- `SecurityServlet` – A servlet used to drive the demonstrations

All of these classes will be members of the `packt` package in the EJB module except for the servlet which will be placed in the `servlet` package of the WAR module.

How to do it...

Create a Java EE application called `SecurityApplication` with an EJB and a WAR module. Add a `packt` package to the EJB module and an entity called `Voucher` to the package.

Add five private instance variables to hold a minimal amount of travel information: `name`, `destination`, `amount`, `approved`, and an `id`. Also, add a default and a three argument constructor to the class to initialize the `name`, `destination`, and `amount` fields. The `approved` field is also set to `false`. The intent of this field is to indicate whether the voucher has been approved or not. Though not shown below, also add getter and setter methods for these fields. You may want to add other methods such as a `toString` method if desired.

```
@Entity
public class Voucher implements Serializable {
    private String name;
    private String destination;
    private BigDecimal amount;
    private boolean approved;
    @Id
    @GeneratedValue(strategy = GenerationType.AUTO)
    private Long id;

    public Voucher() {

    }

    public Voucher(String name, String destination,
        BigDecimal amount) {
        this.name = name;
        this.destination = destination;
        this.amount = amount;
        this.approved = false;
    }
    ...

}
```

Next, add an `AbstractFacade` class described in *Chapter 4, EJB Persistence* and a `VoucherFacade` class derived from it. The `VoucherFacade` class is shown below. As with other facade classes found in previous chapters, the class provides a way of accessing an entity manager and the base class methods of the `AbstractFacade` class.

```
@Stateless
public class VoucherFacade extends AbstractFacade<Voucher> {
    @PersistenceContext(unitName = "SecurityApplication-ejbPU")
    private EntityManager em;

    protected EntityManager getEntityManager() {
        return em;
    }
```

```
    public VoucherFacade() {
        super(Voucher.class);
    }

}
```

Next, add a stateful EJB called `VoucherManager`. Inject an instance of the `VoucherFacade` class using the **@EJB** annotation. Also add an instance variable for a `Voucher`. We need a `createVoucher` method that accepts a name, destination, and amount arguments, and then creates and subsequently persists the `Voucher`. Also, add get methods to return the name, destination, and amount of the voucher.

```
@Stateful
public class VoucherManager {
    @EJB
    VoucherFacade voucherFacade;

    Voucher voucher;

    public void createVoucher(String name, String destination,
        BigDecimal amount) {
        voucher = new Voucher(name, destination, amount);
        voucherFacade.create(voucher);
    }

    public String getName() {
        return voucher.getName();
    }

    public String getDestination() {
        return voucher.getDestination();
    }

    public BigDecimal getAmount() {
        return voucher.getAmount();
    }
    ...
}
```

Next add three methods:

1. `submit` – This method is intended to be used by an employee to submit a voucher for approval by a manager. To help explain the example, display a message showing when the method has been submitted.

2. `approve` – This method is used by a manager to approve a voucher. It should set the `approved` field to `true` and return `true`.

3. `reject` – This method is used by a manager to reject a voucher. It should set the approved field to `false` and return `false`.

```
@Stateful
public class VoucherManager {

  . . .
  public void submit() {
    System.out.println("Voucher submitted");
  }

  public boolean approve() {
    voucher.setApproved(true);
    return true;
  }

  public boolean reject() {
    voucher.setApproved(false);
    return false;
  }
}
```

To complete the application framework, add a package called `servlet` to the WAR module and a servlet called `SecurityServlet` to the package. Use the **@EJB** annotation to inject a `VoucherManager` instance field into the servlet.

In the try block of the `processRequest` method, add code to create a new voucher and then use the `submit` method to submit it. Next, display a message indicating the submission of the voucher.

```
public class SecurityServlet extends HttpServlet {

  @EJB
  VoucherManager voucherManager;

  protected void processRequest(HttpServletRequest request,
    HttpServletResponse response)
    throws ServletException, IOException {
      response.setContentType("text/html;charset=UTF-8");
      PrintWriter out = response.getWriter();
      try {
        voucherManager.createVoucher("Susan Billings",
          "SanFrancisco", BigDecimal.valueOf(2150.75));
        voucherManager.submit();
        out.println("<html>");
        out.println("<head>");
```

```
            out.println("<title>Servlet SecurityServlet</title>");
            out.println("</head>");
            out.println("<body>");
            out.println("<h3>Voucher was submitted</h3>");
            out.println("</body>");
            out.println("</html>");

        } finally {
            out.close();
        }
    }
    ...
}
```

Execute the `SecurityServlet`. Its output should appear as shown in the following screenshot:

How it works...

In the `Voucher` entity, notice the use of `BigDecimal` for the `amount` field. This `java.math` package class is a better choice for currency data than `float` or `double`. Its use avoids problems which can occur with rounding as discussed in *Chapter 12, How to support currency* recipe. The **@GeneratedValue** annotation, used with the `id` field, is discussed in *Chapter 4, Creating an entity facade* recipe.

In the `VoucherManager` class, notice the injection of the stateless `VoucherFacade` session EJB into a stateful `VoucherManager` EJB. Each invocation of a `VoucherFacade` method may result in the method being executed against a different instance of `VoucherManager`. This is the correct use of a stateless session EJB. The injection of a stateful EJB into a stateless EJB is not recommended.

See also

The next recipe, *Configuring the server to handle security*, enables the server to support security for this application.

Configuring the server to handle security

Enabling a server to handle security involves configuring the actual server and configuring the deployment file. In order for the server to handle the application, the application needs to specify certain application security attributes in a deployment descriptor file. This recipe addresses these issues.

Getting ready

Before a Java EE application can use security, the EE server must be configured to handle security. The configuration process involves several steps:

1. Enabling the security manager
2. Selecting a realm
3. Adding users and groups to the realm
4. Optional: Enabling the default principal to role mapping

The actual steps are server-specific. On the application side, this process involves modifying a deployment file. For the `SecurityApplication`, we will modify the `web.xml` file. This process involves:

1. Setting the realm
2. Setting the login configuration
3. Adding the security role
4. Setting the security constraint
5. Enabling the security constraint

How to do it...

The first step is to enable the security manager. Typically, a server administration console is provided as part of the Java EE server and allows the administrator to configure the server. The actual use of the console is server-specific. Here, we will illustrate the process using GlassFish.

For this recipe, you will need to access the administrator console and enable the security manager. This is often simply a checkbox selection. In addition, either use an existing realm or create one if you are comfortable dealing with realms.

The actual realm to use is dependent on the Java EE server you are using. In Glassfish, the file realm is normally available and easy to use. This example will use the file realm but you can choose a different realm for your implementation.

Enabling the security manager and selecting the file realm in Glassfish is shown in the following screenshot:

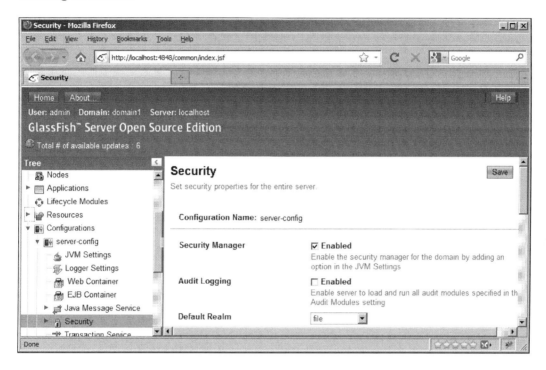

Next, add the following users and associate them with the groups: employee and manager. For each user assign a simple password to use when logging on.

- sally – employee
- mary – manager and employee

From GlassFish, under the Security element select **Realms** and then the **file** realm. Select the **Manage Users** button found at the top of the window. From this window add these two users as shown in the following screenshot:

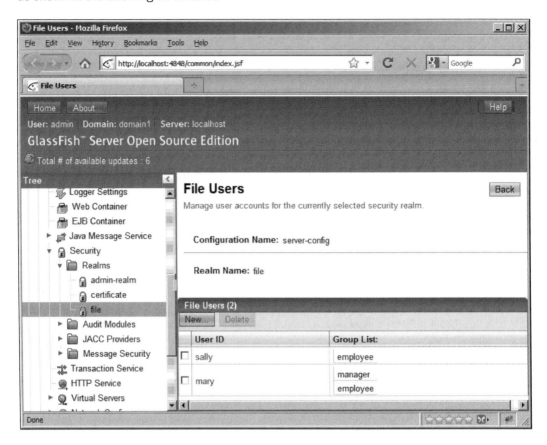

Some servers have the capability to automatically associate a group name with a role if they are identical. This will avoid having to perform explicit mapping. Should your server support this option, then go ahead and exercise it. In addition, the server may require you to restart the server before some of these configuration actions take effect. The following screenshot shows the mapping enabled in GlassFish.

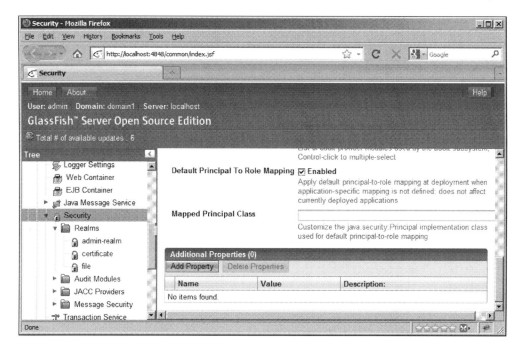

The next step involves modifying a deployment file. For the `SecurityApplication`, we will modify the `web.xml` file. Your development environment may provide a wizard or similar set of dialog boxes to configure the deployment file. Sometimes it is necessary to manually create and modify the `web.xml`. It all depends on the development environment.

The basic settings we will use include:

- ▸ Setting the login configuration to basic authentication
- ▸ Setting the realm to file
- ▸ Setting the initial security role
- ▸ Setting the security constraint to the URL pattern
- ▸ Enabling the security constraint
- ▸ Optionally mapping groups to roles

When the user makes a request which requires authentication, there are several possible authentication techniques available on most servers including:

- ▸ None – No authentication of users will be performed
- ▸ Digest – A cryptographic hash of the user ID and password are used
- ▸ Client certificate – Authentication is based on the client's public key certificate
- ▸ Basic – The server authenticates using a user ID and password
- ▸ Form – The developer provides a customized login screen

For simplicity's sake we will use basic authentication. With this technique, the user is prompted for a user ID and a password that the server uses to authenticate the user. This approach may not be the best for many applications as it is not as secure as other approaches. It sends the user information as Base64 encoded which allows the user ID and password to be easily decoded. However, if used in conjunction with a secure transport mechanism such as SSL, the approach becomes more secure.

Modify the `<login-config>` element of the `web.xml` file to specify the basic authentication method and the file realm as shown below. This can be done manually or using a development environment tool. In NetBeans, the edit window for the file supports this task.

```
<login-config>
  <auth-method>BASIC</auth-method>
  <realm-name>file</realm-name>
</login-config>
```

The roles used in the `SecurityApplication` include employee and manager. Initially, the employee role should be added.

```
<security-role>
  <description/>
  <role-name>employee</role-name>
</security-role>
```

A security constraint also needs to be added to the application. This constraint will specify that when the `SecurityServlet` is accessed, the server needs to prompt the user for a user ID and password. This is accomplished using the `<security-constraint>` XML element.

Nested within this element is a `<web-resource-collection>` element. It includes a `<web-resource-name>` element to hold the name of the resource and the `<url-pattern>` element to specify the resource to authenticate. The name of the resource can be any reasonable descriptive name you choose. The URL pattern should match those pages the security constraint should be applied to. The following code specifies a constraint for our servlet:

```
<security-constraint>
  . . .
  <web-resource-collection>
    <web-resource-name>SecurityApplicationResouces
      </web-resource-name>
    <description/>
    <url-pattern>/SecurityServlet</url-pattern>
  </web-resource-collection>
  . . .
</security-constraint>
```

To enable the security constraint, the `<role-name>` element is added to the `<auth-constraint>` element. Use a role name of employee.

```
<security-constraint>
  . . .
    <auth-constraint>
      <description/>
      <role-name>employee</role-name>
    </auth-constraint>
</security-constraint>
```

Roles need to be mapped to users and groups. As an application developer, it is not necessary to know the names of the users or groups of a realm. In fact, this information may not be known at the time the application is developed. The application may be deployed, and redeployed, to any number of different servers and the group names used by the servers may vary. Mapping the roles to the realm is the responsibility of the deployer. In some circumstances, the deployer and the developer may be one and the same. This is often true during the testing process and within smaller organizations.

If the server has been configured to automatically map groups to roles, it is not necessary to perform this mapping explicitly in a deployment file. If explicit mapping is required, the mapping of roles to groups is performed using the `<security-role-mapping>` element of the runtime deployment descriptor. This descriptor may be in one of several files depending on how the application is deployed (`sun-application.xml`, `sun-web.xml`, or `sun-ejb-jar.xml`). For example, roles can be mapped to either a single user or to a group. Here, the employee role is mapped to a single user: "sally" and the manager group is mapped to the group: "manager".

```
<security-role-mapping>
  <role-name>employee</role-name>
  <principal-name>sally</principal-name>
</security-role-mapping>

<security-role-mapping>
  <role-name>manager</role-name>
  <group-name>manager</group-name>
</security-role-mapping>
```

The use of explicit mapping is not used here as the server was configured to automatically map groups to roles where the name of the role and the group is identical. This allows us to conveniently skip this step. In Glassfish, the `sun-web.xml` contains the `<security-role-mapping elements>`.

This configures the application. Next, execute the application. The results should be the same as in the previous application since no additional security restrictions have been incorporated.

How it works...

We had to configure the server to handle the security requirements of our application. We also needed to modify the `web.xml` file to work with the server. These steps involved enabling security and coordinating the realm, roles, and groups. It was also necessary to specify which web pages were subjected to security constraints using the `<security-constraint>` element.

See also

The next recipe, *Understanding and declaring roles*, adds roles to the application and demonstrates how access to methods is controlled. Subsequent recipes use this framework to demonstrate the implementation of security for EJBs.

Understanding and declaring roles

Roles are defined within an application in one of two ways: using the **@DeclareRoles** annotation and the **@RolesAllowed** annotation. In this recipe we will detail the **@DeclareRoles** annotation while the **@RolesAllowed** annotation will be introduced but developed further in the *Controlling security using declarations* recipe.

Getting ready

The two basic steps used to configure roles involve:

1. Using the **@DeclareRoles** annotation to specify the roles used by the class
2. Adding the **@RolesAllowed** annotation to restrict access to methods

The **@DeclareRoles** annotation, as its name implies, declares the roles used by the application and is applied at the class level. That is, these are the roles to be used with the annotated EJB. The annotation can only be used once per class.

The **@RolesAllowed** annotation is used to specify which methods are accessible by the roles declared within the annotation. If the roles listed in this annotation are not found in the **@DeclareRoles** annotation, the roles are automatically declared.

How to do it...

The **@DeclareRoles** annotation simply declares roles to be used by the EJB. This annotation can only be used at the class level. It does not specify any permission granted for the class or methods within the class.

The annotation takes either a single string argument or an array of string arguments. The following first example declares a single role while the second specifies two roles for a class.

```
@DeclareRoles ("employee")
@DeclareRoles ({"employee", "manager"})
```

Add the second **@DeclareRoles** annotation example to the `VoucherManager` class.

```
@Stateful
@DeclareRoles ({"employee", "manager"})
public class VoucherManager {
  ...
}
```

Execute the application. You should not see any difference in its behavior.

Next, add a **@RolesAllowed("employee")** annotation to the `VoucherManager`'s `submit` method.

```
@Stateful
@DeclareRoles ({"employee", "manager"})
public class VoucherManager {
  ...
  @RolesAllowed("employee")
  public void submit() {
    System.out.println("Voucher submitted");
  }
  ...
}
```

This annotation will be elaborated upon in the next recipe. However, the use of the annotation restricts use of the method to only those users who are members of the employee role.

Execute the application. Since we are using basic authentication (see *Configuring the server to handle security* recipe) you should be prompted to log on. Use "**sally**" as the username and "**password**" as the password. The following screenshot illustrates the dialog box used by GlassFish.

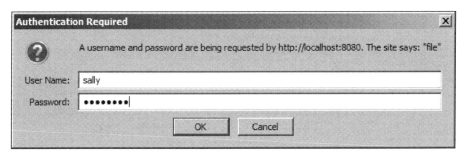

The output of the application should appear as shown in the following screenshot:

How it works...

The **@RolesAllowed** annotation restricted access to the submit method to only those users belonging to the employee role. An exception was thrown otherwise. Since we were using basic authentication, the server-provided login dialog box was used.

Note, if you resubmit the request, the user is not prompted for a name or password. If you want to force the use of the login again, the HttpSession's invalidate method or HttpServletRequest's logout method can be used to close a session. However, this does not always work in a testing environment and frequently it is necessary to close the browser and open it up again to force the authentication of a user.

See also

The next recipe, *Controlling security using Declarations*, goes into more depth regarding the use of the **@RolesAllowed** annotation and other annotations used to control access to classes and methods.

Controlling security using declarations

Declarative security allows users, defined by roles, to access methods of a class. This is accomplished using a series of annotations to permit either certain roles to use a method, to permit all roles to use a method, or to deny access for all roles.

Getting ready

The application developer needs to determine which users (roles) should be permitted to access which methods. Once this has been determined, the classes and methods are annotated to affect these decisions.

Declarative security can be achieved using any of several annotations including **@RolesAllowed**, **@PermitAll**, and **@DenyAll** annotations. Each of these annotations has restrictions on where they can be used.

Annotation	Use With	Description
@PermitAll	Bean, Method	Allows access by all users
@DenyAll	Method	No roles are permitted access to the method
@RolesAllowed	Bean, Method	A list of roles permitted access

The steps used to control access include:

1. Specifying the role permitted using one of the above annotations
2. Applying the annotation at the desired level

How to do it...

The **@RolesAllowed** is configured with either a single string or an array of strings. These strings are the names of the roles allowed access to the EJB or a method. When applied to a method, the assignment will override any class level assignment. Here the use of both an array and a single role are specified.

```
@RolesAllowed({"bankemployee", "bankcustomer"})
@RolesAllowed("bankemployee")
```

In the `VoucherManager` EJB, add an **@RolesAllowed** annotation to both the `approve` and `reject` methods. Specify a role of manager.

```
@RolesAllowed("manager")
public boolean approve() {
  voucher.setApproved(true);
  return true;
}

@RolesAllowed("manager")
public boolean reject() {
  voucher.setApproved(false);
  return false;
}
```

Next, modify the `SecurityServlet`'s `processRequest` method's try block to create a voucher and approve it using the `approve` method. Also, display a message to indicate whether the voucher was approved or not and add a catch block at the end of the try block to handle any access exceptions. The `javax.ejb.EJBAccessException` is thrown when an access restriction is violated.

```
voucherManager.createVoucher("Susan Billings", "SanFrancisco",
  BigDecimal.valueOf(2150.75));
boolean voucherApproved = voucherManager.approve();
...
if(voucherApproved) {
  out.println("<h3>Voucher was approved</h3>");
} else {
    out.println("<h3>Voucher was not approved</h3>");
  }
  ...
catch(EJBAccessException e) {
  System.out.println("Access exception");
}
```

Execute the servlet and enter "mary" as the user. The application should execute normally with the voucher being approved since "mary" is authorized to use the `approve` method as shown in the following screenshot:

Close the browser and re-execute the servlet. This time, use "sally" as the user. Since "sally" is not authorized to use the approve method, an `EJBAccessException` is thrown.

INFO: Access exception

The **@PermitAll** annotation permits access to the EJB or a specific method by all roles. Anyone is able to access and use such methods. This is the default annotation for methods. For example, the `VoucherManager`'s `getName` method is not annotated. Add the following statement to the `SecurityServlet` immediately after the code which displays the voucher approval message.

```
out.println("<h3>Voucher name: " + voucherManager.getName() +
  "</h3>");
```

Execute the servlet using "mary". The voucher's username is displayed as illustrated in the following screenshot:

If we add the **@PermitAll** annotation to the getName method we will see no change in behavior. So what is the use of this annotation?

At the class level, one or more roles may have been declared using the **@DeclareRoles** annotation. The **@PermitAll** annotation can be used to permit a method to be used by some role other than those declared at the class level. For example, use the following annotations for the VoucherManager EJB:

```
@Stateful
@DeclareRoles("manager")
@RolesAllowed("manager")
public class VoucherManager {
    ...
}
```

In the SecurityServlet, remove the code dealing with the submit method.

```
try {
    out.println("<html>");
    out.println("<head>");
    out.println("<title>Servlet SecurityServlet</title>");
    out.println("</head>");
    out.println("<body>");

    voucherManager.createVoucher("Susan Billings", "SanFrancisco",
    BigDecimal.valueOf(2150.75));

    out.println("<h3>Voucher name: " + voucherManager.getName() +
        "</h3>");
```

```
        out.println("</body>");
        out.println("</html>");

    }
    catch(EJBAccessException e) {
      System.out.println("Access exception");
    }
    finally {
      out.close();
    }
```

Next, use the **@RolesAllowed("manager")** annotation only for the `VoucherManager`'s `approve` and `reject` methods. Do not use annotations for any of the other methods. If the servlet is executed using a user in the manager role ("mary"), the application executes cleanly. However, if you log in as "sally", an exception occurs because "sally" is no longer an authorized user. This is to be expected.

Add the **@PermitAll** annotation to the `createVoucher` and `getName` methods. Re-execute the application using "sally". This time the application should execute correctly. While we have only specified the manager role for the class, the **@PermitAll** annotation allows other groups to use those methods.

The **@DenyAll** annotation denies access to all roles and users. However, this annotation has limited utility. If access to the method should be denied to all users, then it can easily be removed from the EJB.

How it works...

The **@PermitAll**, **@DenyAll**, and **@RolesAllowed** annotations provided an easy-to-use mechanism for controlling access to methods based upon the user's role. When an unauthorized user attempted to access a method, an exception was thrown which was caught and dealt with.

However, sometimes it is necessary to allow an unauthorized user access to a method under certain conditions. The need for this access and how to achieve it is detailed in the next recipe.

Propagating identity

In certain situations, the identity of the user may need to be changed to enable a different, possibly more powerful, role. Consider the following analogy:

If you are familiar with the way most operating systems work, a user is not permitted to directly read or write to a file. Low-level access to the file is restricted. When a user needs to read or write to a file, the operating system will verify the individual's access rights to the file and then temporarily grant read/write access privileges to the user. The user assumes a higher level of privilege on a temporary basis.

This is analogous to the use of the **@RunAs** annotation. It allows a new role to be temporarily assigned to the methods of an EJB.

Getting ready

The steps used to propagate an identity include:

1. Executing a method of an EJB using one role which invokes a method of a second EJB
2. Executing the method of the second EJB using a different, more restrictive role as specified by the **@RunAs** annotation

When a method of the second EJB is invoked from the first EJB, the identity (principal) is passed with the invocation as part of the security context. The **@RunAs** annotation is used to temporarily assign a new role to the current principal. When the second class' methods are invoked, the new role is assumed.

This annotation is applied at the class level. The annotation has a single argument, a string containing the name of the role. Only one role can be assumed at a time.

```
@RunAs("manager")
```

When the **@RunAs** annotation is used, it is normally used in conjunction with the **@DeclareRoles** annotation.

How to do it...

We will add another class to the `packt` package to demonstrate the use of the **@RunAs** annotation. Let's assume when a voucher is submitted it should be verified. If it fails verification, then an exception can be thrown. In this example, we will not throw an exception so as to keep it simple. An additional restriction, which we will use to illustrate this technique, requires the methods of this verification EJB to run in the manager role.

Add a class to the `packt` package called `VoucherVerification`. Annotate the class with the **@RunAs** annotation using a value of "manager". In the class, inject a `SessionContext` object using the **@Resource** annotation. Add a `submit` method which passes and returns `void`. In the method, add code to use the `SessionContext` variable to return a principal object. This principal represents the user who invoked the method. The `getCallerPrincipal` method returns a `Principal` object. Follow the call with a `println` method invoking the `getName` method of the principal to display the principal's name.

```
@Stateless
@DeclareRoles("manager")
@RunAs("manager")
public class VoucherVerification {
    @Resource
    private SessionContext sessionContext;

    public void submit() {
        Principal principal = sessionContext.getCallerPrincipal();
        System.out.println("Principal: " + principal.getName());
        // Perform verification checks

    }
}
```

Modify the `VoucherManager` class to inject an instance of the `VerificationManager` class. Modify its `submit` method to call the `VerificationVoucher`'s submit method.

```
public class VoucherManager {
    ...
    @EJB
    VoucherVerification voucherVerification;
    ...
    @RolesAllowed("employee")
    public void submit() {
        System.out.println("Voucher submitted");
        voucherVerification.submit();
    }
    ...
}
```

Modify the `SecurityServlet` try block to appear as follows:

```
out.println("<html>");
out.println("<head>");
out.println("<title>Servlet SecurityServlet</title>");
out.println("</head>");
out.println("<body>");
```

```
voucherManager.createVoucher("Susan Billings", "SanFrancisco",
  BigDecimal.valueOf(2150.75));
voucherManager.submit();

out.println("<h3>Voucher name: " + voucherManager.getName() +
  "</h3>");

out.println("</body>");
out.println("</html>");
```

Execute the application using the user, "mary", first and then "sally". The output from the `println` method reflects the different users.

INFO: Voucher submitted

INFO: Principal: mary

INFO: Voucher submitted

INFO: Principal: sally

Even though the user, "sally", is not a manager, the `submit` method is still executed.

How it works...

The `VoucherManager`'s `submit` method executed using the role of employee. However, we decided the `VoucherValidation`'s `submit` method needed to run in the manager role. Allowing an employee to temporarily use the manager role was achieved using the **@RunAs** annotation.

The use of the **@RunAs** annotation should be used with care. Sufficient checks should be made to ensure the selected method is executed only when any restrictions placed on its use have been met. In a sense, we are augmenting declarative security with a set of criteria to meet special conditions.

Controlling security programmatically

Programmatic security is based upon the **Java Authentication and Authorization Service (JAAS)** API. It should be used when declarative annotation is not adequate to affect the level of security desired. This can occur when access is time-based. For example, a user may only be allowed to access certain services during normal business hours such as when the stock market is open.

Getting ready

Programmatic security is affected by adding code within methods to determine who the caller is and then allowing certain actions to be performed based on their capabilities. There are two `EJBContext` interface methods available to support this type of security: `getCallerPrincipal` and `isCallerInRole`. The `SessionContext` object implements the `EJBContext` interface. The `SessionContext`'s `getCallerPrincipal` method returns a `Principal` object which can be used to get the name or other attributes of the user. The `isCallerInRole` method takes a string representing a role and returns a Boolean value indicating whether the caller of the method is a member of the role or not.

The steps for controlling security programmatically involve:

1. Injecting a `SessionContext` instance
2. Using either of the above two methods to effect security

How to do it...

To demonstrate these two methods we will modify the `SecurityServlet` to use the `VoucherManager`'s approve method and then augment the `approve` method with code using these methods.

First modify the `SecurityServlet` try block to use the following code. We create a voucher as usual and then follow with a call to the `submit` and `approve` methods.

```
out.println("<html>");
out.println("<head>");
out.println("<title>Servlet SecurityServlet</title>");
out.println("</head>");
out.println("<body>");

voucherManager.createVoucher("Susan Billings", "SanFrancisco",
  BigDecimal.valueOf(2150.75));
voucherManager.submit();
boolean voucherApproved = voucherManager.approve();

if(voucherApproved) {
  out.println("<h3>Voucher was approved</h3>");
} else {
    out.println("<h3>Voucher was not approved</h3>");
  }

out.println("<h3>Voucher name: " + voucherManager.getName() +
  "</h3>");

out.println("</body>");
out.println("</html>");
```

Next, modify the `VoucherManager` EJB by injecting a `SessionContext` object using the **@Resource** annotation.

```
public class VoucherManager {
    ...
    @Resource
    private SessionContext sessionContext;
```

Let's look at the `getCallerPrincipal` method first. This method returns a `Principal` object (`java.security.Principal`) which has only one method of immediate interest: `getName`. This method returns the name of the principal.

Modify the `approve` method so it uses the `SessionContext` object to get the `Principal` and then determines if the name of the principal is "mary" or not. If it is, then approve the voucher.

```
public boolean approve() {
    Principal principal = sessionContext.getCallerPrincipal();
    System.out.println("Principal: " + principal.getName());
    if("mary".equals(principal.getName())) {
      voucher.setApproved(true);
      System.out.println("approve method returned true");
      return true;
    } else {
        System.out.println("approve method returned false");
        return false;
    }
}
```

Execute the `SecurityApplication` using "mary" as the user. The application should approve the voucher with the output as shown in the following screenshot:

Execute the application again with a user of "sally". This execution will result in an exception.

INFO: Access exception

The `getCallerPrincipal` method simply returns the principal. This frequently results in the need to explicitly include the name of a user in code. The hard coding of user names is not recommended. Checking against each individual user can be time consuming. It is more efficient to check to see if a user is in a role.

The `isCallerInRole` method allows us to determine whether the user is in a particular role or not. It returns a Boolean value indicating whether the user is in the role specified by the method's string argument. Rewrite the `approve` method to call the `isCallerInRole` method and pass the string "`manager`" to it. If the return value returns `true`, approve the voucher.

```
public boolean approve() {
  if(sessionContext.isCallerInRole("manager")) {
    voucher.setApproved(true);
    System.out.println("approve method returned true");
    return true;
  } else {
    System.out.println("approve method returned false");
    return false;
  }
}
```

Execute the application using both "mary" and "sally". The results of the application should be the same as the previous example where the `getCallerPrincipal` method was used.

How it works...

The `SessionContext` class was used to obtain either a `Principal` object or to determine whether a user was in a particular role or not. This required the injection of a `SessionContext` instance and adding code to determine if the user was permitted to perform certain actions.

This approach resulted in more code than the declarative approach. However, it provided more flexibility in controlling access to the application. These techniques provided the developer with choices as to how to best meet the needs of the application.

There's more...

It is possible to take different actions depending on the user's role using the `isCallerInRole` method. Let's assume we are using programmatic security with multiple roles.

```
@DeclareRoles ({"employee", "manager","auditor"})
```

We can use a `validateAllowance` method to accept a travel allowance amount and determine whether it is appropriate based on the role of the user.

```
public boolean validateAllowance(BigDecimal allowance) {
    if(sessionContext.isCallerInRole("manager")) {
        if(allowance.compareTo(BigDecimal.valueOf(2500)) <= 0) {
            return true;
        } else {
            return false;
        }
    } else  if(sessionContext.isCallerInRole("employee")) {
        if(allowance.compareTo(BigDecimal.valueOf(1500)) <= 0) {
            return true;
        } else {
            return false;
        }
    } else  if(sessionContext.isCallerInRole("auditor")) {
        if(allowance.compareTo(BigDecimal.valueOf(1000)) <= 0) {
            return true;
        } else {
            return false;
        }
    } else {
        return false;
    }
}
```

The `compareTo` method compares two `BigDecimal` values and returns one of three values:

▸ -1 – If the first number is less than the second number

▸ 0 – If the first and second numbers are equal

▸ 1 – If the first number is greater than the second number

The `valueOf` static method converts a number to a `BigDecimal` value. The value is then compared to `allowance`. This data type is discussed in more detail in _Chapter 12, How to support currency_ recipe.

8
Interceptors

In this chapter, we will cover:

- ▶ Creating the Registration Application
- ▶ Defining and using interceptors
- ▶ Using the `InvocationContext` to verify parameters
- ▶ Using interceptors to enforce security
- ▶ Using interceptors to handle transactions
- ▶ Using interceptors to handle application statistics
- ▶ Using lifecycle methods in interceptors

Introduction

Most applications have cross-cutting functions which must be performed. These cross-cutting functions may include logging, managing transactions, security, and other aspects of an application. Interceptors provide a way to achieve these cross-cutting activities.

The use of interceptors provides a way of adding functionality to a business method without modifying the business method itself. The added functionality is not intermeshed with the business logic resulting in a cleaner and easier to maintain application.

Aspect Oriented Programming (AOP) is concerned with providing support for these cross-cutting functions in a transparent fashion. While interceptors do not provide as much support as other AOP languages, they do offer a good level of support.

Interceptors can be:

- Used to keep business logic separate from non-business related activities
- Easily enabled/disabled
- Provide consistent behavior across an application

Interceptors are specific methods invoked around a method or methods of a target EJB. We will use the term target, to refer to the class containing the method(s) an interceptor will be executing around.

The interceptor's method will be executed before the EJB's method is executed. When the interceptor method executes, it is passed as an `InvocationContext` object. This object provides information relating to the state of the interceptor and the target. Within the interceptor method, the `InvocationContext`'s method `proceed` can be issued that will result in the target's business method being executed or, as we will see shortly, the next interceptor in the chain. When the business method returns, the interceptor continues execution. This permits execution of code before and after the execution of a business method.

Interceptors can be used with:

- Stateless session EJBs
- Stateful session EJBs
- Singleton session EJBs
- Message-driven beans

The **@Interceptors** annotation defines which interceptors will be executed for all or individual methods of a class. Interceptor classes use the same lifecycle of the EJB they are applied to, in the case of stateful EJBs, which means the interceptor could be passivated and activated. In addition, they support the use of dependency injection. The injection is done using the EJB's naming context.

More than one interceptor can be used at a time. The sequence of interceptor execution is referred to as an interceptor chain. For example, an application may need to start a transaction based on the privileges of a user. These actions should also be logged. An interceptor can be defined for each of these activities: validating the user, starting the transaction, and logging the event. The use of interceptor chaining is illustrated in the *Using interceptors to handle application statistics* recipe.

Lifecycle callbacks such as **@PreDestroy** and **@PostConstruct** can also be used within interceptors. They can access interceptor state information as discussed in the *Using lifecycle methods in interceptors* recipe.

Interceptors are useful for:

- ▸ Validating parameters and potentially changing them before they are sent to a method
- ▸ Performing security checks
- ▸ Performing logging
- ▸ Performing profiling
- ▸ Gathering statistics

An example of parameter validation can be found in the *Using the InvocationContext to verify parameters* recipe. Security checks are illustrated in the *Using interceptors to enforce security* recipe. The use of interceptor chaining to record a method's hit count and the time spent in the method is discussed in the *Using interceptors to handle application statistics* recipe. Interceptors can also be used in conjunction with timer services, however this discussion is deferred to *Chapter 9, Using interceptors with timers* recipe.

The recipes in this chapter are based largely around a conference registration application as developed in the first recipe. It will be necessary to create this application before the other recipes can be demonstrated.

Creating the Registration Application

A `RegistrationApplication` is developed in this recipe. It provides the ability of attendees to register for a conference. The application will record their personal information using an entity and other supporting EJBs. This recipe details how to create this application.

Getting ready

The `RegistrationApplication` consists of the following classes:

- ▸ `Attendee` – An entity representing a person attending the conference
- ▸ `AbstractFacade` – A facade-based class as detailed in *Chapter 4, EJB Persistence*
- ▸ `AttendeeFacade` – The facade class for the `Attendee` class
- ▸ `RegistrationManager` – Used to control the registration process
- ▸ `RegistrationServlet` – The GUI interface for the application

The steps used to create this application include:

1. Creating the `Attendee` entity and its supporting classes
2. Creating a `RegistrationManager` EJB to control the registration process
3. Creating a `RegistrationServlet` to drive the application

The `RegistrationManager` will be the primary vehicle for the demonstration of interceptors.

How to do it...

Create a Java EE application called `RegistrationApplication`. Add a `packt` package to the EJB module and a `servlet` package in the application's WAR module.

Next, add an `Attendee` entity to the `packt` package. This entity possesses four fields: `name`, `title`, `company`, and `id`. The `id` field should be auto generated. Add getters and setters for the fields. Also add a default constructor and a three argument constructor for the first three fields. The major components of the class are shown below without the getters and setters.

```
@Entity
public class Attendee implements Serializable {
    private String name;
    private String title;
    private String company;
    private static final long serialVersionUID = 1L;
    @Id
    @GeneratedValue(strategy = GenerationType.AUTO)
    private Long id;

    public Attendee() {

    }

    public Attendee(String name, String title, String company) {
        this.name = name;
        this.title = title;
        this.company = company;
    }

}
```

Next, add an `AttendeeFacade` stateless session bean which is derived from the `AbstractFacade` class. Details of the `AbstractFacade` can be found in the *Chapter 4, Creating an entity facade* recipe. The `AbstractFacade` class is not shown here.

```
@Stateless
public class AttendeeFacade extends AbstractFacade<Attendee> {
    @PersistenceContext(unitName = "RegistrationApplication-ejbPU")
    private EntityManager em;

    protected EntityManager getEntityManager() {
        return em;
```

```
    }

  public AttendeeFacade() {
    super(Attendee.class);
  }

}
```

Add a `RegistrationManager` stateful session bean to the `packt` package. Add a single method, `register`, to the class. The method should be passed three strings for the name, title, and company of the attendee. It should return an `Attendee` reference. Use dependency injection to add a reference to the `AttendeeFacade`. In the `register` method, create a new `Attendee` and then use the `AttendeeFacade` class to create it. Next, return a reference to the `Attendee`.

```
@Stateful
public class RegistrationManager {

  @EJB
  AttendeeFacade attendeeFacade;

  Attendee attendee;

  public Attendee register(String name, String title,
    String company) {
    attendee = new Attendee(name, title, company);
    attendeeFacade.create(attendee);
    return attendee;
  }
}
```

In the `servlet` package of the WAR module, add a servlet called `RegistrationServlet`. This servlet will follow the same structure as detailed in the *Chapter 1, Accessing a session bean using dependency injection* recipe. Use dependency injection to add a reference to the `RegistrationManager`. In the try block of the `processRequest` method, use the `register` method to register an attendee and then display the attendee's name.

```
public class RegistrationServlet extends HttpServlet {
  @EJB
  RegistrationManager registrationManager;

  protected void processRequest(HttpServletRequest request,
    HttpServletResponse response)
    throws ServletException, IOException {
      response.setContentType("text/html;charset=UTF-8");
      PrintWriter out = response.getWriter();
```

```
try {

    out.println("<html>");
    out.println("<head>");
    out.println("<title>Servlet RegistrationServlet</title>");
    out.println("</head>");
    out.println("<body>");
    Attendee attendee = registrationManager.register("Bill
        Schroder", "Manager", "Acme Software");
    out.println("<h3>" + attendee.getName() + " has been
        registered</h3>");
    out.println("</body>");
    out.println("</html>");

} finally {
    out.close();
}

}
...
}
```

Execute the servlet. The output should appear as shown in the following screenshot:

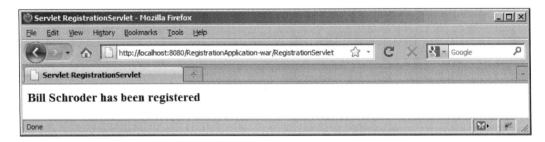

How it works...

The `Attendee` entity holds the registration information for each participant. The `RegistrationManager` session bean only has a single method at this time. In later recipes we will augment this class to add other capabilities. The `RegistrationServlet` is the client for the EJBs.

See also

See *Chapter 1, Accessing a session bean using dependency injection* recipe for details on the creation of a servlet and *Chapter 4, Creating an entity facade* recipe for details about the entity facade.

Defining and using interceptors

In this recipe, we will examine the process of creating and using a simple interceptor. An interceptor method will be invoked before a target method is executed. When the target method returns, additional code within the interceptor can be executed. This approach is useful for performing orthogonal tasks and for manipulating the parameters sent to a method and/or returned from a method.

Getting ready

There are two major steps in the creation and use of an interceptor:

1. Creating a class containing an **@AroundInvoke** annotated method
2. Specifying the target method using the **@Interceptors** annotation

To use an interceptor, we must first create it and then specify where it will be used. The **@AroundInvoke** annotation designates a method as an interceptor method. The method that follows must have a specific signature as shown here:

```
public Object methodName(InvocationContext context) throws Exception
```

The interceptor method can be declared either within the target class or in a separate class.

How to do it...

Add a class called `SimpleInterceptor` to the `packt` package. Within this class add a method called `simpleMethod` which is preceded with the **@AroundInvoke** annotation. Within the method display the name of the target method, invoke the target method with the `proceed` method and then display the target method name again as shown here:

```
public class SimpleInterceptor {
  @AroundInvoke
  public Object simpleMethod(InvocationContext context) throws
    Exception{
    System.out.println("SimpleInterceptor entered: " +
      context.getMethod().getName());
    Object result =  context.proceed();
    System.out.println("SimpleInterceptor exited: " +
      context.getMethod().getName());
    return result;
  }
}
```

The second step is to indicate where the interceptor is to be used. It can be applied in one of three places. Here it is used at the class level using the **@Interceptors** annotation. Add an **@Interceptors** annotation to the `RegistrationManager` class. Notice the annotation takes the interceptor class as its argument. In this example, only the business methods of the `RegistrationManager` class will be intercepted and handled by the `SimpleInterceptor`.

```
@Stateful
@Interceptors(SimpleInterceptor.class)
public class RegistrationManager {
    . . .
}
```

Execute the servlet. It should behave the same way it did earlier but you should notice the following messages being displayed in the server or development environment console window:

INFO SimpleInterceptor entered: register

INFO: register

INFO: SimpleInterceptor exited: register

How it works...

The interceptor will be executed before the EJB's method is executed. The sequence of actions an interceptor will take depends on the specific interceptor. However, this list details possible actions:

- ▸ Perform any processing needed before the target method is invoked (possibly modifying the target method parameters)
- ▸ Invoke the target using the `proceed` method
- ▸ Perform post target processing (possibly modifying the target method's return value)
- ▸ If no exceptions have been thrown, return the target method's result

The interceptor is responsible for invoking the target. If the interceptor does not invoke the target, then it must still return a result or throw an exception. The `InvocationContext`'s `proceed` method invokes the target method. When the interceptor returns, it will normally use the return value of the target method. The target method can be invoked zero or more times.

In the method, `simpleMethod`, an `InvocationContext` object was passed that contains information regarding the invocation such as the name of the target method. This object's `getMethod` returns another object representing the target method whose `getName` method will return the target method's name. We used this technique twice: once before the `proceed` method was called and once after the target method returned. Notice the `proceed` method returned a value we stored in `result` which was then returned by the interceptor.

Interceptors can be defined either:

- ▸ Inside of the class where they will be used, or
- ▸ In an interceptor class

Binding an interceptor to a class or a method can be done using either annotations or a deployment descriptor. The use of a deployment descriptor is detailed in *Chapter 11, Using deployment descriptors for business interceptors* recipe.

There's more...

Interceptors can be created in three different ways:

1. For all EJBs in an EJB module
2. For all of the methods of a class
3. For a specific method

Interceptors can also be declared within the target class itself. In addition, more than one interceptor class can be specified in the **@Interceptors** annotation. Here we have three interceptors defined for use with the `register` method.

```
@Interceptors({LogInterceptor.class, SecurityInterceptor.class,
    TransactionInterceptor.class})
public Attendee register(String name, String title, String company) {
    ...
}
```

These interceptors will be executed in the order they appear in the annotation.

Creating an Interceptor for all EJBs in an EJB module

We can associate an interceptor with all of the EJBs of an application by adding an `<interceptor-binding>` element to the application's EJB jar. Java EE 6 application no longer requires deployment descriptors as annotations have largely taken their place. However, there are certain situations where they are still needed. One of these situations is when we want to use a default interceptor.

You will probably have to create an `ejb-jar.xml` file for your application. This process is development-environment specific. For example, in NetBeans, right-click on the EJB module for your project in the **Project Explorer** and select **New ... Standard Deployment Descriptor**. This will create the `ejb-jar.xml` file.

The process of associating an interceptor with all of the EJBs of an application involves:

1. Adding an `<interceptors>` element to define the interceptor
2. Adding an `<assembly-descriptor>` element to associate the interceptor with all of the methods of the application
3. Creating the interceptor class

Once you have created the `ejb-jar.xml`, add an `<interceptors>` element to declare your default interceptor. Within the element add one `<interceptor>` element for each interceptor. In this case, there is only one. The `<interceptor-class>` element is needed to specify the name of the interceptor class.

```
<interceptors>
  <interceptor>
    <interceptor-class>packt.DefaultInterceptor</interceptor-class>
  </interceptor>
</interceptors>
```

Next, add an `<interceptor-binding>` element inside of an `<assembly-descriptor>` element to bind the interceptor to all of the EJBS in the module. The `<ejb-name>` element uses an asterisk to specify all EJBs in the module. The `<interceptor-class>` element specifies the name of the interceptor.

```
<assembly-descriptor>
  <interceptor-binding>
    <ejb-name>*</ejb-name>
    <interceptor-class>packt.DefaultInterceptor</interceptor-class>
  </interceptor-binding>
</assembly-descriptor>
```

One possible version of the `ejb-jar.xml` file follows:

```
<?xml version="1.0" encoding="UTF-8"?>

<ejb-jar xmlns = "http://java.sun.com/xml/ns/javaee"
  version = "3.1"
  xmlns:xsi = "http://www.w3.org/2001/XMLSchema-instance"
  xsi:schemaLocation = "http://java.sun.com/xml/ns/javaee
  http://java.sun.com/xml/ns/javaee/ejb-jar_3_1.xsd">
  <interceptors>
    <interceptor>
      <interceptor-class>packt.DefaultInterceptor</interceptor-class>
    </interceptor>
  </interceptors>
<assembly-descriptor>
  <interceptor-binding>
```

```
        <ejb-name>*</ejb-name>
        <interceptor-class>packt.DefaultInterceptor</interceptor-class>
    </interceptor-binding>
</assembly-descriptor>
</ejb-jar>
```

We need to create the default interceptor before we can run our application. Add a new class to the `packt` package called `DefaultInterceptor`. It should be very similar to the `SimpleInterceptor` except for the use of the method name `defaultMethod` and there will be no need to use the **@Interceptors** annotation at the class level. Add `println` methods to indicate we are executing from the default interceptor.

```
public class DefaultInterceptor {
  @AroundInvoke
  public Object defaultMethod(InvocationContext context) throws
    Exception{
    System.out.println("Default Interceptor: Invoking method: " +
      context.getMethod().getName());
    Object result =  context.proceed();
    System.out.println("Default Interceptor: Returned from method: "
      + context.getMethod().getName());
    return result;
  }
}
```

Execute the application. Once again we should not see any difference in the output of the servlet. However, the output in the console will reflect the execution of both the `SimpleInterceptor` and the `DefaultInterceptor` as shown here:

INFO: Default Interceptor: Invoking method: register

INFO SimpleInterceptor entered: register

INFO: register

INFO: Default Interceptor: Invoking method: create

INFO: Default Interceptor: Returned from method: create

INFO: SimpleInterceptor exited: register

INFO: Default Interceptor: Returned from method: register

Notice the `DefaultInterceptor` begins execution before the `SimpleInterceptor` and completes after it. This is an example of an interceptor chain. One interceptor is executed followed by another and then by the target method. The order of interceptor chaining is detailed in the *Using interceptors to handle application statistics* recipe.

Using XML notation means we can change the interceptor used without recompiling the source code. This is of particular value if the interceptor is concerned with "system" type functions such as counting the number of times an application is accessed.

Creating an interceptor for all methods of a class

If the intent is to use the same interceptor for all methods of an EJB, then we simply apply the **@Interceptors** annotation to the class as we did with the `SimpleInterceptor`.

```
@Stateful
@Interceptors({SimpleInterceptor.class})
public class RegistrationManager {
```

If we don't want a class level interceptor to be executed for a particular method, we can use the **@ExcludeClassInterceptors** annotation with the method. This annotation has no arguments and will not use any interceptors declared at the class level.

```
@ExcludeClassInterceptors
public Attendee register(String name, String title,
  String company) {
...
}
```

Execute the application using this annotation. The output should be the same except you should not see the `SimpleInterceptor` being used with the `register` method.

Creating an interceptor for a specific method

Interceptors can also be declared at the method level. The **@Interceptors** annotation is used the same way but precedes the method declaration instead of the class declaration. The basic steps include:

1. Defining an interceptor to use
2. Annotating the method with the **@Interceptors** annotation

To illustrate this type of interceptor, add a new interceptor class called, `MethodInterceptor` to the `packt` package. It will be very similar to the previous interceptors except it uses a method name of `methodLevel`. Add `println` methods to indicate we are executing from this interceptor.

```
public class MethodInterceptor {
  @AroundInvoke
  public Object methodLevel(InvocationContext context) throws
    Exception{
    System.out.println("Method Interceptor: Invoking method: " +
      context.getMethod().getName());
    Object result =  context.proceed();
```

```
      System.out.println("Method Interceptor: Returned from method: " +
        context.getMethod().getName());
      return result;
    }
  }
```

Add the **@Interceptors** annotation to the RegistrationManager's register method specifying the MethodInterceptor class.

```
    @Interceptors({MethodInterceptor.class})
    public Attendee register(String name, String title,
      String company) {
    ...
    }
```

Execute the servlet. If the DefaultInterceptor and SimpleInterceptor are still being used, then you will see all three executing.

INFO: Default Interceptor: Invoking method: register

INFO: SimpleInterceptor entered: register

INFO: Method Interceptor: Invoking method: register

INFO: register

INFO: Default Interceptor: Invoking method: create

INFO: Default Interceptor: Returned from method: create

INFO: Method Interceptor: Returned from method: register

INFO: SimpleInterceptor exited: register

INFO: Default Interceptor: Returned from method: register

Declaring an interceptor in the target class

An interceptor method can be declared within a target class in the same way as in a separate class using the **@AroundInvoke** annotation. The interceptor will be applied to all methods of the EJB unless specified otherwise.

Add a new method to the RegistrationManager class called, internalMethod. Place the **@AroundInvoke** annotation in front of it. The method should have the same structure as previous interceptors but with the new method name and different println methods.

```
    @AroundInvoke
    public Object internalMethod(InvocationContext context) throws
      Exception{
```

```
        System.out.println("internalMethod: Invoking method: " +
          context.getMethod().getName());
        Object result =  context.proceed();
        System.out.println("internalMethod: Returned from method: " +
          context.getMethod().getName());
        return result;
    }
```

Execute the servlet. Assuming the previous interceptors are still in place, your output should be as follows:

INFO: Default Interceptor: Invoking method: register

INFO: SimpleInterceptor entered: register

INFO: Method Interceptor: Invoking method: register

INFO: internalMethod: Invoking method: register

INFO: register

INFO: Default Interceptor: Invoking method: create

INFO: Default Interceptor: Returned from method: create

INFO: internalMethod: Returned from method: register

INFO: Method Interceptor: Returned from method: register

INFO: SimpleInterceptor exited: register

INFO: Default Interceptor: Returned from method: register

Using the InvocationContext to verify parameters

The InvocationContext interface is used to support information handling within and between interceptors. It is passed as the single argument to a method annotated with the **@AroundInvoke** annotation. It possesses several methods which can assist in the handling of interceptors. In this recipe we will focus on those methods which provide access to the target method's parameter list and use them to manipulate the parameters.

Getting ready

The basic approach for using an interceptor to validate a target method's parameters involves:

1. Accessing the target's parameters using the `getParameters` method
2. Validating and possibly modifying the parameters
3. Using the `setParameters` method to apply any changes to the parameters
4. Invoking the `proceed` method

How to do it...

To keep the example simple, we will perform a simple validation. We will call the `RegistrationManager`'s `register` method and make sure the parameters do not have any leading or trailing blanks.

First, add a new interceptor to the `packt` package called `ValidationInterceptor`. Call its method `validateParameters` as shown below. In this method we use the `println` method to display the execution sequence of the interceptor and the parameters as they are modified.

```java
public class ValidationInterceptor {
  @AroundInvoke
  public Object validateParameters(InvocationContext context) throws
    Exception{
    System.out.println("ValidationInterceptor");

    Object parameters[] = context.getParameters();
    for(int i=0; i<parameters.length; i++) {
      System.out.println("Before: ["+(String)parameters[i] + "]");
      parameters[i] = ((String)parameters[i]).trim();
      System.out.println("After: ["+(String)parameters[i]+"]");
    }
    context.setParameters(parameters);

    Object result =  context.proceed();
    return result;
  }
}
```

Next, precede the `RegistrationManager`'s `register` method with the interceptor annotation.

```java
@Interceptors(ValidationInterceptor.class)
```

In addition, change the output of the `RegistrationServlet` to create an attendee that has a combination of leading and trailing blanks for its arguments.

```
Attendee attendee = registrationManager.register(" Bill Schroder ",
    "Manager", "Acme Software");
out.println("<h3>" + attendee.getName() + " has been
    registered</h3>");
```

Execute the servlet and examine the console output. Depending on the interceptors in place, your output should be similar to the following:

INFO: ValidationInterceptor

INFO: Before: [Bill Schroder]

INFO: After: [Bill Schroder]

INFO: Before: [Manager]

INFO: After: [Manager]

INFO: Before: [Acme Software]

INFO: After: [Acme Software]

How it works...

When the interceptor is first executed we used the `getParameters` method to retrieve the parameters passed to the target method. The `String` method `trim` was used to remove any leading or trailing blanks for each parameter. The `setParameters` method was then used to pass these new values to the target method. The target method was then invoked with the `proceed` method. Additional `println` methods have be included to help illustrate the execution sequence.

The `InvocationContext` interface provides information about the state of a chain of interceptors and the target. During the execution of this invocation chain, it can be useful to maintain state information. The `InvocationContext` interface has seven methods useful for this purpose as listed in the following table. The interceptor has complete access to the target method's name and its parameters.

Method	Return Value	Description
getContextData	java.util.Map	The Map containing the context data.
getMethod	java.lang.reflect.Method	The object represents the method for which the interceptor was executed
getParameters	Objects[]	The array represents the arguments passed to the method
getTarget	Object	A reference to the target
getTimer	Object	A reference to the Timer object for the target if present
proceed	Object	Control is passed to the next interceptor in the chain or the business method if there are no more interceptors. The return value comes from the next method in the interceptor chain
setParameters	void	It is passed an array of objects which will be passed to the target's method

There's more...

The InvocationContext interface has a number of other useful methods. The getContextData method is used to pass information between interceptors. This is illustrated in the *Using interceptors to handle application statistics* recipe.

Here we will examine two other methods:

- ▸ Using getTarget to return information about the target
- ▸ Using getMethod to return information about the target's method

Using getTarget to return information about the target

The getTarget method returns a reference to the target. Add this statement to the beginning of the validateParameters method. It returns a reference to the RegistrationManager.

```
System.out.println("ValidationInterceptor");
System.out.println(context.getTarget());
```

One possible output appears as follows:

INFO: ValidationInterceptor

INFO: packt._RegistrationManager_Serializable@101b74e

This reference can be used to access fields and methods of the class. For example, to execute a method we could use code similar to the following:

```
((RegistrationManager)context.getTarget()).methodName();
```

Using getMethod to return information about the target's method

The getMethod returns a java.lang.reflect.Method object which is useful if you need more detailed information about the method such as the annotations used, exceptions thrown, and parameter types to mention a few.

For example, to determine which annotations are used with the target method, insert the following code at the beginning of the validateParameters method. The getAnnotations method returns an array of annotations used with the method. Using a for each statement and println method we can display this list.

```
System.out.println("ValidationInterceptor");
Annotation annotations[] = context.getMethod().getAnnotations();
for(Annotation annotation: annotations) {
  System.out.println(annotation);
}
```

The output below shows only one annotation being used at this time.

INFO: ValidationInterceptor

INFO: @javax.interceptor.Interceptors(value=[class packt.ValidationInterceptor])

See the Reflection API (java.lang.reflect) to further explore the capabilities of the Method class.

Using interceptors to enforce security

While security is an important aspect of many applications, the use of programmatic security can clutter up business logic. The use of declarative annotations has come a long way in making security easier to use and less intrusive. However, there are still times when programmatic security is necessary. When it is, then the use of interceptors can help remove the security code from the business logic.

Getting ready

The process for using an interceptor to enforce security involves:

1. Configuring and enabling security for the application server
2. Adding a **@DeclareRoles** to the target class and the interceptor class
3. Creating a security interceptor

How to do it...

Configure the application to handle security as detailed in *Chapter 7, Configuring the server to handle security* recipe. Add the **@DeclareRoles**("employee") to the RegistrationManager class.

Add a SecurityInterceptor class to the packt package. Inject a SessionContext object into the class. We will use this object to perform programmatic security. Also use the **@DeclareRoles** annotation.

Next, add an interceptor method, verifyAccess, to the class. Use the SessionContext object and its isCallerInRole method to determine if the user is in the "employee" role. If so, invoke the proceed method and display a message to that effect. Otherwise, throw an EJBAccessException.

```
@DeclareRoles("employee")
public class SecurityInterceptor {

  @Resource
  private SessionContext sessionContext;

  @AroundInvoke
  public Object verifyAccess(InvocationContext context) throws
    Exception {
  System.out.println("SecurityInterceptor: Invoking method: " +
    context.getMethod().getName());
  if (sessionContext.isCallerInRole("employee")) {
    Object result = context.proceed();
    System.out.println("SecurityInterceptor: Returned from method: "
      + context.getMethod().getName());
    return result;
  } else {
      throw new EJBAccessException();
    }
  }
}
```

Execute the application. The user should be prompted for a username and password as shown in the following screenshot. Provide a user in the employee role.

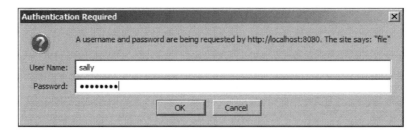

The application should execute to completion.

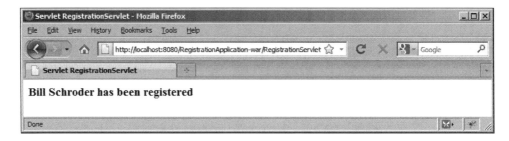

Depending on the interceptors in place, you will console output similar to the following:

INFO: Default Interceptor: Invoking method: register

INFO: SimpleInterceptor entered: register

INFO: SecurityInterceptor: Invoking method: register

INFO: InternalMethod: Invoking method: register

INFO: register

INFO: Default Interceptor: Invoking method: create

INFO: Default Interceptor: Returned from method: create

INFO: InternalMethod: Returned from method: register

INFO: SecurityInterceptor: Returned from method: register

INFO: SimpleInterceptor exited: register

INFO: Default Interceptor: Returned from method: register

How it works...

The **@DeclareRoles** annotation was used to specify that users in the employee role are associated with the class. The `isCallerInRole` method checked to see if the current user is in the employee role. When the target method is called, if the user is authorized then the `InterceptorContext`'s `proceed` method is executed. If the user is not authorized, then the target method is not invoked and an exception is thrown.

See also

Programmatic security is detailed in *Chapter 7, Configuring the server to handle security* recipe.

Using interceptors to handle transactions

Transaction processing is used in many applications. However, the implementation of transactions can clutter up business logic. The use of declarative annotations can make transaction processing easier to use. But there are still times when programmatic transaction is necessary such as with long running transactions. When it is, interceptors can be useful.

Getting ready

The essential steps to use interceptors for handling transactions include:

1. Creating a transaction interceptor
2. Annotating the target class to use bean-managed transactions
3. Annotating the target method with the transaction interceptor

The *Handling transactions manually* recipe in *Chapter 6* explains how to implement bean managed transactions.

How to do it...

To illustrate the use of interceptors to effect transaction processing, add a `TransactionInterceptor` class to the `packt` package. Using dependency injection, inject a `UserTransaction` object.

Next, add a `verifyAccess` method using the **@AroundInvoke** annotation. Within the method, begin the transaction, invoke the `proceed` method and then commit the transaction.

```
public class TransactionInterceptor {

    @Resource
```

```
    private UserTransaction userTransaction;

    @AroundInvoke
    public Object verifyAccess(InvocationContext context) throws
      Exception {
      userTransaction.begin();
      System.out.println("Beginning transaction");
      Object result = context.proceed();
      System.out.println("Committing the transaction");
      userTransaction.commit();
      return result;
    }
}
```

In the RegistrationManager class, add the **@TransactionManagement** annotation at the class level and specify bean-managed transactions. Also add an EntityManager instance for your application.

```
@TransactionManagement(TransactionManagementType.BEAN)
public class RegistrationManager {
    . . .
    @PersistenceContext(unitName = "RegistrationApplication-ejbPU")
    private EntityManager entityManager;
```

Next, add a method called bulkRegister. The intent of this method is to provide a way of adding multiple attendees all from the same company at one time. It is passed an array of names and titles along with the company name. It then iterates through the arrays adding one attendee at a time. Add the **@Interceptor** annotation to the method using the transaction interceptor.

```
@Interceptors({TransactionInterceptor.class})
public void bulkRegister(String names[], String titles[],
  String company) {
  for(int i=0; i<names.length; i++) {
    attendeeFacade.create(new Attendee(names[i],
      titles[i],company));
  }
}
```

Modify the RegistrationServlet to test the interceptor. Add two arrays for the names and titles along with a company variable. Initialize the arrays then invoke the bulkRegister method.

```
String names[] = {"John", "Paul", "Karen"};
String titles[] = {"Lead", "Programmer", "Adminsitrator"};
String company = "Acme Software";
registrationManager.bulkRegister(names, titles, company);
```

Execute the servlet. Depending on which interceptors are in place for the application, you should see an output sequence reflecting this registration process.

INFO: Beginning transaction

INFO: InternalMethod: Invoking method: bulkRegister

INFO: Default Interceptor: Invoking method: create

INFO: Default Interceptor: Returned from method: create

INFO: Default Interceptor: Invoking method: create

INFO: Default Interceptor: Returned from method: create

INFO: Default Interceptor: Invoking method: create

INFO: Default Interceptor: Returned from method: create

INFO: InternalMethod: Returned from method: bulkRegister

INFO: Committing the transaction

How it works...

When the `bulkRegister` method was called, the `verifyAccess` method of the `TransactionInterceptor` class was called first. The method started a transaction using the `begin` method and then invoked the target method, `bulkRegister`, with the `proceed` method. When this method returned, the transaction was committed using the `commit` method.

There's more...

Transaction processing can be more complex than illustrated in the previous example. When a method is invoked, it may or may not be part of another transaction. Exceptions may be thrown which force the roll back of a transaction. These and potentially other issues must be taken into consideration when using an interceptor to handle transactions.

To illustrate the issues involved, the following table outlines the steps needed to handle container-based transactions based on the transaction attribute of the target method. Pre-processing refers to those activities which should be performed before the `proceed` method is executed. The post-processing activities are those which should be performed when the `proceed` method returns.

Transaction attribute	Pre-processing	Post-processing
Required	Create a new transaction if one is not present	Rollback the transaction and throw a `TransactionRolledbackException` if the transaction is marked for rollback or an exception is thrown. Otherwise commit the transaction.
Mandatory	If no transaction exists throw an exception	Rollback the transaction and throw a `TransactionRolledbackException` if the transaction is marked for rollback or an exception is thrown.
RequiresNew	Create a new transaction	Rollback the transaction and throw a `TransactionRolledbackException` if the transaction is marked for rollback or an exception is thrown. Otherwise commit the transaction.

See also

The *Handling transactions manually* recipe in Chapter 6 covers bean-managed transactions in more depth.

Using interceptors to handle application statistics

The gathering of application statistics is a common requirement. It may be desirable to determine how many times a method is executed or how much time is spent in a method. This recipe illustrates collecting both of these types of statistics using a chain of interceptors.

Getting ready

The process for developing and using interceptors for an application's statistics is similar to previous techniques and include:

1. Creating a class to maintain the application's statistics
2. Creating interceptors to support the gathering of the statistics
3. Using the **@Interceptors** annotation to designate a target method

In this recipe we will create two interceptors. The first will keep track of the number of times a method is executed and the second will keep track of the amount of time spent in a method. We will apply the interceptors against the `RegistrationManager`'s `register` method. If we need to keep track of statistics for more than one method, then a more sophisticated version of the statistic class would need to be created.

How to do it...

In both of the interceptors we will be using an instance of the `ApplicationStatistics` class to record information about the application. Since only one instance of this class is needed at a time, we will develop it as a singleton. Add the class to the `packt` package along with three member variables:

- ▸   `instance` – Used to implement the singleton pattern
- ▸   `count` – Keeps track of how many times a method is executed
- ▸   `totalTime` – Keeps track of the total amount of time spent in a method

To implement the singleton, add a private default constructor to the class. This means there are no constructors available to create an instance of the class. Add a static `getInstance` method that creates a single instance of the class and returns the instance.

```
public class ApplicationStatistics {
    private static ApplicationStatistics instance;
    private static int count;
    private long totalTime;


    public static ApplicationStatistics getInstance() {
        if(instance == null) {
            instance = new ApplicationStatistics();
        }
        return instance;
    }

    ...
}
```

Add four methods to the class:

- ▸   `getCount` – Returns the value of count
- ▸   `increment` – Increments the count
- ▸   `increaseTotalTime` – Adds a time to `totalTime`
- ▸   `getTotalTime` – Returns `totalTime`

```
    public int getCount() {
        return count;
    }

    public void increment() {
        this.count++;
    }
```

```
      public void increaseTotalTime(long time) {
        totalTime += time;
      }

      public long getTotalTime() {
        return this.totalTime;
      }


    }
```

Next, create two interceptors: `HitCounterInterceptor` and
`TimeInMethodInterceptor`. Both of these interceptors will use the
`ApplicationStatistics` class.

In the `HitCounterInterceptor` class, add an instance variable for
`ApplicationStatistics` and a method called `incrementCounter`. In this method,
obtain an instance of the `ApplicationStatistics` using its `getInstance` method and
then invoke its `increment` method. Next, call the `proceed` method and then return the
result of the method.

```
    public class HitCounterInterceptor {

      ApplicationStatistics applicationStatistics;

      @AroundInvoke
      public Object incrementCounter(InvocationContext context) throws
        Exception {
        System.out.println("HitCounterInterceptor - Starting");
        applicationStatistics = ApplicationStatistics.getInstance();
        applicationStatistics.increment();
        Object result = context.proceed();
        System.out.println("HitCounterInterceptor - Terminating");
        return result;
      }
    }
```

In the `TimeInMethodInterceptor` class, add an instance variable for
`ApplicationStatistics` and a method called `recordTime`. In this method,
obtain an instance of the `ApplicationStatistics` using its `getInstance` method.
We will use the `System` class' `currentTimeMillis` method to get a start and an
ending time. The difference between these two times will be used as an argument to
the `ApplicationStatistics`'s `increaseTotalTime` method. As we did in the
`HitCounterInterceptor` interceptor, call the `proceed` method and then return
the result of the method.

```
public class TimeInMethodInterceptor {

  ApplicationStatistics applicationStatistics;

  @AroundInvoke
  public Object recordTime(InvocationContext context) throws
    Exception {
    System.out.println("TimeInMethodInterceptor - Starting");
    applicationStatistics = ApplicationStatistics.getInstance();
    long startTime = System.currentTimeMillis();
    Object result = context.proceed();
    long endTime = System.currentTimeMillis();
    applicationStatistics.increaseTotalTime(endTime-startTime);
    System.out.println("TimeInMethodInterceptor - Terminating");
    return result;
  }
}
```

In the RegistrationManager class, add an interceptor annotation to the register method for the two interceptors.

```
@Interceptors({HitCounterInterceptor.class,
  TimeInMethodInterceptor.class})
  public Attendee register(String name,
    String title, String company) {
```

Modify the RegistrationServlet to get an instance of the ApplicationStatistics class and then create an attendee. Display the number of attendees and time spent in the register method.

```
ApplicationStatistics applicationStatus =
  ApplicationStatistics.getInstance();

  . . .
Attendee attendee = registrationManager.register("Bill Schroder",
  "Manager", "Acme Software");
out.println("<h3>" + attendee.getName() + " has been
  registered</h3>");
out.println("<h3>Number of attendees: " +
  applicationStatus.getCount() + "</h3>");
out.println("<h3>Total Time: " + applicationStatus.getTotalTime() +
  "</h3>");
```

Execute the servlet. Its output will appear similar to the following screenshot:

The server console should illustrate the execution order of the interceptors:

INFO: HitCounterInterceptor - Starting

INFO: TimeInMethodInterceptor - Starting

INFO: register

INFO: TimeInMethodInterceptor - Terminating

INFO: HitCounterInterceptor - Terminating

How it works...

Notice the **@Interceptors** annotation for the `register` method included both interceptors. This is an example of interceptor chaining which will be discussed in the next section. Also note, the use of the `currentTimeMillis` method may not be accurate enough for some applications.

There's more...

There are three other topics regarding interceptor chaining we need to address:

- Using the `getContextData` method
- Understanding interceptor chaining
- Excluding interceptors

Using the getContextData method

The `InvocationContext` interface has a `getContextData` method that can be used to pass information between interceptors. This can be illustrated through simple modification of `HitCounterInterceptor` and `TimeInMethodInterceptor`.

A `java.util.Map` object is returned from the `getContextData` method. We can add data to the map in one interceptor and retrieve it in a later interceptor. In this example, we will pass the count value generated in the `HitCounterInterceptor`. While this can be retrieved easily from the `ApplicationStatistics` class, using this is a simple way of demonstrating the use of the map.

In the `HitCounterInterceptor` add these two lines of code before the invocation of the `proceed` method. This retrieves the map and then assigns the count value to the key "count".

```
Map<String,Object> data = context.getContextData();
data.put("count", applicationStatistics.getCount());
```

In the `TimeInMethodInterceptor`, add this code at the beginning of the `recordTime` method. The map is retrieved and the "count" element is returned.

```
Map<String,Object> data = context.getContextData();
System.out.println("ContextData count: " + data.get("count"));
```

When the application executes, you will see the value display in the console window.

INFO: HitCounterInterceptor

INFO: TimeInMethodInterceptor

INFO: ContextData count: 2

Understanding interceptor chaining

When multiple interceptors are used, understanding the order of execution of the interceptors can be important. The rules for determining the order of interceptor execution are:

- The default interceptors, specified in the `ejb.jar` file, will be executed first
- Interceptors are executed in the order in which they are declared
- EJB level interceptors are executed before method level interceptors
- Interceptors defined within the target class are executed last
- The interceptors of the super class of an EJB or interceptor classes are executed before the derived classes are.

We can see this in the execution sequence for the interceptors of this recipe. Consider the use of the following interceptors for the `RegistrationManager` class:

```
// DefaultInterceptor declared in the ejb-jar.xml file

@Interceptors(SimpleInterceptor.class)
public class RegistrationManager {
  ...
  @Interceptors({HitCounterInterceptor.class,
  TimeInMethodInterceptor.class})
  public Attendee register(String name, String title,
    String company) {
  ...
  @AroundInvoke
  public Object internalMethod(InvocationContext context) throws
  Exception{
  ...
}
```

The output sequence illustrates the execution order for the `register` method. Comments have been added to clarify the sequence.

INFO: Default Interceptor: Invoking method: register	**// Default interceptor**
INFO: SimpleInterceptor entered: register	**// Defined at class level**
INFO: HitCounterInterceptor	**// Method level – first in list**
INFO: TimeInMethodInterceptor	**// Method level – second in list**
INFO: internalMethod: Invoking method: register	**// Class interceptor**
INFO: register	

...

The use of super classes is not illustrated here; however any interceptors of the EJB super class or an interceptor super class are executed before the derived class interceptors are executed. A super class interceptor for a class level interceptor will be executed before the super class of a method level interceptor.

Excluding interceptors

Sometimes it may be desirable to ignore certain interceptors. There are two annotations whose use will exclude the annotated method from execution:

- ▶ **@ExcludeDefaultInterceptors**
- ▶ **@ExcludeClassInterceptors**

The **@ExcludeDefaultInterceptors** annotation is used at the class level and will exclude default interceptors. The **@ExcludeClassInterceptors** annotation is used at the method level and will exclude annotations declared at the class level.

Use these interceptors with the `RegistrationManager` class as outlined below to exclude the use of the `DefaultInterceptor` and `SimpleInterceptor`.

```
@Interceptors(SimpleInterceptor.class)
@ExcludeDefaultInterceptors
public class RegistrationManager {
  ...
  @Interceptors({HitCounterInterceptor.class,
    TimeInMethodInterceptor.class})
  @ExcludeClassInterceptors
  public Attendee register(String name, String title,
    String company) {
  ...
  @AroundInvoke
  public Object internalMethod(InvocationContext context) throws
    Exception{
  ...
}
```

The output reflects the use of only the `HitCounterInterceptor`, `TimeInMethodInterceptor` and internal interceptors.

INFO: HitCounterInterceptor

INFO: TimeInMethodInterceptor

INFO: internalMethod: Invoking method: register

INFO: register

...

Using lifecycle methods in interceptors

Methods marked with annotations such as **@PreDestroy** and **@PostConstruct** are lifecycle methods. They are invoked during various phases in the lifecycle of an EJB. The **@PrePassivate** and **@PostActivate** annotations are also life cycle methods for stateful session beans. Each EJB type has a different set of lifecycle events. These lifecycle methods can also be used in interceptors.

Getting ready

We will be reusing the `SimpleInterceptor` class as defined in the *Defining and using interceptors* recipe. In this recipe, we will add a **@PostConstruct** annotation to illustrate the incorporation of lifecycle methods.

How to do it...

Modify the `SimpleInterceptor` and add a `constructed` method annotated with **@PostConstruct**. In the method, use the `println` method to display a simple message indicating the execution of the method.

```
public class SimpleInterceptor {

    @PostConstruct
    private void constructed(InvocationContext invocationContext) {
        System.out.println("SimpleInterceptor constructed: ");
    }

    @AroundInvoke
    public Object simpleMethod(InvocationContext context) throws
        Exception {
        System.out.println("SimpleInterceptor entered: " +
            context.getMethod().getName());
        Object result = context.proceed();
        System.out.println("SimpleInterceptor exited: " +
            context.getMethod().getName());
        return result;
    }
}
```

Execute the servlet using the interceptor declared at the class level for the `RegistrationManager` class. The output will show the `constructed` method being executed before the interceptor's `simpleMethod` is executed.

INFO: SimpleInterceptor constructed:

INFO: SimpleInterceptor entered: register

How it works...

Since the `SimpleInterceptor`'s `constructed` method executes when the instance is created, it will execute before its `simpleMethod` executes for a target. Adding lifecycle methods to an interceptor can enhance the utility of the interceptor.

A lifecycle method is annotated with one of several possible lifecycle annotations. These methods must return `void` and normally are passed `void`. However, if they are used in an interceptor, then they have an `InvocationContext` argument.

9

Timer Services

In this chapter, we will cover:

- ▶ Setting up the `ReportsApplication`
- ▶ Creating and using declarative timers
- ▶ Creating and using programmatic timers
- ▶ Understanding calendar-based scheduling
- ▶ Using the timer interface
- ▶ Using persistent and non-persistent timers
- ▶ Creating timers upon application deployment
- ▶ Using interceptors with timers

Introduction

Many business functions are periodic in nature. For example, reports need to be generated, statistics need to be computed, and administrative cleanup tasks need to be performed; all on a regular basis. The EJB container's timer server supports time-delayed, asynchronous callbacks to an EJB to address these needs. An EJB will register with the timer service and a method will be called back.

Timers can be created for all EJB types except for a stateful session bean. Java EE 6 supports two types of timers: automatic and programmatic. Automatic timers are created using annotations. Programmatic timers are created using methods of the `TimerService` interface.

The callback methods of an EJB may be called:

- At a specific time
- After an elapsed period of time
- At specific intervals

The signature of a callback must use one of these two signatures:

- `void methodName()`
- `void methodName(Timer timer)`

The second signature provides access to the `Timer` object that provides additional control and information about the timer. There is no restriction on the method's access modifier. It can be public, private, protected, or package level. However, the method cannot be declared as final or static and cannot throw application exceptions. The use of the `Timer` interface is discussed in the *Using the timer interface* recipe.

A callback method for an automatic timer is defined using either:

- **@Timeout** annotation, or
- **@Schedule** annotation

The *Understanding calendar-based scheduling* recipe discusses how to create a schedule for a timer. Once created, a timer can be cancelled using the `cancel` method. When it is cancelled, the callback method is no longer called.

Sometimes it is necessary to perform auxiliary operations such as logging or security when a callback method is executed. The use of interceptors, as detailed in the *Using interceptors with timers* recipe, facilitates this need.

Timers can be persistent or non-persistent. Persistent timers are able to survive application and server crashes. The *Using persistent and non-persistent timers* recipe covers this topic in more depth.

An application called, `ReportsApplication`, will be used in this chapter to illustrate the use of timers. The *Setting up the ReportsApplication* recipe details the steps needed to create the application.

A timer can be created in any number of different circumstances. The second and third recipes detail how to create a timer automatically and programmatically respectively. In the *Creating timers upon application deployment* recipe, singleton EJBs are used to create timers.

If a timer is involved in a transaction and an exception occurs, the transaction can be rolled backed. If a transaction is rolled back, then the creation of any timers will also be rolled back. If the timer is cancelled and its transaction is rolled back, then the cancellation of the timer is rolled back.

The timer service is not designed for use as part of a real-time application. The time duration used by the service is measured in milliseconds which is often inadequate for a real-time application. The timer service is designed for use with business applications where a time unit precision of hours, minutes, or seconds is sufficient.

Many of the examples used in this chapter are based on the "current" time. Feel free to change the time specified in the examples to a more appropriate value based on your needs.

Setting up the ReportsApplication

The recipes used in this chapter are built around a `ReportsApplication`. To keep the demonstration of timers simple, a `SystemReportManager` class is created which issues reports detailing the memory usage of the current JVM. The actual report generated is secondary to learning how to create and use timers. Reporting on JVM memory usage is easy and simple, and its use does not distract from the explanation of timers.

Getting ready

We will create a Java 6 EE application called `ReportsApplication`. As usual, we will use a `packt` package to hold our classes and a `servlet` package to hold the servlet used to drive the application. We will add a simple `SystemReportManager` class to generate reports and a `ReportsServlet` to drive many of the timers.

How to do it...

Create a new Java 6 EE application called `ReportsApplication`. In the EJB module add a `packt` package. In the WAR module add a package called `servlet`. Next, add a stateless EJB called `SystemReportManager` to the `packt` package. Create a method called `getMemoryReport`. This method returns a string representing the memory utilized by the current JVM. Within the method add a `StringBuilder` variable called `report`. We will build a string containing memory utilization data acquired using the `java.lang.Runtime` class. It has three methods of interest:

- `totalMemory` – Returns the amount of JVM's total memory
- `maxMemory` – Returns the maximum amount of memory to be used
- `freeMemory` – Returns the amount of JVM's free memory

Use the `report` variable to build a report and then return it as shown here:

```
@Stateless
public class SystemReportManager {

  long duration = 1000;
```

```
    public String getMemoryReport() {
      StringBuilder report = new StringBuilder();
      GregorianCalendar reportCalendar = new GregorianCalendar();
      Date reportDate = reportCalendar.getTime();
      Runtime runtime = Runtime.getRuntime();

      DateFormat dateFormat =
        DateFormat.getDateTimeInstance(DateFormat.MEDIUM,
        DateFormat.MEDIUM);
      report.append("\n").append(dateFormat.format(reportDate));
      report.append("\nTotal Memory: ").append(runtime.totalMemory());
      report.append("\n");
      report.append("Maximum Memory: ").append(runtime.maxMemory());
      report.append("\n");
      report.append("Free Memory: ").append(runtime.freeMemory());
      report.append("\n");

      return report.toString();
    }
  }
}
```

Next, create a servlet called `ReportsServlet` in the WAR module. Use dependency injection to create an instance of the `SystemReportManager`. Modify the try block of the `processRequest` method to call the `getMemoryReport` method.

```
  public class ReportsServlet extends HttpServlet {

    @EJB
    SystemReportManager systemReportManager;

    protected void processRequest(HttpServletRequest request,
      HttpServletResponse response)
      throws ServletException, IOException {
        response.setContentType("text/html;charset=UTF-8");
        PrintWriter out = response.getWriter();
        try {
          out.println("<html>");
          out.println("<head>");
          out.println("<title>Servlet ReportsServlet</title>");
          out.println("</head>");
          out.println("<body>");
          out.println("<h3>" + systemReportManager.getMemoryReport() +
            "</h3>");
          out.println("</body>");
          out.println("</html>");
```

```
        } finally {
            out.close();
        }
    }

    protected void doGet(HttpServletRequest request,
      HttpServletResponse response)
      throws ServletException, IOException {
        processRequest(request, response);
    }

    protected void doPost(HttpServletRequest request,
      HttpServletResponse response)
      throws ServletException, IOException {
        processRequest(request, response);
    }

}
```

Execute the servlet. The output should be similar to the following screenshot:

How it works...

The `getMemoryReport` method used a `Runtime` object to get JVM memory usage information. A date was created using the `GregorianCalendar` class as detailed in *Chapter 12, Using time within an EJB* recipe. All of this was pulled together in a `StringBuilder` object and returned as a string.

Creating and using declarative timers

Declarative timers, also called automatic timers, offer a technique to declare a timer using annotations. The **@Schedule** annotation accepts a set of arguments defining a timer event. The annotation specifies the time the event is to occur and declares the callback method. This technique provides an easy to use and intuitive way of scheduling application tasks.

Getting ready

The process of creating a declarative timer includes:

1. Creating a method to perform some task

2. Adding the **@Schedule** or **@Schedules** annotation to a method

The argument of the **@Schedule** consists of a set of time elements that correspond to fields of a `ScheduleExpression` object. These fields specify when and how often a timer callback will be made. Multiple timers can be assigned to a method using the **@Schedules** annotation.

The callback method will frequently be passed a single `Timer` object. The `Timer` object passed can be used to obtain additional information about the timer.

How to do it...

Add a method to the `SystemReportManager` class called `displayMemoryReport`. Annotate the method with the **@Schedule** annotation as shown below. This set of arguments defines a timer that will call back the `displayMemoryReport` every 10 seconds. The use of the calendar-based timer is explained in more detail in the *Understanding calendar-based scheduling* recipe. In the method, add `println` statements to display the execution of the method and the results of the `getMemoryReport` method.

```
@Schedule(second = "0,10,20,30,40,50", minute="*", hour = "*")
public void displayMemoryReport(Timer timer) {
  System.out.println("SystemReportManager: displayMemoryReport
    occurred");
  System.out.println(getMemoryReport());
}
```

Deploy the application. There is no need to execute the application as the timer starts when the EJB is loaded. The output should be similar to the following. While it is not complete, your output should show the execution of the callback method every 10 seconds.

INFO: SystemReportManager: displayMemoryReport occurred

INFO: Jan 5, 2011 4:22:50 PM

Total Memory: 270569472

Maximum Memory: 518979584

Free Memory: 149789352

INFO: SystemReportManager: displayMemoryReport occurred

INFO: Jan 5, 2011 4:23:00 PM

Total Memory: 270569472

Maximum Memory: 518979584

Free Memory: 148865080

INFO: SystemReportManager: displayMemoryReport occurred

INFO: Jan 5, 2011 4:23:10 PM

Total Memory: 270569472

Maximum Memory: 518979584

Free Memory: 147933616

How it works...

The **@Schedule** annotation consisted of a list of 10 second increments which specified when the report was generated. The asterisk in the minute and hour fields indicated that it should execute every minute and hour. This resulted in the `displayMemoryReport` executing every 10 seconds. It displayed memory usage information obtained from the `getMemoryReport` method.

There's more...

In addition to the single use of the **@Schedule** annotation, we can use **@Schedule** annotations with multiple methods in an EJB. In addition, we can apply more than one **@Schedule** annotation to a method using the **@Schedules** annotation.

Using @Schedule with multiple methods

More than one method of an EJB can be annotated with **@Schedule**. Here, a second method called `clearStatistics` has been added and is called once a minute.

```
@Schedule(second = "0", minute="*", hour = "*")
public void clearStatistics(Timer timer) {
  System.out.println("clearStatistics executed");
}
```

When the application deploys you should see the execution of both of the callback methods.

INFO: SystemReportManager: displayMemoryReport occurred

INFO: Jan 5, 2011 4:32:50 PM

Total Memory: 270569472

Maximum Memory: 518979584

Free Memory: 143028648

INFO: clearStatistics executed

INFO: SystemReportManager: displayMemoryReport occurred

INFO: Jan 5, 2011 4:33:00 PM

Total Memory: 270569472

Maximum Memory: 518979584

Free Memory: 141976424

Using @Schedules with a single method

The **@Schedules** annotation allows us to assign multiple timers to the same method. This annotation has an argument consisting of an array of **@Schedule** annotations. In this example, the `displayMemoryReport` method is annotated with the **@Schedules** annotation and two **@Schedule** annotations. They specify that the callback method should be executed every minute and at 20 and 30 seconds after the minute.

```
@Schedules(
  {@Schedule(second = "0", minute="*", hour = "*"),
  @Schedule(second = "20,30", minute="*", hour = "*")})
public void displayMemoryReport(Timer timer) {
  System.out.println("SystemReportManager: displayMemoryReport
    occurred");
  System.out.println(getMemoryReport());
}
```

When deployed, your output should appear similar to the following:

INFO: SystemReportManager: displayMemoryReport occurred

INFO: Jan 5, 2011 4:43:00 PM

Total Memory: 270569472

Maximum Memory: 518979584

Free Memory: 146682928

INFO: SystemReportManager: displayMemoryReport occurred

INFO: Jan 5, 2011 4:43:20 PM

Total Memory: 270569472

Maximum Memory: 518979584

Free Memory: 144880096

INFO: SystemReportManager: displayMemoryReport occurred

INFO: Jan 5, 2011 4:43:30 PM

Total Memory: 270569472

Maximum Memory: 518979584

Free Memory: 144050896

See also

The use of calendar-based expressions is detailed in the *Understanding calendar-based scheduling* recipe. Instead of using declarative annotations, programmatic timers can also be created as explained in the next recipe.

Creating and using programmatic timers

Timers can be created using methods of the `TimerService` interface. This interface supports methods for creating timers which generate events at a specific time, after an elapsed time, after a specific interval, or according to a schedule. This approach provides the client with the ability to initiate a timer.

Getting ready

There are two basic steps needed to create a programmatic timer:

1. Using a `TimerService` instance to create the timer, and
2. Declaring a callback method using the **@Timeout** annotation

As we will see, there are several `TimerService` interface methods available to create a timer. Most of these will be explored in the *There's more* section of this recipe. Initially, we will use the `createSingleActionTimer` method to create a simple one-time timer. When a timer is created, a callback method must be identified. With programmatic timers, the **@Timeout** annotation is used to mark the method as the callback method. This annotation can only be used once per class.

How to do it...

The simplest way of getting a `TimerService` instance is to use dependency injection. In the `SystemReportManager`, use the **@Resource** annotation to inject a `TimerService` object. Also, add a long variable called `duration` and initialize it to 1000.

```
@Resource
TimerService timerService;
long duration = 1000;
```

Next, add a method called `createTimer`. The method is passed and returns **void**. In the method, use the `TimerService` method, `createSingleActionTimer`, to create a timer. This method has two arguments:

▶ First argument – A `long` number specifying the number of milliseconds to wait until the timer event occurs

▶ Second argument – A `TimerConfig` object containing timer configuration information

Use the `duration` variable as the first argument and create a new `TimerConfig` object as the second argument. The use of the `TimerConfig` argument is explored in the *Using the timer interface* recipe and holds additional timer-related information.

```
public void createTimer() {
  timerService.createSingleActionTimer(duration, new
    TimerConfig());
}
```

Next, we will create a callback method called `timeout`. Use the **@Timeout** annotation with the method. In the method, display a message indicating the method has executed and then display the value returned from the `getMemoryReport` method.

```
@Timeout
public void timeout(Timer timer) {
   System.out.println("timeout: timeout occurred");
   System.out.println("getMemoryReport: " + getMemoryReport());
}
```

In the `ReportsServlet`, comment out the statement which calls the `getMemoryReport` method. Instead, add the following statement which calls the `createTimer` method:

```
systemReportManager.createTimer();
```

Execute the `ReportsServlet`. Its output should closely match the following:

INFO: timeout: timeout occurred

INFO: getMemoryReport:

Total Memory: 266604544

Maximum Memory: 518979584

Free Memory: 149822400

How it works...

A `TimerService` object was injected into the EJB and later used in the `createTimer` method to create the timer. This `createTimer` method had a duration argument of one second which meant that the timer would not fire until approximately one second after its creation. The timer method, `timeout`, was designated using the **@Timeout** annotation. The `createTimer` method was called from the `ReportsServlet`.

There's more...

The `TimerService` interface has several methods to create timers. Each of these methods returns a `Timer` object representing the timer except for the `getTimers` method which returns a `Collection` of `Timer`s. They differ in how they specify the time of the callback event.

All timers created with these methods are persistent by default. The control of a timer's persistent is detailed in the *Using persistent and non-persistent timers* recipe. Also, timers can be cancelled using the `Timer`'s `cancel` method.

The methods of the `TimerService` interface supports three types of events:

- ▸ Single event – The event occurs only once
- ▸ Interval events – Events occur at regular recurring intervals
- ▸ Calendar events – Events occur based on the value of a `ScheduleExpression`

In addition, the `getTimer` method allows us to obtain a list of currently scheduled timers for the EJB.

Single event timers

Single event timers result in the callback method executing only once. There are two `createSingleActionTimer` methods supporting this type of event. In addition, there are two `createTimer` methods supporting single events.

Let's look at the `createSingleActionTimer` methods first. Both of its methods have two arguments. The first argument is either a `Date` object or a `long` value. The second argument is a `TimerConfig` object used to hold additional timer-related information.

The event will occur at the time specified by the `Date` object. Using the `long` argument specifies the event will occur in that number of milliseconds in the future.

To demonstrate the use of the `Date` parameter, replace the body of the `SystemReportManager`'s `createTimer` method with the following code. When the code is executed, a callback should be made on January 5, 2014 at 11:12. Depending on the current time, you may or may not want to wait for this event.

```
GregorianCalendar reportCalendar = new GregorianCalendar(2014,
    Calendar.JANUARY, 5, 11, 12);
Date reportDate = reportCalendar.getTime();
timerService.createSingleActionTimer(reportDate, new
    TimerConfig());
```

Like the `createSingleActionTimer`, the `createTimer` methods have two arguments. The first is either a `Date` or a `long` value and behaves the same way as the `createSingleActionTimer` methods. Its second argument is a `Serializable` argument whose value is associated with the timer and can be retrieved by the `Timer`'s `getInfo` method. The use of this argument is explored in the *Using the timer interface* recipe.

The code sequence below achieves the same result as the previous example. The `Serializable` object is set to `null` in this case.

```
GregorianCalendar reportCalendar = new GregorianCalendar(2014,
    Calendar.JANUARY, 5, 11, 12);
Date reportDate = reportCalendar.getTime();
timerService.createTimer(reportDate, null);
```

Interval event timers

The `createIntervalTimer` method can also be used to create timers which execute at intervals. In addition, there are two versions of the `createTimer` method that will do the same thing.

Both versions of the `createIntervalTimer` method take three arguments. The first argument is either a `Date` or a delay value specifying the time the first callback is to occur. The second argument is a `long` value which determines the time between subsequent callbacks. The last argument is a `TimerConfig` object.

The following example results in a series of callbacks which occur one second after the timer is created and are repeated every three seconds.

```
timerService.createIntervalTimer(1000, 3000, new TimerConfig());
```

Two of the `createTimer` methods support the creation of interval timers. These methods also have three arguments which are the same as those of the `createIntervalTimer` except for the last argument. The last argument is a `Serializable` object whose value becomes part of the `Timer`. The `Timer`'s `getInfo` method can be used to retrieve this information as detailed in the _Using the timer interface_ recipe.

Here, the previous interval timer is duplicated using the `createTimer` method. A `null` value is passed as the `Serializable` object.

```
timerService.createTimer(1000, 3000, null);
```

Calendar event timers

The callback event in a calendar-based timer is controlled by a `ScheduleExpression` object. This expression is detailed in the _Understanding calendar-based scheduling_ recipe. The overloaded `createCalendarTimer` method supports the creation of this type of timer.

The first of the two overloaded methods has a single argument: `ScheduleExpression`. The expression represented by this object specifies when the callback will occur. The second version of the method has two arguments with the first being the `ScheduleExpression` object and the second being a `TimerConfig` object which conveys additional information to the timer.

Replace the body of the `createTimer` method with a call to the `createCalendarTimer` method as shown below. A `ScheduleExpression` is created first and initialized to January 5, 2014 at 14:7:40.

```
ScheduleExpression scheduleExpression = new ScheduleExpression();
scheduleExpression.year(2014);
scheduleExpression.month(1);
scheduleExpression.dayOfMonth(5);
scheduleExpression.hour(14);
scheduleExpression.minute(7);
```

```
scheduleExpression.second(40);
timerService.createCalendarTimer(scheduleExpression, new
  TimerConfig());
```

When the method is executed, a callback will be made at the specified time.

Getting a collection of scheduled timers

Periodically, it may be desirable to determine which timers have been scheduled. The `TimerService`'s `getTimers` method returns a collection of currently scheduled timers. Replace the body of the `createTimer` method with the following code sequence. In this sequence, two `Timer` objects are created. The first is for January 1, 2012 and the second is for January 1, 2013. This is followed by the use of the `getTimers` method and a `for` loop to display the timer's schedule expressions.

```
ScheduleExpression scheduleExpression = new ScheduleExpression();
scheduleExpression.year(2012);
scheduleExpression.month(1);
scheduleExpression.dayOfMonth(1);
timerService.createCalendarTimer(scheduleExpression, new
  TimerConfig());

scheduleExpression = new ScheduleExpression();
scheduleExpression.year(2013);
scheduleExpression.month(1);
scheduleExpression.dayOfMonth(1);
timerService.createCalendarTimer(scheduleExpression, new
  TimerConfig());

Collection<Timer> timers = timerService.getTimers();
for(Timer timer : timers) {
  System.out.println(timer.getSchedule());
}
```

The execution of the code will result in output similar to the following:

INFO: ScheduleExpression [second=0;minute=0;hour=0;dayOfMonth=1;month=1;dayOfWe ek=*;year=2013;timezoneID=null;start=null;end=null]

INFO: ScheduleExpression [second=0;minute=0;hour=0;dayOfMonth=1;month=1;dayOfWe ek=*;year=2012;timezoneID=null;start=null;end=null]

Understanding calendar-based scheduling

Calendar-based scheduling is used with the **@Schedule** annotation and with the `ScheduleExpression` class. It provides an alternative approach for specifying the time when a callback should be made. The calendar-based timer expressions are similar to those used by the UNIX Cron facility.

Using a calendar expression we can express one of several types of events:

- A single event in time
- A repeating set of times
- A time interval

This approach provides a more powerful technique for expressing a point in time.

Getting ready

A calendar expression can be expressed using the **@Schedule** annotation or using a `ScheduleExpression` object. These two approaches are closely related. In fact, the `Timer` class has an `isCalendarTimer` and a `getSchedule` method. If the timer was created using calendar scheduling, then the `getSchedule` method returns a `ScheduleExpression` object representing the schedule. These methods are illustrated in the _Using the timer interface_ recipe.

The **@Schedule** annotation takes a series of comma delimited settings to express a time or set of times. Each setting corresponds to a unit of time such as hour or minute. A simple repeating event occurring every minute can be expressed using the **@Schedule** annotation as follows:

```
@Schedule(second="0", minute = "*", hour = "*")
```

The `ScheduleExpression` class represents a time or set of times. It possesses a number of methods to set the time. This class is used in conjunction with the `TimerService`'s `createCalendarTimer` method.

Let's examine the attributes used with the **@Schedule** annotation first. The table below, summaries the attribute names, default values and permissible values. The table is adapted from Table 16.1 found at `http://ze-zo0m.ru/javaeesuntutorial6/bnboy.html`. The * represents all possible values. String constants are case-insensitive.

Attribute	Default Value	Permissible Values
second	0	0-59
minute	0	0-59
hour	0	0-23
dayOfMonth	*	1-31
		-7 through -1 (day before the last day of the month)
		"Last" or
		{"1st", "2nd", "3rd", "4th", "5th", "Last"} {"Sun", "Mon", "Tue", "Wed", "Thu", "Fri", "Sat"}
month	*	1-12
		{"Jan", "Feb", "Mar", "Apr", "May", "Jun", "Jul", "Aug", "Sep", "Oct", "Nov", Dec"}
dayOfWeek	*	0-7 (0 and 7 are both Sunday)
		{"Sun", "Mon", "Tue", "Wed", "Thu", "Fri", "Sat"}
year	*	Four digit calendar year
timezone	Container's default time zone	String found in the tz database

The tz database is also known as the zoneinfo database and is a collection of the world's time zones. The database can be found at `http://www.twinsun.com/tz/tz-link.htm`.

How to do it...

The following expression consists of a series of attribute assignments. The combination of these assignments defines a particular time. Let's examine some of the more straightforward expressions. Here, the weekly time statements are generated every Sunday at 1 AM.

```
@Schedule(hour="1", dayOfWeek="Sun")
public void generateWeeklyTimeStatement() {...}
```

In this example, weekly meeting notices are sent out at 3 PM every Wednesday.

```
@Schedule(hour="15", dayOfWeek="3")
public void sendWeeklyMeetingReminder() {...}
```

We could use the following expression to invoke the `computeStackAverages` method at 1 AM Europe/Stockholm time on the first day of each month.

```
@Schedule(hour="1", dayOfMonth="1", timezone=" Europe/Stockholm")
public void computeStackAverages() {...}
```

The `ScheduleExpression` class has methods corresponding to the attribute fields listed previously. For example, to set the month of an expression to the month of March, the `month` method can be used.

```
scheduleExpression = new ScheduleExpression();
scheduleExpression.month("Mar");
```

Also, `ScheduleExpression` has additional methods which further constrain the schedule based on an optional start date and/or end date using the `start` and `end` methods. In this example, the `timeout` method is executed starting on January 10, 2013 at noon.

```
GregorianCalendar reportCalendar = new GregorianCalendar(2013,
   Calendar.JANUARY, 10, 12, 0);
Date startDate = reportCalendar.getTime();
scheduleExpression = new ScheduleExpression();
scheduleExpression.start(startDate);
scheduleExpression.second(0);
scheduleExpression.minute("*");
scheduleExpression.hour("*");
timerService.createCalendarTimer(scheduleExpression, new
TimerConfig());
   ...

@Timeout
public void timeout(Timer timer) {
   System.out.println("timeout: timeout occurred");
   System.out.println("getMemoryReport: " + getMemoryReport());
}
```

How it works...

The **@Schedule** annotation was used with one or more attributes which were used to control when the event would occur. When a `ScheduleExpression` object was used, methods were used to set the value for the corresponding attributes. As seen with the `start` method, it is possible to further constrain the schedule.

There's more...

Another open source scheduler is Quartz. It has inspired several parts of the EJB 3.1 timers and can be used outside of the Java EE environment. More information about Quartz can be found at `http://www.quartz-scheduler.org/`.

There are several other features of schedule expression that should be addressed including:

- Using lists in schedule expressions
- Using ranges in schedule expressions
- Using increments in schedule expressions

An optional information string can be used with the annotation. This feature is discussed in the *Using the timer interface* recipe.

Using lists in schedule expressions

The use of lists provides a means of specifying multiple callback times. For a given field, a list can be specified by separating values with commas. For example, to cause the `displayMemoryReport` to be executed at 5, 10, and 15 seconds after each minute, the **@Schedule** annotation could be configured as follows:

```
@Schedule(second = "5,10,15", minute = "*", hour = "*")
public void displayMemoryReport(Timer timer) {
  System.out.println("SystemReportManager: displayMemoryReport
    occurred");
  System.out.println(getMemoryReport());
}
```

One possible output follows:

INFO: Jan 5, 2011 7:57:05 PM

Total Memory: 270569472

Maximum Memory: 518979584

Free Memory: 156212800

INFO: SystemReportManager: displayMemoryReport occurred

INFO: Jan 5, 2011 7:57:10 PM

Total Memory: 270569472

Maximum Memory: 518979584

Free Memory: 155517272

INFO: SystemReportManager: displayMemoryReport occurred

INFO: Jan 5, 2011 7:57:15 PM

Total Memory: 270569472

Maximum Memory: 518979584

Free Memory: 155134888

INFO: SystemReportManager: displayMemoryReport occurred

INFO: Jan 5, 2011 7:58:05 PM

Total Memory: 270569472

Maximum Memory: 518979584

Free Memory: 150765240

Using ranges in schedule expressions

A range can also be used to specify a multiple set of callback times. A range is created using the dash character to separate start and end values. Here, the displayMemoryReport is called on a daily basis at midnight except for Saturdays and Sundays.

```
@Schedule(minute = "0", hour = "0", dayOfWeek="Mon-Fri")
public void displayMemoryReport(Timer timer) {
  System.out.println("SystemReportManager: displayMemoryReport
    occurred");
  System.out.println(getMemoryReport());
}
```

Using increments in schedule expressions

Increments are used to express a progression of time starting at some value and repeated at regular intervals. An increment expression consists of an initial value separated by a forward slash and then followed by an interval value. The first value specifies the initial value with subsequent times determined by adding the interval value repeatedly to the initial value. It can only be used with second, minute, and hour and the values must fall within the acceptable range for each unit.

In this example, the `displayMemoryReport` executes at 15 seconds after the minute and then every 20 seconds.

```
@Schedule(second = "15/20", minute = "*", hour = "*")
public void displayMemoryReport(Timer timer) {
  System.out.println("SystemReportManager: displayMemoryReport
    occurred");
  System.out.println(getMemoryReport());
}
```

Your output should be similar to the following:

INFO: SystemReportManager: displayMemoryReport occurred

INFO: Jan 5, 2011 8:06:15 PM

Total Memory: 270569472

Maximum Memory: 518979584

Free Memory: 93179256

INFO: SystemReportManager: displayMemoryReport occurred

INFO: Jan 5, 2011 8:06:35 PM

Total Memory: 270569472

Maximum Memory: 518979584

Free Memory: 91437032

INFO: SystemReportManager: displayMemoryReport occurred

INFO: Jan 5, 2011 8:06:55 PM

Total Memory: 270569472

Maximum Memory: 518979584

Free Memory: 89611656

INFO: SystemReportManager: displayMemoryReport occurred

INFO: Jan 5, 2011 8:07:15 PM

Total Memory: 270569472

Maximum Memory: 518979584

Free Memory: 87862224

See also

The *Creating and using programmatic timers* recipe illustrates the use of the
`ScheduleExpression` class in the creation of a timer.

Using the timer interface

The `Timer` interface has a number of methods that can be used by the callback method to
assist in the execution of the callback. This interface is useful to obtain information about the
timer event and in passing information to the event. The use of these methods is illustrated in
this recipe.

Getting ready

The basic steps involve:

1. Obtaining an instance of the `Timer` object
2. Using the `Timer` interface methods

The **@Schedule** annotated method is passed an instance of the `Timer` object. For
programmatic timers, the **@Timeout** annotated method is passed the `Timer` object. These
callback methods can subsequently use this object to control the callback. The `Timer`
interface's methods of interest to us include:

- `getInfo` – Returns information provided by the caller when the timer was created
- `getNextTimeout` – Returns a `Date` object representing the time when the callback
  method will be executed next
- `getSchedule` – Returns a `ScheduleExpression` for the timer
- `getTimeRemaining` - Returns the number of milliseconds until the callback method
  will be called back
- `isCalendarTimer` – Returns `true` if the timer is a calendar-based timer
- `isPersistent` – Returns `true` if the timer is persistent

How to do it....

To demonstrate the use of the `Timer` interface, add a `getTimerData` method which is
passed a `Timer` object. In the method, call each of the previous `Timer` interface methods.
Use these methods to build a string to return at the completion of the method.

```
public String getTimerData(Timer timer) {
    StringBuilder timerData = new StringBuilder();
    timerData.append("\nInfo: ").append(timer.getInfo());
```

```
    timerData.append("\nNext timeout:
      ").append(timer.getNextTimeout());
    timerData.append("\nSchedule: ").append(timer.getSchedule());
    timerData.append("\nTime remaining:
      ").append(timer.getTimeRemaining());
    timerData.append("\nCalendar timer: ").append(timer.
      isCalendarTimer());
    timerData.append("\nPersistent: ").append(timer.isPersistent());
    return timerData.toString();
}
```

Next, modify the displayMemoryReport's **@Schedule** annotation so it is call backed once a second. Also, invoke the getTimerData method with the timer variable.

```
@Schedule(second="0", minute="*", hour = "*")
public void displayMemoryReport(Timer timer) {
  System.out.println("SystemReportManager: displayMemoryReport
    occurred");
  System.out.println(getMemoryReport());
  System.out.println(getTimerData(timer));
}
```

When the application is deployed, your output will appear similar to the following:

INFO: Jan 5, 2011 8:38:00 PM

Total Memory: 270569472

Maximum Memory: 518979584

Free Memory: 107203800

INFO: Info: null

Next timeout: Wed Jan 05 20:39:00 CST 2011

Schedule: ScheduleExpression [second=0;minute=*;hour=*;dayOfMonth=*;month=*;dayO fWeek=*;year=*;timezoneID=null;start=null;end=null]

Time remaining: 59320

Calendar timer: true

Persistent: true

Notice that the `getInfo` method returns `null`. If we wanted to pass additional information to the callback method, we could use the information attribute, `info`, and assign it a value. Here, a simple string is assigned. The `displayMemoryReport` has been modified below to not display the timer data if the string is set to `NoTimerData`.

```
@Schedule(second="0", minute="*", hour = "*", )
public void displayMemoryReport(Timer timer) {
  System.out.println("SystemReportManager: displayMemoryReport
    occurred");
  System.out.println(getMemoryReport());
  if(!"NoTimerData".equals(timer.getInfo())) {
    System.out.println(getTimerData(timer));
  }
}
```

The output should not display the timer data. This data should be `Serializable` in the case of a persistent timer. Should a failure occur, it will be necessary to restore the timer and any data associated with it.

How it works...

We created a `getTimerData` method that used several of the `Timer` interface methods. The output of these methods was concatenated to a `StringBuilder` object and returned as a string to the `displayMemoryReport` method. In the last example, we used the **info** attribute to control whether timer information was displayed or not.

There's more...

Information can also be added to the `Timer` object when a timer is created programmatically. The `createCalendarTimer` method has a `TimerConfig` argument. Using its `setInfo` method, we can assign a string or any other object which implements the `Serializable` interface.

In addition, two of the `createTimer` methods support the creation of interval timers. The last argument of these methods is a `Serializable` object whose value becomes part of the `Timer`. The `Timer`'s `getInfo` method can be used to retrieve this information.

Using the TimerConfig object to pass information

Here, we pass a string to the timer. In the `createTimer` method, add the following code to create a timer. The timer is set up to call back the timeout method every 10 seconds. The `setInfo` method is passed the string, "information".

```
scheduleExpression = new ScheduleExpression();
scheduleExpression.second("0/10");
scheduleExpression.minute("*");
```

```
scheduleExpression.hour("*");
TimerConfig timerConfig =  new TimerConfig();
timerConfig.setInfo("information");
timerService.createCalendarTimer(scheduleExpression,timerConfig);
```

The memory usage report should be displayed every 10 seconds with the timer data.

Using the Serializable object to pass information

In the *Single event timers* section of the *Creating and using programmatic timers* recipe, a timer was created using the createTimer method. Its second argument is an object that implements the Serializable interface. This object is associated with the timer and can be retrieved by the Timer's getInfo method.

Replace the SystemReportManager's createTimer method with the following code. Here, we create a calendar to use with the createTimer method. Modify the date to reflect a time convenient for you. Next, create an ArrayList which is initialized with three strings. In this case, they are intended to present font information. Using the createTimer method, pass the reportDate and the ArrayList as its parameters.

```
public void createTimer() {
  GregorianCalendar reportCalendar = new GregorianCalendar(2011,
    Calendar.JANUARY, 6, 19, 56);
  Date reportDate = reportCalendar.getTime();
  ArrayList<String> list = new ArrayList<String>();
  list.add("capitalize");
  list.add("center");
  list.add("arial");
  timerService.createTimer(reportDate, list);
}
```

Modify the timeout method to use the getInfo method to return a list of strings and then display the list.

```
@Timeout
public void timeout(Timer timer) {
  ArrayList<String> list = (ArrayList<String>) timer.getInfo();
  System.out.println("List Elements");
  for(String element : list) {
    System.out.println(element);
  }
}
```

When the application is executed your output should display the following:

INFO: List Elements

INFO: capitalize

INFO: center

INFO: arial

Using persistent and non-persistent timers

Timers can be either persistent or non-persistent. In this recipe, we will learn more about what persistence means and how to create either a persistent or non-persistent timer.

Getting ready

A persistent/non-persistent timer is created using the **@Schedule** annotation and setting its `persistent` attribute to `true`/`false`. If programmatic timers are being used, the `TimerConfig`'s `setPersistent` method is passed an argument of `true`/`false`.

Persistent timers are able to survive application and server crashes. When the system recovers, any persistent timers will be recreated and missed callback events will be executed. When replay of missed timer events is not desired, then a non-persistent timer should be used. For example, we probably do not want to send out meeting notices for a meeting which has already been held.

A persistent timer survives when:

- ▸ The container crashes
- ▸ The server shuts down
- ▸ From activation/passivation

How to do it...

By default, timers are persistent. A non-persistent timer is created using the **@Schedule** annotation and setting its `persistent` attribute to `false`.

```
@Schedule(second="0", minute="*", hour = "*", info="",
  persistent=false)
```

Programmatic calendar-based timers can be created using the `createCalendarTimer` method. The second argument of this overloaded method is a `TimerConfig` argument. By passing `false` to its `setPersistent` method we can create a non-persistent timer.

```
TimerConfig timerConfig =  new TimerConfig();
timerConfig.setPersistent(false);
...
timerService.createCalendarTimer(scheduleExpression, timerConfig);
```

How it works...

Timers are persistent by default. However, by setting the persistent attribute to `false` or using the `setPersistent` method with a `false` argument we saw how they can be made non-persistent. You may want to stop and then restart to server to verify how these settings work.

There's more...

There is only one instance of a persistent timer per application regardless of the number of JVMs the application is deployed to. Non-persistent timers are created within their JVM.

From a callback method, the `Timer`'s `isPersistent` method can be used to determine whether the timer is persistent or not. This method is illustrated in the *Using the timer interface* recipe.

Creating timers upon application deployment

Sometimes it is useful to create a timer as soon as the application is deployed. Many applications have actions that need to occur on a regular basis. Creating timers for these actions at application start up is a convenient way of addressing this need.

One way to achieve this is to use a singleton EJB. Here we will programmatically create a timer that generates a JVM memory report after the application has been deployed.

Getting ready

The steps to achieve the creation of timers in this fashion include:

1. Creating a singleton session bean using the **@Startup** annotation
2. Marking a method with the **@PostConstruct** annotation
3. Creating timers from this method

We will create a singleton EJB and then use the **@PostConstruct** annotation with a method which creates the timer. In this method, we will also create an instance of the `SystemReportManager` so we can get ready access to the report.

How to do it...

Create a singleton EJB called `ReportsSingleton`. Details on how singletons work is found in the *Singleton session bean* and *Using multiple singleton beans* recipes of *Chapter 2, Session Beans*. Use the **@Startup** annotation to request immediate instantiation of the EJB when the application is loaded.

```
@Singleton
@Startup
public class ReportsSingleton {

    ...
}
```

First, set up three instance variables for the application:

- `timerService` – Use resource injection to create an instance of the `TimerService`
- `duration` – A long value set to 1000 milliseconds specifying the delay before the report is generated
- `systemReportManager` – Use dependency injection to create an instance of the `SystemReportManager`

```
@Resource
TimerService timerService;
long duration = 1000;
@EJB
SystemReportManager systemReportManager;
```

Create a method called `initialization` which returns `void` and is passed `void`. Add the **@PostConstruct** annotation to the method. In the method, add a `println` method to show the method is executing. Next, use the `createSingleActionTimer` method to create a timer.

```
@PostConstruct
public void initialization() {
    System.out.println("ReportsSingleton initialization");
    timerService.createSingleActionTimer(duration, new
        TimerConfig());
}
```

The last step is to create the **@Timeout** method. Name the method, `timeout`, and use the `getMemoryReport` to display the memory used.

```
@Timeout
public void timeout(Timer timer) {
    System.out.println("timeout occurred");
    System.out.println("\n" + systemReportManager.getMemoryReport());
}

}
```

Deploy the application. The output should appear similar to the following:

INFO: ReportsSingleton initialization

INFO: Loading application ReportsApplication#ReportsApplication-war.war at ReportsApplication-war

INFO: ReportsApplication was successfully deployed in 420 milliseconds.

INFO: timeout occurred

INFO: Total Memory: 235073536

Maximum Memory: 518979584

Free Memory: 91557120

How it works...

Annotating the singleton with the **@Startup** annotation resulted in the creation of the singleton when the application was deployed. The **@PostConstruct** annotated method, `initialization`, was executed after the singleton was created. Within this method we created a new timer event that executed one second later. The `timeout` method was executed at that time.

See also

The use of the `createSingleActionTimer` method and **@Timeout** annotation is explained in more detail in the *Creating and using programmatic timers* recipe.

Using interceptors with timers

Interceptors provide a convenient way of incorporating required functionality of an application into the application without cluttering up the business logic. For example, security and logging operations may be required when certain methods of an application execute. Code could be added directly to the method to perform these actions. However, they are tangential to the method itself and can obscure the business logic of the method.

An interceptor is a technique permitting the addition of this functionality, but places the code implementing the functionality outside of the actual function. When the method executes, the interceptor is executed first. Within the interceptor, its code can be executed before and after the body of the target method is executed. Interceptors are discussed in more detail in *Chapter 8, Interceptors*.

Getting ready

The essential steps include:

1. Creating the interceptor
2. Performing the required processing in the interceptor

Interceptors can be declared within a separate class or within the current class. Here, we will use the current class. To use interceptors with timeouts, the **@AroundTimeout** annotation is used to declare an interceptor method. There are no restrictions on the name of the method, but it must be passed an `InvocationContext` object and must return an `Object`.

The interceptor is invoked before the target callback method is invoked. The target method is called from within the interceptor using the `InvocationContext`'s `proceed` method. Placing interceptor code before and after this call allows the interceptor to perform its functions before and after the target method executes.

The `InvocationContext` has a `getTimer` method which returns the `Timer` object associated with the callback method. There are also other `InvocationContext` methods available which can be used in support of the interceptor such as those accessing the target method's parameters. The interceptor normally returns the object returned by the `proceed` method. This is necessary to propagate any target method return values.

How to do it...

To demonstrate the use of a timer interceptor, add a method to the `SystemReportManager` class called `interceptorTimeout`. The method is passed an `InvocationContext` object, returns an `Object` and can potentially throw an `Exception`. Use the **@AroundTimeout** annotation before the method. To clearly see the behavior of the method, add `println` statements to show when the method starts and when it is about to return. Next, add a call to get the target method's `Timer` object and display its schedule. Follow this with the use of the `proceed` method.

```
@AroundTimeout
public Object interceptorTimeout(InvocationContext
  invocationContext) throws Exception {
  System.out.println("interceptTimeout executing");
  Timer timer = (Timer)invocationContext.getTimer();
  System.out.println("Timer: " + timer.getSchedule());
  Object object = invocationContext.proceed();
  System.out.println("interceptTimeout returning");
  return object;
}
```

Use the following `displayMemoryReport` method developed in the *Using the timer interface* recipe:

```
@Schedule(second="0", minute="*", hour = "*")
public void displayMemoryReport(Timer timer) {
  System.out.println("SystemReportManager: displayMemoryReport
    occurred");
  System.out.println(getMemoryReport());
  System.out.println(getTimerData(timer));
}
```

The output of this sequence should be similar to the following:

INFO: interceptorTimeout executing

INFO: Timer: ScheduleExpression [second=0;minute=*;hour=*;dayOfMonth=*;month=*;dayOfWeek=*;year=*;timezoneID=null;start=null;end=null]

INFO: SystemReportManager: displayMemoryReport occurred

INFO: Jan 6, 2011 1:11:00 PM

Total Memory: 276893696

Maximum Memory: 518979584

Free Memory: 99677928

INFO: Info: null

Next timeout: Thu Jan 06 13:12:00 CST 2011

Schedule: ScheduleExpression [second=0;minute=*;hour=*;dayOfMonth=*;month=*;dayO fWeek=*;year=*;timezoneID=null;start=null;end=null]

Time remaining: 59898

Calendar timer: true

Persistent: true

INFO: interceptorTimeout returning

How it works...

We created an interceptor called `interceptorTimeout` and annotated it with the **@AroundTimeout** annotation. When the interceptor executed, the start of the interceptor and the `Timer`'s schedule was displayed. Next, the `timeout` method was executed using the `proceed` method. When the `proceed` method returned, its return value was assigned to the `object` variable. This value was returned by the interceptor method after a message was displayed indicating the interceptor was terminating. The timer was triggered by the `displayMemeoryReport` method using the **@Schedule** annotation.

There's more...

When the interceptor executes, it is part of the same transaction and uses the same security context as that of the target method. In addition, it may throw any exception which may be thrown by the target method. It can also suppress these exceptions if appropriate.

See also

Chapter 8, _Interceptors_ covers the use and capabilities of interceptors in more depth.

10
Web Services

In this chapter, we will cover:

- ▸ Creating an EJB-based web service using JAX-WS
- ▸ Creating an EJB-based web service using JAX-RS
- ▸ Using an MDB as part of a web service

Introduction

A Web Service is an application which provides functionality for a client. Clients are typically web browsers but can also be standard applications. The communication between a client and a service is facilitated through standard protocols that connect to end-points created for the services. The term, endpoint, refers to a specific location used to access the web service.

From a Java perspective, web services can be divided into two broad categories. The first category is the **Java API for XML Web Services (JAX-WS)** and is based on XML and the **Simple Object Access Protocol (SOAP)**. The capabilities of a service are published in an XML-based **Web Services Description Language (WSDL)**. It supports message-oriented and remote procedure call type services. This approach is more complex but provides support for applications in terms of transactions, security, and other features.

The second category is **Representational State Transfer)(RESTful)** web services as supported by JAX-RS. This type of service is useful for simpler applications having less stringent demands placed upon them. It is good for stateless services where caching can be used to improve its performance.

The first two recipes address using JAX-WS and JAX-RS respectively. The third recipe, *Using an MDB as part of a web service*, examines an approach for using an MDB in support of a web service.

A Java Web Service application called `CustomerApplication` is used to demonstrate the creation of web services in this chapter. The application simply returns the number of customers in a given region. The session EJB `CustomerManager` supports this basic functionality. These classes are developed in the first recipe.

There is a lot more to web services than is covered in this chapter. The intent here is to provide examples of web services as they relates to EJBs and many of the commonly used features of web services.

Creating an EJB-based web service using JAX-WS

In this recipe, we will demonstrate how to create a JAX-WS application based on a stateless session EJB. There are several variations on how this can be done, however, they all use a class as the web service and embed other session EJBs to provide the web service's functionality. Stateless and singleton session beans can be used as endpoints. As of EJB 3.1, stateful session beans can also be used for endpoints.

Getting ready

The two fundamental steps involved in the creation of a JAX-WS web service include:

- Creating an EJB which provides the application's functionality
- Creating a Web Service (JAX-WS) which utilizes the EJB

The creation of the EJB is detailed in earlier chapters, particularly *Chapter 2, Session Beans* that deals with session EJBs. The focus of this recipe is how to create the web service. To create a web service endpoint based on JAX-WS we need to:

1. Use the **@WebService** annotation to designate a class as an endpoint
2. Annotate the methods of the service with the **@WebMethod** annotation

Within the web service class methods we need to use the supporting EJB to implement the service's functionality.

To demonstrate the creation of a web service, we will use a `CustomerManager` class which provides simple customer information. The EJB will support two methods: `getCustomerCount` and `getCustomerCountByRegion`. These methods are simple by design so as not to distract from the details of creating the web service.

How to do it...

Create a Java Web Application called `CustomerApplication`. In NetBeans this type of project is found in the **Java Web** category of the **New Project** wizard. Go ahead and add three packages to the project's **Source Packages** folder though we will only be using two of them in this recipe.

- ▸ `packt` – Holds the `CustomerManager` class
- ▸ `jaxws` – Used for the JAX-WS web service class
- ▸ `jaxrs` – Used in the next recipe to hold the RESTful application classes

Next, create the `CustomerManager` stateless session bean in the `packt` package. Add two methods:

- ▸ `getCustomerCount` – This method is passed `void` and returns an integer
- ▸ `getCustomerCountByRegion` – This method also returns an integer but is passed a string representing the region of interest.

To keep the application simple, the `getCustomerCount` will always return 27. Implement the `getCustomerCountByRegion` method such that when passed the string, "West", it will return 12 and when passed the string, "East", it will return 15. Otherwise, we will return 0 keeping the method simple. One possible implementation follows:

```
@Stateless
public class CustomerManager {

  public int getCustomerCount() {
    return 27;
  }

  public int getCustomerCountByRegion(String region) {
    if("West".equals(region)) {
      return 12;
    } else  if("East".equals(region)) {
        return 15;
      } else {
        return 0;
      }
  }
}
```

This completes our session EJB. Now let's see what we need to do to create the actual web service. The basic steps we will use include:

1. Create an **@WebService** annotated class
2. Inject the supporting EJB
3. Create **@WebMethod** annotated methods to expose the desired web service functionality

Classes that act as a web service endpoint are designated with the **@WebService** annotation. A **Service Endpoint Interface (SEI)** is an interface that declares the endpoint's methods. An explicit interface is not required but can be specified using the **@WebService endpointInterface** element.

Create a class called Customer in the jaxws package. Annotate it using the **@WebService** annotation. In the class inject an instance of the CustomerManager class and add getCustomerCount and getCustomerCountByRegion methods mimicking those of the CustomerManager class.

Add the **@WebMethod** annotation to these two methods. In the getCustomerCount method, use the CustomerManager's getCustomerCount as the return value. In the getCustomerCountByRegion method, use the region parameter as the argument to the CustomerManager's getCustomerCountByRegion method and return this value.

```
@WebService()
public class Customer {
  @EJB
  private CustomerManager customerManager;

  @WebMethod
  public int getCustomerCount() {
    return customerManager.getCustomerCount();
  }

  @WebMethod
  public int getCustomerCountByRegion (String region) {
    return customerManager.getCustomerCountByRegion(region);
  }

}
```

To test this service, use the URL, `http://localhost:8080/CustomerApplication/` `CustomerService?Tester` with a browser. This should result in output similar to the following screenshot:

Execute both methods. Notice the resulting output shows a SOAP Request and SOAP Response further down in the browser's window. In the case of the second method, notice the name of the argument is **arg0**.

<?xml version="1.0" encoding="UTF-8"?>

<S:Envelope xmlns:S="http://schemas.xmlsoap.org/soap/envelope/">

  <S:Header/>

  <S:Body>

    <ns2:getCustomerCountByRegion xmlns:ns2="http://jaxws/">

      <arg0>West</arg0>

    </ns2:getCustomerCountByRegion>

  </S:Body>

</S:Envelope>

In the *There's more* section we will see how we can control this name and other aspects of the service.

How it works...

The **@WebService** annotation designated the class as a web service endpoint. Its **serviceName** element provided the name of the service as known to a client. In this case it was `CustomerService` as used in the URL. Notice while our class name is `Customer`, the string, "Service" was automatically appended to the class name. The **@WebMethod** designates a method available as part of the service. When these methods are invoked, they used the corresponding methods provided by the injected EJB `CustomerManager`.

The `getCustomerCount` method returned 27. We could have developed a more sophisticated application using a database and entity classes, however, the added sophistication would have distracted from the creation of the web service.

Actually, this additional functionality is where JAX-WS becomes more important. When issues such as security and transaction processing are an important part of an application, JAX-WS is a better choice than JAX-RS.

There's more...

Here we will address the web service-related annotations in more depth:

  ▶ Variations of the **@WebService** annotation
  ▶ Using the **@WebMethod** annotation
  ▶ Using the **@WebParam** annotation

Variations of the @WebService annotation

The **@WebService** annotation has several elements permitting us to control the names used with the service. Here we are only interested in the **serviceName** element. Using this element allows us to use a name other than the default name provided for us, "CustomerService". Notice while our class name is `Customer`, the string, "Service" is automatically appended to the class name. The **serviceName** element allows us to change the name of the service.

Modify the **@WebService** as shown below:

```
@WebService(serviceName="Customer")
```

Use the following URL in place of the old one:

```
http://localhost:8080/CustomerApplication/Customer?Tester
```

Notice the behavior is the same.

Using the @WebMethod annotation

Business methods of the web service interface must be declared as `public` and cannot be declared as `static` or `final`. They are annotated with the **@WebMethod** annotation to designate them as endpoint methods.

Parameters of these methods must be JAXB-compatible. **The Java Architecture for XML Binding (JAXB)** is an API used to simplify access to XML documents. This API provides an alternative to using the **Simple API for XML (SAX)** or the **Document Object Module (DOM)** to access an XML document. A list of JAXB-compatible data types is found at: `http://download.oracle.com/javaee/5/tutorial/doc/bnazq.html#bnazs`.

To control the name of the method as exposed by the web service, we can use the **operationName** element of the **@WebMethod** annotation. For example, use the following **@WebMethod** annotation for the `getCustomerCount` method:

```
@WebMethod(operationName="getTotalCount")
```

When the application is executed you should see the new method name in the browser.

Using the @WebParam annotation

As pointed out earlier, the name of the `getCustomerCountByRegion`'s argument is **arg0**. While this is not necessarily a problem, we can control this name using the **@WebParam** annotation. Modify the `getCustomerCountByRegion` method as shown below. This annotation specifies the web name of the parameter to be "region".

```
public int getCustomerCountByRegion(@WebParam(name = "region")
    String region) {
```

When the application is executed you should see the new parameter name in the SOAP Request message as shown here:

```
<?xml version="1.0" encoding="UTF-8"?>

<S:Envelope xmlns:S="http://schemas.xmlsoap.org/soap/envelope/">

  <S:Header/>

  <S:Body>

    <ns2:getCustomerCountByRegion xmlns:ns2="http://jaxws/">

      <region>West</region>

    </ns2:getCustomerCountByRegion>

  </S:Body>

</S:Envelope>
```

The first three recipes in *Chapter 2*, *Session Beans* provide more detail about the use and creation of session EJBs.

Creating an EJB-based web service using JAX-RS

A RESTful web service is useful for applications which do not require the use of transactions, security and other features that can adversely impact its performance. JAX-RS supports the creation of RESTful applications. These types of services are typified through the use of HTTP commands such as **GET** and **POST**. In this recipe, we will use annotations that identify methods of a service corresponding to these commands.

Getting ready

The two basic steps involved in creating a JAX-RS web service include:

1. Creating an EJB which provides the application's functionality
2. Creating a Web Service (JAX-RS) which utilizes the EJB

We will reuse the `CustomerManager` class as described in the first recipe to provide our service's functionality.

The focus of this recipe is how to create the Web Service. To create a web service endpoint we need to:

1. Use the **@Path** annotation to designate a class as an endpoint
2. Annotate the methods of the service with one of several annotations depending on the service provided by the method
3. Use a supporting EJB to implement the desired functionality of the service

How to do it...

We will create our JAX-RS web service by adding two classes to the `jaxrs` package. The classes will use the two `CustomerManager` methods. Start by creating a stateless session EJB called `Customer` in the `jaxrs` package.

Sometime during the process of creating the `Customer` using NetBeans, you may be prompted with the following dialog box. When encountered, select the first option and proceed. In other development environments you may have to take different steps. The `ApplicationConfig` class created here is detailed in a later section of this recipe.

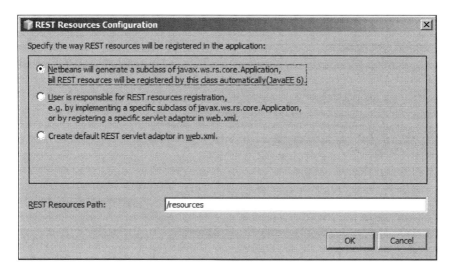

In this version of the `Customer` class, we will provide a simple method which responds to an HTTP **GET** request and returns an HTML string containing the number of customers returned by the `CustomerManager`'s `getCustomerCount` method.

Annotate the class with an **@Path** annotation as shown below. Inject an instance of the **CustomerManager** class as an instance variable and add a method called `doGet` which uses this class. Annotate the method with a **@GET** and **@Produces** annotation.

```
@Path("customer")
@Stateless
public class Customer {
  @EJB
  private CustomerManager customerManager;

  @GET
  @Produces("text/html")
  public String doGet() {
    return "<h3>Customer Count: " +
      customerManager.getCustomerCount() + "</h3>";
  }

}
```

To test the service after it has been deployed, use the following URL in a browser:
`http://localhost:8080/CustomerApplication/resources/customer`. The
"resources" part of the URL will be explained shortly. The browser output should appear
as shown in the following screenshot:

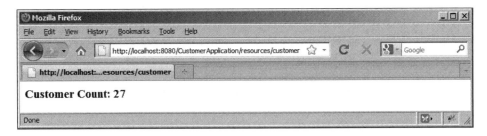

From this example, you can see how easy it is to respond to a user's request. When the use of
an EJB is needed to support this type of interaction, JAX-RS provides a good solution.

How it works...

The **@Path** annotation was used to designate the class as a web service endpoint. Its value,
the string, "customer" was used as part of the path used to access this web page. This was
reflected in the URL.

A JAX-RS application responds to standard HTTP commands such as **GET** and **POST**. To
respond to a **GET** request, we added the `doGet` method. The **@GET** annotation specified
the method as the one to execute when the HTTP **GET** command arrived. The **@Produces**
annotation means the data returned by the method is HTML. The body of the method returned
a simple HTML string reflecting the return value of the `getCustomerCount` method.

There's more...

Notice in the URL the use of the string **resources**. JAX-RS uses an `Application` derived
class in support of applications. How this works is detailed next. In addition, we will look into
the use of the **GET** command in more depth and also see how to use HTML **FORM** data.

Understanding the Application class

As we saw earlier, NetBeans generated an `ApplicationConfig` class which extends the
`javax.ws.rs.core.Application` class. The purpose of the class is to manage all of the
resources used by the application. The `ApplicationConfig` class provided by NetBeans
provides default support for all the basic operations.

The `ApplicationConfig` class is shown below and is annotated with the **@ApplicationPath** annotation. It is found under the **Generated Sources (rest)** folder of the application. The string used specifies the root name of the application as we saw reflected in the URL.

```
package org.netbeans.rest.application.config;
/**
 * This class is generated by the Netbeans IDE,
 * and registers all REST root resources created in the project.
 * Please, DO NOT EDIT this class !
 */
@javax.ws.rs.ApplicationPath("resources")
public class ApplicationConfig extends javax.ws.rs.core.Application {
}
```

Using the GET command with parameters

The `getCustomerCountByRegion` method is passed a string representing the region of interest. So how do we handle requests when parameters need to be passed? The answer involves using the **@QueryParam** and **@DefaultValue** annotations. The **@QueryParam** annotation associates the name of an HTML parameter with a parameter of the method responding to the **GET** command. The **@DefaultValue** annotation specifies a default value for the parameter.

Add a new stateless EJB called `CustomerByRegion` to the `jaxrs` package. Inject an instance of the `CustomerManager` class.

```
@Path("customerByRegion")
@Stateless
public class CustomerByRegion {

  @EJB
  private CustomerManager customerManager;


  ...
}
```

Add a `doGet` method using the **@GET** and **@Produces** annotations as we did with the `Customer` class. However, use the following parameter list and inside of the method use the `getCustomerCountByRegion` method.

```
@GET
@Produces("text/html")
public String doGet(
  @DefaultValue("East") @QueryParam("region") String region) {
    return "<h3>Customer Count: " +
      customerManager.getCustomerCountByRegion(region) + "</h3>";
}
```

The **@QueryParam** annotation associates the HTML parameter "region" with the methods parameter `region`. A default value of "East" is also assigned using the **@DefaultValue** annotation.

To test the method, use the following URL. Notice the use of the name as specified by the **@Path** annotation. The question mark is used to indicate that a parameter is being passed. In this case, the parameter is **region** and is assigned a value of **West**.

```
http://localhost:8080/CustomerApplication/resources/customerByRegion?
region=West
```

Your output should appear as shown in the following screenshot:

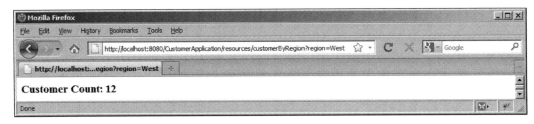

Using the POST command with form data

The **POST** command is an alternative to the **GET** command and is also used to send information to the server. The **GET** command encodes form data into the URL while the **POST** command places data within the HTTP message body. The **POST** command can also be used to retrieve information passed as part of an HTML **FORM** tag.

To illustrate the use of this command, create an `index.html` file as shown below. This file contains a **FORM** tag with an `input` element allowing the user to enter a region name. The **FORM** tag has two fields of interest. The first is the `action` field. This specifies the URL to use when the user presses the submit button. In this case it specifies the `Customer` class we developed at the beginning of this recipe. The second field is the **method** field. This specifies the HTTP command to use. Here we specify the use of the **POST** command.

```html
<html>
  <head>
    <title></title>
    <meta http-equiv="Content-Type" content="text/html;
      charset=UTF-8">
  </head>
  <body>
    <form action="/CustomerApplication/resources/customer"
      method="post" >
      Region<input name="region" value="East"><br>
      <input type="submit">
    </form>
  </body>
</html>
```

However, in order to use the **POST** command we need to add a supporting method to the
`Customer` class. Add a `doPost` method to the `jaxr`'s `Customer` class as shown below.
In this simple method, we return the number of customers based on the region.

```
@POST
@Produces("text/html")
@Consumes("application/x-www-form-urlencoded")
public String doPost(@FormParam("region") String region) {
   return "<h3>Customer Count: " +
      customerManager.getCustomerCountByRegion(region) + "</h3>";
}
```

This method uses the **@Produces** annotation as we had used earlier. It also uses a
@Consumes annotation which determines the type of input accepted by the method. In this
case we use "application/x-www-form-urlencoded". This means the method accepts data
encoded by an HTML **FORM**. The server will generate an exception if the wrong type of
data is sent.

The **@FormParam** annotation associates the **FORM**'s **region** parameter with the
method's `region` parameter. The `region` parameter is used as an argument of the
`getCustomerCountByRegion` method.

Use the URL `http://localhost:8080/CustomerApplication/index.html` to test the
application. The following screenshot shows the expected output:

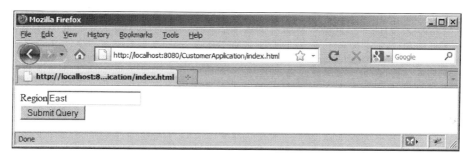

Selecting the **Submit** button should result in output as shown in the following screenshot:

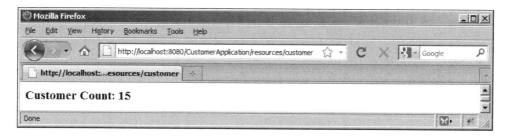

Using an MDB as part of a web service

An MDB can be used in the support of a web service. When the need exists to asynchronously perform some action, a web client can send information to a web service which then repackages it in a message. The message can then be sent to a queue for processing at a later date. A framework for this type of task is presented here.

The use of asynchronous session beans can also be used to support this type of operation. The use of asynchronous methods is discussed in *Chapter 2, Using an asynchronous method to create a background process* recipe.

Getting ready

Essentially we will reuse parts of the recipes in *Chapter 3, Message-Driven Beans* dealing with Message-Driven Beans (MDB), specifically the *Handling a text-based message* recipe. There are two steps in this process.

1. Creating an MDB
2. Adding code to the web service to create a message and send it to the queue

In this example, we will create an MDB called `AddMessage`. The `onMessage` method, which handles a dequeued message, will simply display the text message in the console window. We will then modify the `jaxrs.Customer`'s `doPost` method developed in the previous recipe to create the message. Together, this will demonstrate the approach.

In order for this approach to work, we need to setup a queue in the server. The step used to create the queue is server-specific. Refer to your server's documentation to set up a queue. In this example, we will use a queue called `jms/Customer`.

How to do it...

Add an MDB called `AddMessage`, which implements the `MessageListener` interface, to the `packt` package. Use the following **@MessageDriven** annotation to specify the use of the `jms/Customer` queue. Details of this annotation can be found in the introduction of *Chapter 3, Message-Driven Beans*.

```
@MessageDriven(mappedName = "jms/Customer", activationConfig = {
    @ActivationConfigProperty(propertyName = "acknowledgeMode",
      propertyValue = "Auto-acknowledge"),
    @ActivationConfigProperty(propertyName = "destinationType",
      propertyValue = "javax.jms.Queue")
  })
```

```
public class AddMessage implements MessageListener {

   ...

}
```

Add a public default constructor and an `onMessage` method which is passed a `Message` object. In the `onMessage` method, cast the `message` parameter to a `TextMessage` and then use its `getText` method to retrieve and display the message.

```
public AddMessage() {
}

public void onMessage(Message message) {
   System.out.print("onMessage");
   TextMessage textMessage = (TextMessage) message;
   try {
      System.out.println(textMessage.getText());
   } catch (JMSException e) {
      throw new RuntimeException(e);
   }

}
```

Next we will augment the `jaxrs.Customer` class to send a message to the customer queue. Inject a reference to the `QueueConnectionFactory` and a `Queue`.

```
@Path("customer")
@Stateless
public class Customer {

   @EJB
   private CustomerManager customerManager;

   @Resource(mappedName="jms/CustomerFactory")
   private QueueConnectionFactory queueConnectionFactory;

   @Resource(mappedName="jms/Customer")
   private Queue queue;
```

Add the following code to the `jaxr`'s `Customer`'s `doPost` method before its `return` statement.

```
try {
  String message = region + " passed";

  Connection connection =
    queueConnectionFactory.createConnection();
  Session session = connection.createSession(false,
    Session.AUTO_ACKNOWLEDGE);
  MessageProducer messageProducer = (MessageProducer)
    session.createProducer(queue);
  TextMessage textMessage = session.createTextMessage();
  textMessage.setText(message);
  messageProducer.send(textMessage);
  System.out.println("Message sent successfully");
} catch (JMSException ex) {
    System.out.println("JMSException in SalutationServlet");
}
```

In your browser load the `index.html` page using the URL: `http://localhost:8080/CustomerApplication/index.html`. The output should appear as shown in the following screenshot:

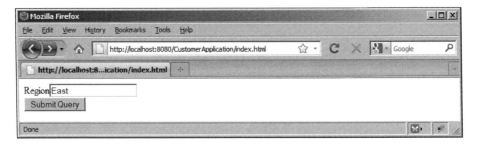

Enter **East** and then press the **Submit Query** button. The output of the browser should be similar to the following screenshot:

In the console window you should see output similar to the following:

INFO: Message sent successfully

INFO: onMessage

INFO: East

How it works...

When the `index.html` **Submit** button was pressed, the **region** parameter was passed to the `doPost` method. Within the `doPost` method, a `TextMessage` was created and sent to the `jms/Customer` queue. The details of these steps are explained in *Chapter 3, Handling a text-based message* recipe.

In the `AddMessage` MDB, the `onMessage` method processed the dequeued message and displayed the text message in the console window. The **@MessageDriven** annotation associated the MDB with the `jms/Customer` queue.

See also

MDBs are discussed in *Chapter 3, Message-Driven Beans*. Of immediate relevance are the introduction and the first recipe which deals with text-based messages.

11
Packaging the EJB

In this chapter, we will cover:

- ▸ Understanding an application's JAR files using the `jar` command
- ▸ Understanding class loading
- ▸ Using deployment descriptors for interceptors
- ▸ Using deployment descriptors for timer interceptors
- ▸ Using deployment descriptors for default interceptors
- ▸ Using deployment descriptors for callback interceptors
- ▸ Using deployment descriptors for transactions
- ▸ Using deployment descriptors for security

Introduction

Before a Java EE application can be used it must be deployed to a server. The process of deployment consists of packaging the components of the application together and then installing these components on a server. Once they are installed, individual classes are loaded into memory. This process can be complicated; however, the deployment descriptors examined in this chapter provide additional opportunities for tailoring an application for specific servers and making applications more portable and maintainable.

The packaging of a Java EE application is accomplished using **Java ARchive (JAR)** files. These files are stored in ZIP format and contain the classes and resources needed by the application. In Java EE, there are specialized versions of the JAR files including EAR, WAR, and EJB-JAR.

The deployment process is controlled by deployment descriptors. These files specify how the application should be installed and how many of the behavioral characteristics of a component, such as how transactions are handled or which roles can access a component. In the context of EJB development roles, the management of deployment descriptors is the responsibility of the application assembler. In a larger organization, an individual may be tasked with the assembly of EJB JAR and WAR files into EAR files. The individual would also be responsible for configuring the deployment descriptors for the application.

Annotations or elements of a deployment descriptor can be used to configure an EJB. Annotations are easy to use but may not be the best choice if application settings change frequently. Hard coding names for JNDI and JMS resources will require the code to be re-compiled if they change. Also, some settings such as specifying default interceptors cannot be done using annotations.

While there is some argument as to which approach is best, you are free as a developer to use the most appropriate approach for your application. In general, annotations are better suited for static environments while deployment descriptors are better suited for dynamic environments. The approaches can be intermixed. When this happens, deployment descriptors override annotations.

Some annotations cannot be overridden:

- @Stateless
- @Stateful
- @MessageDriven
- @Service
- @Consumer

Deployment descriptors are optional in Java EE 5 and later. When a deployment descriptor is not present, the server determines the makeup of the application by examining the contents of the JAR files and using a standard naming convention as detailed in `http://java.sun.com/blueprints/code/namingconventions.html`.

A Java EE application typically consists of many different types of components including EJBs, HTML, JSP, and servlets. EJBs execute from within an EJB container while servlets execute from a web container. These components can be packaged in different JAR files. The various packaging types include:

- CAR – A Client Application Archive file is used to hold the components needed for Java clients not normally managed by a browser
- EAR – The Enterprise Application Archive file contains other EE modules such as the EJB-JAR and WAR modules
- EJB-JAR – The EJB Java Archive file is intended to contain session and message driven beans. Entities may also be packaged in this file and elsewhere.

- ► RAR – The Resource Adaptor Archive file holds resource adapters.

- ► WAR – The Web Application Archive file holds user interface files such as servlets, JSPs, JSF, and similar type classes. Entities and other EJBs can also be packaged in this file.

Entities can be deployed in most JAR files except RAR modules. When entities are packaged in a file, a `persistence.xml` file is frequently placed in the JAR file also.

An important aspect of deployment and the execution of the application is the class loading process. The *Understanding class loading* recipe addresses this issue.

Chapter 8, Interceptors details the creation and use of interceptors. There are several kinds of interceptor methods and these can be configured using a deployment descriptor:

- ► Business method interceptors – Covered in the *Using deployment descriptors for interceptors* recipe

- ► Timeout method interceptors – Detailed in the *Using deployment descriptors for timer interceptors* recipe

- ► Lifecycle callback interceptors – Covered in the *Using deployment descriptors for callback interceptors* recipe

- ► Default interceptors – Covered in the *Using deployment descriptors for default interceptors* recipe

We also examine the use of deployment descriptors for transactions and security in the *Using a deployment descriptor for transactions* and *Using deployment descriptors for security* recipes respectively.

Understanding an application's JAR files using the jar command

The EAR file is a top level JAR file and holds other JAR files. This packaging provides a single JAR file to simplify the deployment process. The use and organization of this JAR and those for EJB and WEB modules is explained in this recipe using the Java JDK `jar` command. While this command is more often used to create a JAR file, it can also be used to examine the structure of an existing JAR file. Upon the creation of a JAR file is it good to be able to verify its contents when a deployment tool performs other than as expected.

Getting ready

There are several different types of files used in the deployment of an application. The following table lists these files along with the internal file which serves as the deployment descriptor.

Type	Typical file name	Deployment descriptor file	Location of deployment descriptor	Contents
CAR	`*-app-client.jar`	`application-client.xml`	`/META-INF` directory of `app-client.jar`	Contains an `application-client.xml` file or a Main-Class declaration in the manifest file.
EAR	`*.ear`	`application.xml`	Standalone	Will contain other JAR files along with manifest
EJB-JAR	`*-ejb.jar`	`ejb-jar.xml`	`/META-INF` directory of `ejb-jar.jar`	Will include an `ejb-jar.xml` file and/or contain EJB annotated classes. May also contain entities along with a `persistence.xml` file
RAR	`*.rar`	`ra.xml`	`/META-INF` directory of `*.rar`	Contains resource adapters.
WAR	`*-war.war`	`web.xml`	`/WEB-INF` directory of `war.jar`	Files such as servlets, JSPs, and JSFs. May also contain entities along with a `persistence.xml` file

The * is normally replaced with the name of the application.

The steps required to use the Java SDK `jar` command include:

1. Opening a command window
2. Setting the `path` environmental variable
3. Executing the `jar` command

How to do it...

The structure of the EAR files is simple. It consists of a MANIFEST.MF manifest file used to describe the contents of the JAR. It also contains an `*-ejb.jar` file and `*-war.jar` files. A JAR file can be created using the `jar.exe` program. Development environments such as NetBeans incorporate the tool into the environment and create the various JAR files transparently.

To use the `jar` command we need to open a command window. On Windows this can be done by selecting **Start | All Programs** and then **Accessories**. Select the **Command Prompt** menu item. A **Command Prompt** window should appear similar to that found in the following screenshot:

The `jar.exe` command file is located in the bin directory of the Java SDK directory. Depending on the version of the SDK installed on your machine, the `path` environmental variable needs to be set to reference this location. This environmental variable is used by the command prompt to locate executable files. The following command set the variable to search the bin directory of the jdk1.6.0_20 version found on the C drive in the `\Program Files (x86)\Java\` directory. The last part of the command preserves the previous path setting.

C:\>set path=C:\Program Files (x86)\Java\jdk1.6.0_20\bin;%path%

Next, navigate to the directory where the JAR file to be examined is found.

Using the `jar` command with the arguments `-tf` allows us to display the contents of a JAR. Using the command against the EAR file for the `SingletonExample` application found in *Chapter 2, Creating a singleton bean* recipe, allows us to examine the file. The following illustrates the use of the command. However, note that the command has been issued at the root level instead of the directory where the JAR file resides. The actual path you use will depend on where the application was developed.

C:\>jar -tf SingletonExample.ear

The file should contain the following items:

META-INF/

  META-INF/MANIFEST.MF

SingletonExample-ejb.jar

SingletonExample-war.war

We can use the `jar` command against the `SingletonApplication-ejb.jar` file and the `SingleApplication-war.war` files also. The contents of the EJB file will contain the following:

META-INF/

> **META-INF/MANIFEST.MF**

> **META-INF/beans.xml**

packt/

> **packt/GameBean.class**

> **packt/PlayerBean.class**

.netbeans_automatic_build

.netbeans_update_resources

The actual contents of your file will be dependent on the development environment you used to create the JAR. In this example, we see NetBeans-specific files. These files are not of immediate interest to us. However, notice the two EJB are packaged as members of the `packt` package.

The WAR file will contain:

META-INF/

> **META-INF/MANIFEST.MF**

WEB-INF/

> **WEB-INF/classes/**

>> **WEB-INF/classes/servlet/**

>> **WEB-INF/classes/servlet/GameServlet.class**

>> **WEB-INF/classes/.netbeans_automatic_build**

>> **WEB-INF/classes/.netbeans_update_resources**

> **WEB-INF/beans.xml**

> **WEB-INF/sun-web.xml**

> **WEB-INF/web.xml**

index.jsp

We can see the NetBeans-specific files and the `GameServlet` class found in the `servlet` package. An `index.jsp` file is also included which is an artifact of the application as generated by NetBeans.

How it works...

The `jar` command executes from a command window. Once the window was brought up it was necessary to set the `path` environmental variable to the directory containing the executable `jar` file. It was then necessary to navigate to the directory where the JAR file of interest was located. The `jar` command was then executed against the file.

Instead of using the `jar` command, we could have also used a windows-based tool such as 7-ZIP. Details of the use of the JAR tool can be found at `http://download.oracle.com/javase/6/docs/technotes/tools/windows/jar.html`.

Also, most JAR files contain a manifest file which details the contents of the JAR or provides additional information about the JAR. Other references to JAR file components can be specified using the **Class-Path** attribute of the JAR file. Details of the JAR file format can be found at `http://download.oracle.com/javase/1.4.2/docs/guide/jar/jar.html`.

See also

Most of the recipes in this chapter address the specific of the deployment descriptor for applications.

Understanding class loading

In this recipe, we will examine how classes are loaded and the class loader hierarchy typically found in a Java EE server. An understanding of this process also explains the dependencies found between modules. In addition, a class not found type of exception is not uncommon. Understanding the loading process will help resolve these types of errors.

Getting ready

Not all of the application's classes are loaded immediately upon deployment of an application. Classes are generally loaded as needed at runtime when a client needs it. When an instance of a class is created, the class must be in memory.

It is not uncommon for an application to generate a `ClassNotfoundException` or a `ClassNoDefException` during execution. Thus, it can be important to understand the class loading process to correct these types of problems. Most environments use what is called Parent-First Delegation class loading process. The basic steps of this process include:

▸ The loader checks its local cache to see if it is available

▸ If not, it asks the parent loader to load the class

▸ If the parent cannot load the class it uses a local source such as a JAR file

By checking for the presence of a class in a cache, the loading process can be sped up. By using the parent loader, we can be confident that malicious classes were not inadvertently loaded. If desired, it is possible to create your own class loader.

How to do it...

The actual loading process is vendor-specific. There are no specifications on how class loading is to be accomplished by a Java EE server. This limitation can make it difficult to port an application to a different server if the order of class loading is important.

One way of determining when a class loads is to use a static initialization block for the class and displaying a message indicating that the class has been loaded. This block is executed only once when the class is loaded. However, this technique can only be applied to those classes whose source code is available. The JVM **-verbose** option can also be used which will show when each class is loaded. However, as the option name implies, the output can be verbose and hard to follow.

How it works...

The overall process of class loading begins when a JVM starts up. The `CLASSPATH` environment variable frequently defines the locations of classes. Essential classes are loaded first and then application-specific classes are loaded as needed. The JVM frequently uses multiple class loaders. For example, the Sun JVM uses a hierarchy of class loaders:

▸ Boot class loader – Loads classes from `$JAVAHOME/jre/rt.jar` which contain the standard JDK classes

▸ Extension class loader – Follows the boot class loader and loads classes from `$JAVAHOME/jre/lib/ext/*.jar`

▸ System class loader – Loads application-specific classes

The boot class loader loads core classes such as those found in `java.lang` and `java.util` packages. The JVM command line argument, **bootclasspath** can be used to direct the JVM to load additional classes.

The extension class loader is concerned with additional classes such as those used in cryptography. It will load files from the $JAVAHOME/jre/lib/ext/ directory and any found in the java.ext.dirs system property.

The system class loader, also called the application class loader, loads the application classes as specified by the CLASSPATH environment variable or a **Class-Path** entry in a JAR file.

Application server-specific class loaders are used by the JVM when the JVM starts up. In the case of the Java EE server, an application server class loader then starts loading classes as specified by the environment variable, $APP_SERVER_HOME/lib.

As mentioned before, the actual loading process is vendor-specific. However, frequently an EJB class loader is used by an application to load its classes. This loader is often the parent of a WAR class loader. This arrangement results in the classes loaded by the EJB class loader being visible to those loaded by the WAR class loader.

When a class loader loads classes, it does so from a code source location. These locations are dependent on the module. The following table details these locations by module.

Type	Code source
EAR	JAR file in its /lib directory
	Those JARs specified in the Class-Path manifest element of the above JAR files
EJB-JAR	Those in the EJB-JAR file
	Those JARs specified in the Class-Path manifest element of the above EJB-JAR file
	Those JARs specified in the Class-Path manifest element of the above JAR files
WAR	WEB-INF/classes
	JARs in the WEB-INF/lib directory
	Those JARs specified in the Class-Path manifest element of WAR
	Those JARs specified in the Class-Path manifest element of the above two JAR categories

There's more...

Session and message-driven beans are normally packaged in an EJB-JAR file. Entities can also be packaged there. There are several ways of packaging classes into a JAR.

One approach uses the jar command, which is executed at a command prompt. Most development environments perform this task automatically, hiding the details of this process. The Apache Ant tool or Maven tool is often used for this purpose.

Helper classes contain functionality that can be useful to one or several classes. The visibility of these helper classes can be controlled. To make them visible to all of the application's modules, package them in the EAR's lib directory. To restrict access to them, place the classes in a separate JAR file and add a **Class-Path** attribute referencing the helper class JAR file in those modules requiring access to them. The **Class-Path** attribute is found in the containing EJB-JAR or WAR module's `Manifest.mf` file. However, when a top level JAR file is processed by a deployment tool it should not contain a **Class-Path** entry.

Using deployment descriptors for interceptors

To specify interceptor methods of an interceptor class, we use the `<interceptors>` element with other elements in the `ejb-jar.xml` file. In this recipe, we examine how this is done. Interceptors are discussed in more detail in *Chapter 8, Interceptors*.

Java EE 6 application no longer requires deployment descriptors as annotations have largely taken their place. However, there are certain situations where they are still needed. One of these situations is when we want to use a default interceptor as detailed in the *Using deployment descriptors for default interceptors* recipe.

Getting ready

The steps to use deployment descriptors include:

1. Adding an `ejb-jar.xml` file to your application
2. Using the `<interceptors>` element to define interceptors
3. Using the `<interceptor-binding>` element to define the interceptor bindings
4. Deploying the application

The interceptor bindings defined in the `ejb-jar.xml` file will override the annotations found in a class. The advantage of using deployment descriptors lies in the ability to control the interceptors without having to modify the EJB source code. This can result in a more portable and malleable application.

How to do it...

To use deployment descriptors for interceptors, you will need to create an `ejb-jar.xml` file in the EJB module under the META-INF directory. This process is development environment-specific. For example, in NetBeans, right-click on the EJB module for your project in the Project Explorer and select **New | Standard Deployment Descriptor**. This will create the `ejb-jar.xml` file.

Consider the `SimpleInterceptor` class defined in *Chapter 8, Defining and Using Interceptor* recipe.

```
public class SimpleInterceptor {
  @AroundInvoke
  public Object simpleMethod(InvocationContext context) throws
    Exception{
  ...
  }
}
```

Using the **@Interceptors** annotation as shown below will result in all methods of the `RegistrationManager` class being intercepted and handled by `SimpleInterceptor`.

```
@Stateful
@Interceptors(SimpleInterceptor.class)
public class RegistrationManager {

  ...
}
```

We can achieve the same result using the `<assembly-binding>` element within the `<assembly-descriptor>` element. First, add an `ejb-jar.xml` file to your application. Add an `<ejb-jar>` element as the root element of the file.

```
<?xml version="1.0" encoding="UTF-8"?>

<ejb-jar xmlns = "http://java.sun.com/xml/ns/javaee"
  version = "3.1"
  xmlns:xsi = "http://www.w3.org/2001/XMLSchema-instance"
  xsi:schemaLocation = "http://java.sun.com/xml/ns/javaee
  http://java.sun.com/xml/ns/javaee/ejb-jar_3_1.xsd">
  ...
</ejb-jar>
```

Within the root element, we will add an `<interceptors>` element followed by an `<assembly-descriptor>` element. The first element is used to declare an interceptor and the second binds the interceptor to an EJB.

```
<?xml version="1.0" encoding="UTF-8"?>

<ejb-jar xmlns = "http://java.sun.com/xml/ns/javaee"
  version = "3.1"
  xmlns:xsi = "http://www.w3.org/2001/XMLSchema-instance"
  xsi:schemaLocation = "http://java.sun.com/xml/ns/javaee
  http://java.sun.com/xml/ns/javaee/ejb-jar_3_1.xsd">
  <interceptors>
    ...
```

```
    </interceptors>
    <assembly-descriptor>
      . . .
    </assembly-descriptor>
  </ejb-jar>
```

The `<interceptor-class>` element is nested inside the `<interceptor>` element. Its value identifies the interceptor class. In this case, it is `packt.SimpleInterceptor`.

```
    <interceptor>
      <interceptor-class>packt.SimpleInterceptor</interceptor-class>
      </interceptor>
    </interceptors>
```

The `<assembly-descriptor>` element contains an `<interceptor-binding>` element. Within this element, the name of the EJB is declared using an `<ejb-name>` element and the name of the interceptor class using an `<interceptor-class>` element. Here the `RegistrationManager` EJB is associated with the `SimpleInterceptor`.

```
    <assembly-descriptor>
      <interceptor-binding>
        <ejb-name>RegistrationManager</ejb-name>
        <interceptor-class>packt.SimpleInterceptor</interceptor-class>
      </interceptor-binding>
    </assembly-descriptor>
```

To specify the use of an interceptor for all classes, use the asterisk wildcard character.

```
    <interceptor-binding>
      <ejb-name>*</ejb-name>
      <interceptor-class>packt.SimpleInterceptor</interceptor-class>
    </interceptor-binding>
```

How it works...

The `ejb-jar.xml` file was used to specify the configuration of the `SimpleInterceptor` for use with the methods of the `RegistrationManager`. The `<interceptors>` element was used to define the interceptor and the `<assembly-descriptor>` element was used to associate the methods of the `RegistrationManager` with the interceptor. When the application is deployed, the server will intercept calls to the `RegistrationManager`'s methods using the `SimpleInterceptor`. This technique provides a way of allowing the deployer to determine when the interceptor should be used without having to use annotations.

There's more...

Interceptors can be bound to:

- ▸ All target classes. These are called default interceptors and are covered in *Using deployment descriptors for default interceptors* recipe
- ▸ One target class (class-level interceptors)
- ▸ Methods of a class (method-level interceptors)

In the previous section, the use of class-level interceptors was illustrated. In addition, we can exclude interceptors for classes and/or methods. We can also control the execution order of interceptors using deployment descriptors.

Using method-level interceptor descriptors

To restrict the use of the interceptor to a specific method of a class, use the `<method-name>` element in conjunction with the `<method>` element. If the method is overloaded, the interceptor is applied to all of the methods. In the following example, we associate the `SimpleInterceptor` with the `RegistrationManager`'s `register` method.

```
...
<interceptor-binding>
  <ejb-name>RegistrationManager</ejb-name>
  <interceptor-class>packt.SimpleInterceptor</interceptor-class>
  <method>
    <method-name>register</method-name>
  </method>
</interceptor-binding>
```

If we need to identify a specific overloaded method, then we use one or more `<method-params>` elements inside of the `<method-params>` element. These immediately follow the `<method-name>` element. The `<method-param>` element contains the data type of the parameter.

While the `register` method is not overloaded, the following illustrates the use of these elements. This matches a `register` method with three string parameters.

```
<interceptor-binding>
  <ejb-name>RegistrationManager</ejb-name>
  <interceptor-class>packt.SimpleInterceptor</interceptor-class>
  <method>
    <method-name>register</method-name>
    <method-params>
      <method-param>java.lang.String</method-param>
      <method-param>java.lang.String</method-param>
      <method-param>java.lang.String</method-param>
    </method-params>
  </method>
</interceptor-binding>
```

If the parameter data type is `void`, then the element is left empty.

```
<method-param></method-param>
```

Excluding interceptors

Interceptors can be assigned at the class level. They will apply to all methods of the class. However, if you wish to exclude an interceptor for a specific method, you can use the **@ExcludeClassInterceptors** annotation or use the `<exclude-class-interceptors>` element in the deployment descriptor.

To demonstrate the use of the deployment descriptor approach, use the **@Interceptors** annotation with the `RegistrationManager` class.

```
@Interceptors(SimpleInterceptor.class)
public class RegistrationManager {
```

Next, modify the `ejb-jar.xml` file to use the `<exclude-class-interceptors>` element. The element uses a `true` or `false` value to exclude or include the class-level interceptors. The following illustrates how to exclude the use of any class-level interceptors for the `RegistrationManager`'s `register` method:

```
<interceptor-binding>
  <ejb-name>RegistrationManager</ejb-name>
  <exclude-class-interceptors>true</exclude-class-interceptors>
  <method>
    <method-name>register</method-name>
  </method>
</interceptor-binding>
```

Default interceptors can also be excluded from a method using the `<exclude-default-interceptors>` element. It works in the same way as the `<exclude-class-interceptors>` element and is illustrated here:

```
<interceptor-binding>
  <ejb-name>RegistrationManager</ejb-name>
  <exclude-default-interceptors>true</exclude-default-interceptors>
  <exclude-class-interceptors>true</exclude-class-interceptors>
  <method>
    <method-name>register</method-name>
  </method>
</interceptor-binding>
```

Controlling the execution order of interceptors

Interceptors are normally executed in the order they are declared in an annotation. However, the order can be controlled in a deployment descriptor using the `<interceptor-order>` element. Within this element the `<interceptor-class>` element specifies the interceptors to use and their order. They are executed in the order they are listed. The following illustrates this technique for the register method where the `SimpleInterceptor` is executed before the `DefaultInterceptor`:

```
<interceptor-binding>
  <ejb-name>RegistrationManager</ejb-name>
  <interceptor-order>
    <interceptor-class>packt.SimpleInterceptor</interceptor-class>
    <interceptor-class>packt.DefaultInterceptor</interceptor-class>
  </interceptor-order>
  <method>
    <method-name>register</method-name>
  </method>
</interceptor-binding>
```

See also

Timer interceptors are discussed in the _Using deployment descriptors for timer interceptors_ recipe and callback interceptors are detailed in the _Using deployment descriptors for callback interceptors_ recipe.

Using deployment descriptors for timer interceptors

The **@AroundTimeout** annotation is used to specify an interceptor method for a timer. The interceptor method will be executed before and after the timer method executes. The creation and use of timers is detailed in _Chapter 9, Timer Services_. In this recipe, we will learn how to specify a timer interceptor using a deployment descriptor.

Getting ready

The process for creating a deployment descriptor for a timer interceptor includes:

1. Creating an `ejb-jar.xml` file for the EJB module
2. Adding an `<around-timeout>` element to the file
3. Deploying the application

We will reuse the code developed in the *Chapter 9, Using interceptors with timers* recipe. In the recipe, the **@Schedule** annotation was used with the SystemReportManager's displayMemoryReport method. This configuration displays the JVM memory utilization every 10 seconds. The **@Schedule** annotation used and the displayMemoryReport method minus its body are shown here:

```
@Schedule(second = "0,10,20,30,40,50", minute="*", hour = "*")
public void displayMemoryReport(Timer timer) {...}
```

The interceptorTimeout method follows:

```
public Object interceptorTimeout(InvocationContext
    invocationContext) throws Exception {
  System.out.println("interceptorTimeout executing");
  Timer timer = (Timer) invocationContext.getTimer();
  System.out.println("Timer: " + timer.getSchedule());
  Object object = invocationContext.proceed();
  System.out.println("interceptorTimeout returning");
  return object;
}
```

How to do it...

Create an ejb-jar.xml if one does not already exist. Add a declaration for the SystemReportManager session EJB using the <enterprise-beans> and <session> elements. Within the <session> element, use the <ejb-name> to specify the SystemReportManager EJB followed by an <around-timeout> element. Within the <around-timeout> element, add a <method-name> element using interceptorTimeout as its value. These elements are listed here:

```
<?xml version="1.0" encoding="UTF-8"?>

<ejb-jar xmlns = "http://java.sun.com/xml/ns/javaee"
   version = "3.1"
  xmlns:xsi = "http://www.w3.org/2001/XMLSchema-instance"
  xsi:schemaLocation = "http://java.sun.com/xml/ns/javaee
  http://java.sun.com/xml/ns/javaee/ejb-jar_3_1.xsd">
  <enterprise-beans>
    <session>
      <ejb-name>SystemReportManager</ejb-name>
      <around-timeout>
        <method-name>interceptorTimeout</method-name>
      </around-timeout>
    </session>
  </enterprise-beans>
</ejb-jar>
```

Redeploy the application. When the deployment is complete, the timer along with its interceptor should execute every 10 seconds.

How it works...

The `ejb-jar.xml` file was used for associating the `interceptorTimeout` method with the `SystemReportManager`'s `displayMemoryReport` method. In the `<session>` element, the `SystemReportManager` was declared using the `<ejb-name>` element. Following this was the `<around-timeout>` element where the interceptor was named. At deployment, the server will associate this interceptor with the `SystemReportManager` methods.

See also

The *Using deployment descriptors for interceptor* recipe covers the general aspects of using interceptors.

Using deployment descriptor for default interceptors

Default interceptors are intended to be executed for every session and message-driven EJB in the EJB module. However, default interceptors can only be declared within the `ejb-jar.xml` deployment descriptor. This recipe will illustrate this technique.

Getting ready

The process for creating a deployment descriptor for default interceptors includes:

1. Creating an `ejb-jar.xml` file for the EJB module
2. Using the `<interceptors>` element to define your interceptors
3. Adding an `<interceptor-binding>` element to bind the interceptor to an EJB
4. Deploying the application

The basic structure of the XML elements is as follows:

```
<interceptors>
  <interceptor>
    <interceptor-class>interceptorClass</interceptor-class>
  </interceptor>
</interceptors>
<assembly-descriptor>
  <interceptor-binding>
    <ejb-name>*</ejb-name>
```

```
    <interceptor-class>interceptorClass</interceptor-class>
  </interceptor-binding>
</assembly-descriptor>
```

The use of the asterisk in this position means the interceptor is to be used with all of the EJBs in the EJB module.

How to do it...

We will use the *Chapter 8, Defining and using interceptors* recipe, to illustrate deployment descriptors. In the `ejb-jar.xml` file, add an `<interceptors>` element to declare your default interceptor. Within the element add one `<interceptor>` element for each interceptor. In this case there is only one. The `<interceptor-class>` element is needed to specify the name of the interceptor class.

```
<interceptors>
  <interceptor>
    <interceptor-class>packt.DefaultInterceptor</interceptor-class>
  </interceptor>
</interceptors>
```

Next, add an `<interceptor-binding>` element inside of an `<assembly-descriptor>` element to bind the interceptor to all of the EJBs in the module. Next, add an `<ejb-name>` element within the `<interceptor-binding>` element and use an asterisk for its value to specify all EJBs in the module. Add the `<interceptor-class>` element next to specify the name of the interceptor.

```
<assembly-descriptor>
  <interceptor-binding>
    <ejb-name>*</ejb-name>
    <interceptor-class>packt.DefaultInterceptor</interceptor-class>
  </interceptor-binding>
</assembly-descriptor>
```

We need to create the default interceptor before we can run our application. Add a new class to the `packt` package called `DefaultInterceptor`. It should be very similar to the `SimpleInterceptor` except for the use of the method name `defaultMethod`. Modify the `println` methods to indicate we are executing from the default interceptor.

```
public class DefaultInterceptor {
  @AroundInvoke
  public Object defaultMethod(InvocationContext context) throws
    Exception{
    System.out.println("Default Interceptor: Invoking method: " +
      context.getMethod().getName());
    Object result =  context.proceed();
```

```
System.out.println("Default Interceptor: Returned from method: "
    + context.getMethod().getName());
return result;
}
```

Execute the application. The output should be similar to the following:

INFO: Default Interceptor: Invoking method: register

INFO SimpleInterceptor entered: register

INFO: register

INFO: Default Interceptor: Invoking method: create

INFO: Default Interceptor: Returned from method: create

INFO: SimpleInterceptor exited: register

INFO: Default Interceptor: Returned from method: register

How it works...

The `ejb-jar.xml` file contained the XML elements used to associate the `DefaultInterceptor` with all of the EJBs of an application. The `DefaultInterceptor` was added to the `packt` package and declared with the `<interceptors>` element. Within the `<assembly-descriptor>` element it was bound to the application's EJBs. Upon execution of the application, the interceptors were invoked as expected.

See also

The *Using deployment descriptors for interceptors* recipe covers the general aspects of using interceptors.

Using deployment descriptors for callback interceptors

Lifecycle callback methods are used to perform special processing during the creation, destruction and other events of an EJB. The callback events available are EJB-specific. In this recipe we will examine the use of deployment descriptors to specify a callback event.

Getting ready

The process for creating a deployment descriptor for interceptors includes:

- ▸ Creating an `ejb-jar.xml` file for the EJB module
- ▸ Using the `<interceptors>` element to define interceptors
- ▸ Adding a lifecycle element to bind the interceptor to an EJB
- ▸ Deploying the application

To illustrate the use of a deployment descriptor for a lifecycle method, we will modify the `RegistrationApplication` along with the `SimpleInterceptor` class developed in the first two recipes of *Chapter 8, Interceptors*. The `SimpleInterceptor` class has a method called `constructed`, as shown below, which we want to be a post construct method. Post construct methods will be executed after its class has been created and after any dependency injection has been performed. We could use the **@PostConstruct** annotation to mark the method as a post construct method. Instead we will use a deployment descriptor.

```
public class SimpleInterceptor {

  private void constructed(InvocationContext invocationContext) {
    System.out.println("SimpleInterceptor constructed: ");
  }
  ...
}
```

How to do it...

Create an `ejb-jar.xml` file. The root element is `<ejb-jar>` as shown here:

```
<?xml version="1.0" encoding="UTF-8"?>
<ejb-jar xmlns = "http://java.sun.com/xml/ns/javaee"
  version = "3.1"
  xmlns:xsi = "http://www.w3.org/2001/XMLSchema-instance"
  xsi:schemaLocation = "http://java.sun.com/xml/ns/javaee
  http://java.sun.com/xml/ns/javaee/ejb-jar_3_1.xsd">
  ...
</ejb-jar>
```

For a post construction life cycle callback, the `<post-construct>` element is used. Add an `<interceptors>` element within the `<ejb-jar>` element. Within this element you can add one or more `<interceptor>` elements to declare interceptors and their callback methods.

Add an `<interceptor>` element and within this element add the following two elements:

- ▸ `<lifecycle-callback-class>` – Used to specify the class
- ▸ `<lifecycle-callback-method>` – Used to specify the method

The following code illustrates the deployment code to affect the use of this lifecycle method.

```
<interceptors>
  <interceptor>
    <interceptor-class>packt.DefaultInterceptor</interceptor-class>
  </interceptor>
  <interceptor>
    <interceptor-class>packt.SimpleInterceptor</interceptor-class>
    <post-construct>
      <lifecycle-callback-class>packt.SimpleInterceptor
        </lifecycle-callback-class>
      <lifecycle-callback-method>constructed
        </lifecycle-callback-method>
    </post-construct>
  </interceptor>
</interceptors>
```

How it works...

In the `ejb-jar.xml` file, the `SimpleInterceptor` was declared using the `<interceptor>` element. As part of this element, the `<post-construct>` element was used to associate the `SimpleInterceptor` with the `constructed` method. At deployment the server will effect these specifications.

There's more...

There are other lifecycle methods which can be configured using a deployment descriptor. A list of common events is found in the following table:

Annotation	Element
@AroundInvoke	<around-invoke>
@PostActivate	<post-activate>
@PostConstruct	<post-construct>
@PreDestroy	<pre-destroy>
@PrePassivate	<pre-passivate>

When multiple lifecycle events are handled by the same class, the lifecycle elements follow each other within the same `<interceptor>` element for the same class. Here post-construct and pre-destroy methods are declared.

```xml
<interceptors>
  <interceptor>
    <interceptor-class>interceptorClass</interceptor-class>
      <post-construct>
        <lifecycle-callback-class>package.interceptorClassName
          </lifecycle-callback-class>
        <lifecycle-callback-method>someMethodName
          </lifecycle-callback-method>
      </post-construct>
      <pre-destroy>
        <lifecycle-callback-class>package.interceptorClassName
          </lifecycle-callback-class>
        <lifecycle-callback-method>someMethodName
          </lifecycle-callback-method>
      </pre-destroy>
  </interceptor>
</interceptors>
```

See also

The *Using deployment descriptors for interceptors* recipe covers the general aspects of using interceptors with business methods.

Using a deployment descriptors for transactions

Transaction types can be specified using annotations or deployment descriptors. In this recipe, we illustrate how to use a deployment descriptor to specify the transaction type for an EJB and its methods.

Getting ready

The process for creating a deployment descriptor for transactions includes:

- Creating an `ejb-jar.xml` file for the EJB module
- Using the `<container-transaction>` element to define interceptors
- Deploying the application

We will base this example on the `PopulationManager` class from the *Chapter 6, Understanding how the TransactionAttributeType affects transactions* recipe. The `PopulationManager` class as shown below, uses container-managed transactions and annotates the `updateCityPopulation` method with **RequiresNew**. The other methods of the class default to **Required**.

```
@Stateful
@TransactionManagement(TransactionManagementType.CONTAINER)
public class PopulationManager implements SessionSynchronization {

  @EJB
  CityFacade cityFacade;

  ...

@TransactionAttribute(TransactionAttributeType.REQUIRES_NEW)
  public void updateCityPopulation(String cityName, long count) {
    // Update city's population
    try {
      cityFacade.changePopulation(cityName, count);
    } catch(IllegalPopulationException e) {
        System.out.println("IllegalPopulationException caught");
      }
    }
  }
}
```

How to do it...

Transaction attributes are specified in the `ejb-jar.xml` file. Create an `ejb-jar.xml` file. The root element is `<ejb-jar>` as shown here:

```
<?xml version="1.0" encoding="UTF-8"?>
<ejb-jar xmlns = "http://java.sun.com/xml/ns/javaee"
  version = "3.1"
  xmlns:xsi = "http://www.w3.org/2001/XMLSchema-instance"
  xsi:schemaLocation = "http://java.sun.com/xml/ns/javaee
  http://java.sun.com/xml/ns/javaee/ejb-jar_3_1.xsd">
  ...
</ejb-jar>
```

Within the `<ejb-jar>` element add an `<assembly-descriptor>` element. Within this element add two `<container-transaction>` elements which will be used to define the transactions.

```
<?xml version="1.0" encoding="UTF-8"?>
<ejb-jar>
  <assembly-descriptor>
    <container-transaction>
      ...
    </container-transaction>
    <container-transaction>
      ...
    </container-transaction>
  </assembly-descriptor>
</ejb-jar>
```

Within the `<container-transaction>` element the `<method>` element is used to specify those methods that transactions will be applied to. This is followed by a `<trans-attribute>` element which contains the transactions type.

The `<method>` element contains an `<ejb-name>` element to specify the name of the EJB and a `<method-name>` element to specify the method. The following example shows the complete `ejb-jar.xml` file which declares the same configuration as obtained from the annotations used earlier.

```
<?xml version="1.0" encoding="UTF-8"?>
<ejb-jar>
  <assembly-descriptor>
    <container-transaction>
      <method>
        <ejb-name>PopulationManager</ejb-name>
        <method-name>*</method-name>
      </method>
      <trans-attribute>Required</trans-attribute>
    </container-transaction>
    <container-transaction>
      <method>
        <ejb-name>PopulationManager</ejb-name>
        <method-name>updateCityPopulation</method-name>
      </method>
      <trans-attribute>RequiresNew</trans-attribute>
    </container-transaction>
  </assembly-descriptor>
</ejb-jar>
```

When the `PopulationServlet` is executed, the application should execute successfully.

To verify that the `ejb-jar.xml` is controlling the transaction type, change the `<trans-attribute>` for the `updateCityPopulation` method to **Mandatory**. Re-executing the application results in an exception being thrown since the method requires a transaction to be present but there is none at this point.

How it works...

In the `ejb-jar.xml` file `<container-transaction>` elements were used to specify the transaction attribute to be used for methods of the application. The default transaction attribute for the `PopulationManager` was declared as **Required** except for the `updateCityPopulation` method which was specified as **RequiresNew**. These associations are applied by the server upon deployment of the application. This permits associations to differ by server.

Using deployment descriptors for security

Several of the security-related annotations can be overridden in a deployment descriptor. This recipe examines how this is done. This can be useful when access to a method may differ depending on the server it is deployed to. Configuring access in a deployment descriptor will provide this type of flexibility.

Getting ready

The process for creating a deployment descriptor for security configuration includes:

- Creating an `ejb-jar.xml` file for the EJB module
- Using the `<enterprise-beans>` element to define the EJB
- Using the `<assembly-descriptor>` to declare security roles and the method permissions
- Deploying the application

Each security role is granted access to a set of classes and methods. This can be achieved through descriptors using the `<method-permission>` element. Roles can be assigned to all of the methods of an EJB or specific methods of an EJB. In this example, all methods of the `VoucherManager` EJB found in the *Chapter 7, Creating the SecurityApplication* recipe, will be accessible by users possessing the **manager** role.

How to do it...

Create an `ejb-jar.xml` file if it does not already exist. Add an `<enterprise-beans>` element to define the `VoucherManager` EJB. The `<session>` element identifies the class as a session EJB and the `<ejb-name>` element holds the name of the EJB.

```
<?xml version="1.0" encoding="UTF-8"?>
<ejb-jar xmlns = "http://java.sun.com/xml/ns/javaee"
  version = "3.1"
  xmlns:xsi = "http://www.w3.org/2001/XMLSchema-instance"
  xsi:schemaLocation = "http://java.sun.com/xml/ns/javaee
  http://java.sun.com/xml/ns/javaee/ejb-jar_3_1.xsd">
    <enterprise-beans>
      <session>
        <ejb-name>VoucherManager</ejb-name>
      </session>
    </enterprise-beans>
  ...
</ejb-jar>
```

Next, add an `<assembly-descriptor>` element to the file. Within this element we will declare security roles and the methods granted access by these roles. First, add the `<security-role>` element which contains a `<role-name>` element and the name `manager`.

```
<?xml version="1.0" encoding="UTF-8"?>
  ...
    <assembly-descriptor>
      <security-role>
        <role-name>manager</role-name>
      </security-role>
  ...
    </assembly-descriptor>
</ejb-jar>
```

Next, add a `<method-permission>` element which we will use to define the method the role can access. Within the element, add a `<role-name>` element with the name `manager`. Follow this with a `<method>` element. This element contains two sub-elements: `<ejb-name>` which should match an EJB defined earlier in the file and a `<method-name>` element containing the name of the method.

```
<?xml version="1.0" encoding="UTF-8"?>
  ...
    <assembly-descriptor>
      <security-role>
        <role-name>manager</role-name>
```

```
    </security-role>
    <method-permission>
      <role-name>manager</role-name>
      <method>
        <ejb-name>VoucherManager</ejb-name>
        <method-name>approve</method-name>
      </method>
    </method-permission>
  </assembly-descriptor>
</ejb-jar>
```

If the <method-name> element contains an asterisk, then all methods of the EJB are accessible by the role.

If the method is overloaded, then the <method-params> needs to be used in conjunction with the <method-param> element to identify the method. While the approve method is not overloaded, these elements have been specified to illustrate the use of these elements.

```
<method-permission>
  <role-name>manager</role-name>
  <method>
    <ejb-name>VoucherManager</ejb-name>
    <method-name>approve</method-name>
    <method-params>
      <method-param></method-param>
    </method-params>
  </method>
</method-permission>
```

Notice the <method-param> element is left empty in the example. This signifies a void argument. If the argument had not been void, then the data type for the parameter would be used such as java.lang.String or long. Each parameter of a method should have a corresponding <method-param> element.

How it works...

The ejb-jar.xml file was used to configure the security roles for the VoucherManager class. Within the <assembly-descriptor> element, the manager security role was declared. The <method-permission> element was then used to associate this role with the VoucherManager's approve method. This configuration was performed by the server upon deployment of the application.

12

EJB Techniques

In this chapter, we will cover:

- ▸ Exception handling and EJBs
- ▸ Using logging within an EJB
- ▸ Using an interceptor for logging and exception handling
- ▸ Creating your own interceptor
- ▸ Using time within an EJB
- ▸ How to support currency
- ▸ Efficient manipulation of strings

Introduction

Java EE applications address a wide range of application types. The use of specific EJB technologies as addressed in earlier chapters is application-specific. There are techniques, while not necessarily EJB-specific, are useful in many EJB applications. This chapter examines a few of these techniques.

We start with exception handling which is an important aspect of any production application. The failure to handle exceptions cleanly can result in an unreliable application. A common technique to assist in dealing with exceptions for simpler applications is to use the `println` method within a `catch` block to display exception-related information. Frequently, stack traces are also displayed to the console. This technique is not advisable in a production application for a number of reasons including:

- ▸ It is not a very elegant approach
- ▸ The console may not be available on a production system

- System managers may redirect `System.out` and `System.err` streams to a null device
- If the system crashes, the console will not be available

Redirecting the console output to a file may not work because these files are frequently overridden by the server. Logging is the preferred technique and is the process of recording events and information about events to provide an audit trail for the execution of the application. This can be useful for determining the root causes of application failures and to provide feedback on how the application is used. While most servers provide a degree of automatic logging, customized logging is often needed to provide sufficient detail to troubleshoot a problem. The essence of this approach is discussed in the *Using logging within an EJB* recipe.

Exceptions can be grouped into three categories:

- JVM exceptions
- Application exceptions
- System exceptions

JVM exceptions are thrown by the JVM and there is little the developer can do to handle them. For example, if the JVM runs out of memory then an exception is thrown. The only reasonable thing to do is to restart the server with potentially additional resources.

Application exceptions generally reflect business logic errors that we can usually handle. If an exception is thrown because the account is low on funds, then we can usually remedy the situation in a controlled and predictable manner. Exceptions of this type are derived from the `java.lang.Exception` class and are called checked exceptions. Checked exceptions must be handled in code otherwise a compile-time error is generated.

System exceptions that derive from the `java.lang.RuntimeException` class are called unchecked exceptions and are not required to be handled in application code. If they are not handled, then the application will terminate.

The EJB container intercepts EJB method invocations and deals with application and system exceptions. When an application exception occurs, the EJB container will not automatically rollback transactions, which might be present, but allows the application to deal with them.

With system exceptions, the EJB container will automatically rollback any transactions and returns an `EJBException` to the client. Servers will automatically log system exceptions, though the format of the logs will differ by vendor.

We have seen interceptors used for a variety of purposes in earlier chapters. Their use for logging and exception handling is illustrated in the *Using an interceptor for logging and exception handling* recipe. While there are many predefined interceptors available, it may be advantageous to create our own. An introduction to creating interceptors is found in the *Creating your own interceptor* recipe.

Dates and times are frequent components of applications. However, the use of time as supported by Java can be confusing. The _Using time within an EJB_ recipe examines several of the more common uses of time and the mistakes made using time.

Likewise, the use of currency and its localization is important. The _How to support currency_ recipe looks at the techniques used to represent currency and provides an introduction to the use of the `BigDecimal` class in support of currency.

Lastly, strings are found in most applications. There are efficient and inefficient ways of representing and manipulating strings. The _Efficient manipulation of strings_ recipe examines these issues.

Exception handling and EJBs

Exception handling is essential to any robust application. Understanding what constitutes a good exception handling technique is important in creating robust applications. In this recipe, we will examine several of these techniques, and see how we can apply them to Java EE applications.

Knowing where to handle exceptions is the key to the proper use of exception handling. The organization of the exception handling code is dependent upon the structure of the application. Exception handling can be viewed from a development and a production standpoint, both of which are important.

When an exception occurs in an EJB that it cannot recover from, it is typically wrapped in an EJBException and then thrown to the caller.

Getting ready

Exceptions are not something we want to avoid, but rather we should embrace them as another tool in our arsenal to create good applications. Exceptions will occur. They may be the result of user input, system problems such as a network being down, or a server crashing, or simply events that were not anticipated during the development of the application.

When an exception occurs, the developer can either have the containing method throw the exception to the caller or handle the exception using try-catch blocks. Throwing the exception back to the caller is appropriate when the caller is in a better position to handle the exception. If the exception can be handled within the method, then try-catch blocks should be used.

In this recipe, we are concerned with how to structure and handle exceptions we catch. However, we may still return the exception to the caller. The basic approach is to use a `try` block followed by one or more `catch` blocks, and optionally, a `finally` block.

```
...
try {
  // Attempt to execute code which might throw an exception
}
catch(Exception1 e) {
    //Handle execption1
}
catch(Exception2 e) {
      //Handle execption2
}
    ...
finally {
      // Clean up actions
}
...
```

The order of the catch blocks is important. The base-most exception should be listed last since the first catch clause that matches the exception will handle the exception thrown. If the base-most exception is listed first, the other derived exceptions will never be executed. A compile-time error may be generated in some situations depending on the inheritance relationship between the exceptions.

How to do it...

Let's examine a situation where we inadvertently lose information about an exception. Consider the following `catch` block which recasts the exception as an `EJBException`. The `EJBException` single string argument is used to pass an error message describing the exception.

```
catch(Exception e) {
   throw new EJBException("Some Exception");
}
```

The problem here is the name of the original exception and where in our code the exception occurred is unknown. It is possible the exception could have been generated at more than one point, and understanding where the exception occurred can be important in recovering from the exception.

A better technique is to wrap the exception context information inside the new exception.

```
catch(exception e) {
   throw new EJBException(e);
}
```

A variation of this is to use the `toString` method when recasting the exception.

```
catch(exception e) {
   throw new EJBException(e.toString());
}
```

The usefulness of this technique depends on what is returned by the `toString` method. The `getMessage` method could have been used but it may not provide much more information than the `toString` version.

```
catch(exception e) {
   throw new EJBException(e.getMessage());
}
```

Frequently, the best approach is to propagate the message and the exception as follows:

```
catch(exception e) {
   throw new EJBException(e.getMessage(),e);
}
```

How it works...

We saw that it is important to avoid losing information about an exception. The first example illustrated how the name of the exception can be lost along with its location. Using the `toString` method to retrieve exception information was shown not to be a reliable technique. The last example illustrates a better technique where the `getMessage` method was used to convey the essence of the problem and the exception itself was propagated to the calling method.

There's more...

There are other aspects to exception handling including:

- Logging exceptions to the console
- Incomplete exception handling
- Exceptions that are ignored

Logging exceptions to the console

Problems can occur when exception information is written to the console.

```
catch(exception e) {
   e.printStackTrace();
   throw new EJBException(e.getMessage(),e);
}
```

The problem here is that the console may not always be available. During the development process, it may work fine. The development server and the application may actually reside on the same machine or the server is easily accessible. In a production environment we may not have access to the server. In addition, the administrators of the server may have redirected `System.out` and `System.err` output to a null file. Worst yet, we may not even know where the server resides.

Logging is a better technique for reporting exceptions as illustrated here:

```
catch(exception e) {
   log.error(e.getMessage), e);
   throw new EJBException(e.getMessage(),e);
}
```

Even better, let the caller decide whether or not to log the exception. This can avoid situations where the same exception is logged twice, once in the current method and again by the caller. In this situation, we may want to get rid of the whole try-catch block and have the current method throw the exception.

Incomplete exception handling

Exception handling can be complicated at times. Consider the following sequence where two files are used:

```
try {
   inputFile = new FileInputStream(someFile);
   outputFile = new OutputFileStream(someOtherFile);
   . . .
}
   catch(exception e) {
   . . .
   }
   finally {
     try {
        inputFile.close();
        outputFile.close();
     }
        catch(IOException e) {
          // Handle exception
        }
   }
```

When using system resources such as files, it is important to release them. In the case of files, they should be closed when the application no longer needs them. The above sequence attempts to close the files whether an exception has occurred or not.

There are a couple of problems with this approach. First, it is possible that the attempt to create the input file will throw an exception. When this occurs, executing the `outFile.close()` statement will throw a `NullPointerException`. Second, if the `inputFile.close()` statement throws an exception, it will skip the `outputFile.close()` statement.

A better way of handling this situation is shown here:

```
try {
    inputFile = new FileInputStream(someFile);
    outputFile = new OutputFileStream(someOtherFile);
    ...
}
catch(exception e) {
    ...
}
finally {
    try {
        if(inputFile != null) {
            inputFile.close();
        } catch(IOException e) {
            // Nothing to do
        }
    }
    try {
        if(outputFile != null) {
            outputFile.close();
        } catch(IOException e) {
            // Nothing to do
        }
    }
}
```

Both file reference variables are checked separately to determine if they are `null`. If they are not, then the file is closed. If an exception occurs trying to close the file, then there is little we can do. Even with this example, depending on how the first catch block is written, we may not be able to determine which line caused the exception.

While we have focused on an IO sequence, any set of operations which require cleanup performed in a finally block, should be examined carefully to determine if the exception handling approach used is complete.

Exceptions that are ignored

Sometimes we may be tempted not to handle or propagate exceptions we know will never be thrown. We may consider the likelihood of the exception occurring so unlikely that if it did happen, we wouldn't know what to do anyway.

```
try {
   ...
}
  catch(SomeException e) {
     // Do nothing
     // This should never happen
  }
```

While the current environment may never generate the exception, who knows what may happen in the future when things change. The implementation of the code throwing the exception may change resulting in the exception being thrown. In addition, we may be wrong and in a very rare set of circumstances the exception may actually be thrown.

If we ignore the exception, then the exception is lost, potentially making it much more difficult to find the error in our application. A better approach is to catch the exception and then throw a runtime exception.

```
try {
   ...
}
  catch(SomeException e) {
     // Should never happen
     throw new RuntimeException(e.getMessage(),e);
  }
```

In addition, it may be desirable to log the exception. This will provide yet another avenue to help us determine the nature of the problem.

See also

The *Using an interceptor for logging and exception handling* recipe uses interceptors to handle exceptions.

Using logging within an EJB

Logging is a useful technique for recording exceptions and significant events which occur during the execution of an application. While there are many different logging APIs available, we will focus on those classes found in the `java.util.logging` package. If you are interested you may find alternate logging technologies such as log4j (`http://logging.apache.org/log4j/1.2/`) or the Simple Logging Facade for Java (SLF4J) (`http://www.slf4j.org/`) to be useful.

Getting ready

The process of creating using a logger involves:

1. Importing the `java.util.logging` package
2. Using the `Logger` class' static method `getLogger` to obtain an instance of a logger
3. Using methods of the `Logger` to record application data
4. Optionally, various filters, handlers, and formatter can be added to control the logging process

Logging involves writing messages to a data store. The logged messages can be controlled using levels and filters. The Logging API has seven predefined logging levels:

Level	Meaning
SEVERE	The highest level normally reserved for critical errors
WARNING	Used for warning type messages
INFO	This message does not necessarily indicate an error but rather conveys general information
CONFIG	Used for configuration-type information
FINE	First of three levels of detail
FINER	Intermediate level of detail
FINEST	Indicates the greatest level of detail

The `Logger`'s overloaded `log` method's first argument is a `Level` value. The value assigned to this argument denotes the level of the log. However, this does not mean the message will be logged. A logger will have a level specified for it and will log all messages at this or a higher level. The `setLevel` method determines the level of logging. Any request using levels below that value will be ignored. In addition, even if the message is accepted for logging, a filter may restrict those messages from being logged.

When the message is logged, it can be processed and formatted to add additional content to the message. For example, a time stamp can be added to the message eliminating the need to include this information in each `log` method call.

A `java.util.logging.Handler` derived class actually writes the message to a data store. A data store can be one of several different types of stores, though files are the most common type. There are two standard `Handler` classes available: `MemoryHandler` and `StreamHandler`. It is possible to create your own handler if needed.

The following figure depicts the structure of the Java Logging API.

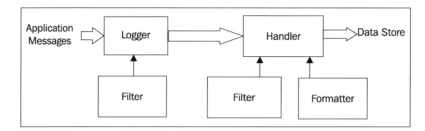

How to do it...

Create a Java EE application called `LoggingApplication`. We will use this application to demonstrate various logging techniques. In the EJB module create a package called `packt` and a stateless session bean called `PhoneNumber`. This EJB consists of a default constructor and four methods. The purpose of the EJB is to validate and format a phone number. Using these elements of the EJB, we will demonstrate logging.

First add a private `logger` variable and a default constructor. Within the constructor, create an instance of a `Logger` using the `getLogger` method and use the instance to log the creation of the `Logger`.

```
@Stateless
public class PhoneNumber {
  private Logger logger;

  public PhoneNumber() {
    logger = Logger.getLogger("phonenumber");
    logger.log(Level.INFO, "Phone number logger created");
  }
  ...
}
```

Next, add a `format` method which accepts three integers representing the three parts of a standard telephone number. Within this method we will call three different validation methods, each of which may throw an exception. If there are no errors, then a simple formatted string is returned and this event is logged at the level `FINEST`. If there are errors, then the exception is logged as a simple message at the level `FINE`. Using different levels allows us to record events in the application based on our interest.

```
public String format(int areaCode, int prefix, int lineNumber) {
  try {
    validateAreaCode(areaCode);
    validatePrefix(prefix);
    validateLineNumber(lineNumber);
```

```
      logger.log(Level.FINEST, "Formatted phone number returned");
      return "(" + areaCode + ")" + prefix + "-" + lineNumber;
    }
    catch(InvalidAreaCodeException e) {
      logger.log(Level.FINE, "InvalidAreaCodeException");
    }
    catch(InvalidPrefixException e) {
      logger.log(Level.FINE, "InvalidPrefixException");
    }
    catch(InvalidLineNumberException e) {
      logger.log(Level.FINE, "InvalidLineNumberException");
    }
    return "";
  }
```

Next, add the three methods used for validation. These methods perform a simple test on their arguments. A more sophisticated test would be needed in a production application.

```
  private boolean validateAreaCode(int areaCode) throws
    InvalidAreaCodeException {
    if (areaCode < 0 || areaCode > 999) {
      throw new InvalidAreaCodeException();
    }
      return true;
  }


  private boolean validatePrefix(int prefix) throws
    InvalidPrefixException {
    if (prefix < 0 || prefix > 999) {
      throw new InvalidPrefixException();
    }
    return true;
  }


  private boolean validateLineNumber(int lineNumber) throws
    InvalidLineNumberException {
    if (lineNumber < 0 || lineNumber > 9999) {
      throw new InvalidLineNumberException();
    }
    return true;
  }

}
```

Add three classes for the three different exceptions.

```
public class InvalidAreaCodeException extends java.lang.Exception {
  public InvalidAreaCodeException() {}
  public InvalidAreaCodeException(String message) {super(message);}
}

public class InvalidLineNumberException extends Exception {
  public InvalidLineNumberException() {}
  public InvalidLineNumberException(String message) {super(message);}
}

public class InvalidPrefixException extends Exception{
  public InvalidPrefixException() {}
  public InvalidPrefixException(String message) {super(message);}
}
```

Create a servlet called LoggingServlet in the servlet package of the Web module. Inject the PhoneNumber EJB and invoke its format method as shown below. Notice the line number is too large.

```
public class LoggingServlet extends HttpServlet {
    @EJB
    PhoneNumber phoneNumber;

    protected void processRequest(HttpServletRequest request,
      HttpServletResponse response)
      throws ServletException, IOException {
        response.setContentType("text/html;charset=UTF-8");
        PrintWriter out = response.getWriter();
        try {

          out.println("<html>");
          out.println("<head>");
          out.println("<title>Servlet LoggingServlet</title>");
          out.println("</head>");
          out.println("<body>");
          out.println("<h1>Phone Number: " + phoneNumber.format(202,
            555, 10003) + "</h1>");
          out.println("</body>");
          out.println("</html>");

        } finally {
            out.close();
          }
      }
}
```

Execute the servlet. The output in part shows the creation of the logger. The **INFO:** prefix is added automatically reflecting the level of the message.

...

INFO: Phone number logger created

The reason the `InvalidLineNumberException` is not displayed is because, by default, the `Logger` is set to the level `INFO`. It will only log those messages at that level or above. Since the exception is logged at the level `FINE`, it does not show up.

To rectify this situation, use the Logger's `setLevel` command after the creation of `logger` with an argument of `Level.ALL`.

```
logger.setLevel(Level.ALL);
```

Re-executing the servlet will produce the expected results.

...

INFO: Phone number logger created

FINE: InvalidLineNumberException

How it works...

The `PhoneNumber` EJB was created to illustrate the logging approach. In its constructor an instance of a `Logger` class was created. The string argument of the `getLogger` method was used to name the `Logger` instance. While it is not discussed here, the Java Logger API provides a sophisticated hierarchy of `Logger`s that can provide a richer set of logging capabilities than presented here.

The `log` method is overloaded. In this example, we used a simple variation of the method. The first argument specified the logging level and the second argument was the message we wanted to log. In the `format` method, exceptions that were caught were logged. The servlet used an invalid line number which resulted in the exception being logged once the appropriate logging level was set using the `setLevel` method.

There's more...

At the beginning of this recipe the creation of a `Logger` was accomplished as follows:

```
@Stateless
public class PhoneNumber {
  private Logger logger;

  public PhoneNumber() {
```

```
        logger = Logger.getLogger("phonenumber");
        logger.log(Level.INFO, "Phone number logger created");
    }
    ...
}
```

However, this approach may not be suitable in all environments. The technique is not thread-safe and we cannot use the logger from a static method. An alternative approach declares the logger as follows:

```
@Stateless
public class PhoneNumber {
    private static final Logger logger =
      Logger.getLogger("phonenumber");

    public PhoneNumber() {
        logger.log(Level.INFO, "Phone number logger created");
    }
    ...
}
```

The `static` keyword means the logger can be used by static and instance methods. Making it `final` results in a single instance of the object and avoids many thread issues as the methods of the `Logger` class are thread-safe.

See also

The *Using an interceptor for logging and exception handling* recipe that follows incorporates logging in an interceptor.

Using an interceptor for logging and exception handling

Interceptors are good for removing extraneous code from a method. In the `format` method developed in the *Using logging within an EJB* recipe, most of the code was concerned with handling exceptions. This recipe shows how an interceptor can be used to greatly simplify the `format` method.

The general process of using an interceptor for logging includes:

1. Accessing the parameters of the target method
2. Using the validation methods to validate the parameters
3. Catching and logging any thrown exceptions

We will also need to modify the target class to accommodate the use of an interceptor.

The process of creating and using an interceptor class is detailed in *Chapter 8, Interceptors*. Here, we will create an interceptor class called `PhoneNumberInterceptor` in the `packt` package. We will also access the target method's parameters using the `getParameters` method as discussed in *Chapter 8, Using the InvocationContext to verify parameters* recipe.

How to do it...

Create the `PhoneNumberInterceptor` class and add a `validatePhoneNumber` method annotated with **@AroundInvoke**.

```
public class PhoneNumberInterceptor {

    @AroundInvoke
    public Object validatePhoneNumber(InvocationContext context) throws
        Exception {
    . . .
    }
    . . .
}
```

Next, copy the current body of the `PhoneNumber`'s `format` method and paste it into the `validatePhoneNumber` method. You will need to make a few tweaks to the code including:

- Moving the declaration of the `result` variable to the top of the method and initializing it to an empty string
- Adding code to get and convert the target method's parameters to integers
- Obtain a reference to the `Logger`
- Replacing the first return statement with a call to the `proceed` method
- Replacing the last return statement so it returns `result`

Use the following declaration for the `result` variable:

```
Object result="";
```

The parameters of the target method are obtained using the `getParameters` method. They are then converted to integers using the `Integer` class's `intValue` method.

```
Object parameters[] = context.getParameters();
int areaCode = new Integer(parameters[0].toString()).intValue();
int prefix = new Integer(parameters[1].toString()).intValue();
int lineNumber = new Integer(parameters[2].toString()).intValue();
```

To use the `logger` variable we use the `InvocationContext`'s `getTarget` method to obtain a reference to the target. This gives us access to `logger`. Notice, that we will get an error until we modify the `PhoneNumber`'s `logger` variable which we will do shortly.

```
Logger logger = ((PhoneNumber) context.getTarget()).logger;
```

The `proceed` method returns control to the target method as explained in *Chapter 8, Interceptors*.

```
result = context.proceed();
```

Notice the interceptor uses the validation methods used in the `PhoneNumber` EJB. Move these to the `PhoneNumberInterceptor`.

Next, we need to rework the `PhoneNumber`'s `format` method developed in the *Using logging within an EJB* recipe. This will involve:

- Changing the protection level of the `logger` variable
- Adding **@Interceptor** annotation to the `format` method
- Returning the formatted string

We need to change the declaration of the `logger` variable so we can access the variable in the interceptor. This default access declaration gives access to the variable to all classes of the package.

```
Logger logger;
```

Add the **@Interceptor** annotation using the `PhoneNumberInterceptor.class` as its value.

```
@Interceptors(PhoneNumberInterceptor.class)
public String format(int areaCode, int prefix, int lineNumber) {
    ...
}
```

Use the following statement as the body of the method:

```
return "(" + areaCode + ")" + prefix + "-" + lineNumber;
```

Execute the application. It should behave the same way as before but with a simpler `format` method. While this technique uses essentially the same code as the original technique, it removes the complexity from the business method. In addition, if the application is structured correctly, other parts of the application may be able to benefit from and reuse the interceptor.

How it works...

We created the `PhoneNumberInterceptor` class to move the validation code out of the `format` method. Adding the **@AroundInvoke** annotation to the `validatePhoneNumber` method resulted in the method being invoked before the `format` method is executed. We used the `getParameters` method to retrieve the phone number and then validated the phone number using the validation methods developed earlier. When an exception was thrown, it was caught and logged. We added the **@Interceptors** annotation to the `format` method so that when executed, the `validatePhoneNumber` interceptor would execute.

See also

The *Exception handling and EJBs* and *Using logging within an EJB* recipes discuss exception handling and logging, respectively.

Creating your own interceptor

Interceptors can be configured to execute before and after a method is executed. This permits moving orthogonal functionality out of the method thus reducing the complexity and clutter of the method. As we have seen in previous chapters, interceptors have been used for a variety of tasks such as handling transactions and security. In this recipe, we will demonstrate the technique for creating our own interceptors to meet any unique requirements of our application.

Getting ready

The process to create and use an interceptor involves:

1. Creating an interceptor binding to define the characteristics of the interceptor
2. Implementing the interceptor class
3. Adding the interceptor to the application

An interceptor binding is used to define the type of interceptor we want to create. The **@InterceptorBinding** annotation precedes a series of annotations used to define the interceptor's characteristics. These can include:

- ▶ **@Target** – Used to specify the type of element the interceptor can be applied to
- ▶ **@Retention** – Identifies when the interceptor is used

The **@Target** annotation can use the attributes: **CONSTRUCTOR, METHOD, FIELD, PARAMETER, LOCAL_VARIABLE, PACKAGE**, and **TYPE**. **TYPE** refers to a class interface or enum.

An annotation is inserted into the source code of an application. It can be processed in one or more of three places: source code, class file, runtime. The place is determined by the annotation's retention policy as specified using the **@Retention** annotation. This annotation is assigned one of three values: **SOURCE, CLASS**, or **RUNTIME**.

We will create an interceptor, **CountInterceptor**, to keep count of the number of times a method is invoked. This is a simple interceptor whose functionality could have been implemented using other techniques. However, using this approach provides a simple demonstration of the interceptor creation process, uncluttered by a more complex interceptor example.

The class that implements the interceptor is annotated with the **@Interceptor** annotation. This is followed by the name of the binding annotation. Within the interceptor class, a method is annotated with **@AroundInvoke**. This method will be executed as appropriate and must return an `Object`. It is passed an `InvocationContext` object that contains information about the target method.

Within the method annotated with **@AroundInvoke**, code can be executed before and after the target method invocation. It is also possible to modify the parameters sent to the target and to modify the target method's return value.

The general organization of the **@AroundInvoke** method is:

- ▸ Execute code before the target method is invoked, possibly using and/or modifying any target method parameters
- ▸ Execute the target method using the `InvocationContext`'s proceed method. The proceed method returns the target method's return value.
- ▸ Execute code possibly modifying the target return value
- ▸ Return an object

How to do it...

Add the `CountInteceptorBinding` code declared below to the `packt` package. It defines the characteristics of the interceptor.

```
@InterceptorBinding
@Retention(RetentionPolicy.RUNTIME)
@Target({ElementType.METHOD, ElementType.TYPE})
public @interface CountInterceptorBinding {
}
```

Next, add the `CountInterceptor` class as shown below to the `packt` package. Declare a static `counter` variable which is incremented and displayed from within the **@AroundInvoke** method `increment`. The target method is then called. Upon return from the target, no other processing occurs and the result from the target method is returned.

```
@Interceptor
@CountInterceptorBinding
public class CountInterceptor {
  private static int counter;

  @AroundInvoke
  public Object increment(InvocationContext context) throws
    Exception {
    counter++;
    System.out.println("counter: " + counter);
    Object result = context.proceed();
    return result;
  }

}
```

To test the interceptor, add the **@Interceptors** annotation in front of the `LoggingApplication`'s `format` method.

```
    @Interceptors({PhoneNumberInterceptor.class,CountInterceptor.
  class})
    public String format(int areaCode, int prefix, int lineNumber) {
    ...
    }
```

Modify the `LoggingServlet` to call the `format` method with a valid phone number and then execute the servlet. The output as seen in the console window should reflect the use of the interceptor.

INFO: Phone number logger created

FINEST: 202 - Formatted phone number returned

INFO: counter: 1

How it works...

We created the `CountInterceptorBinding` annotation permitting the annotation to be retained at runtime. The use of the **@Rentention** annotation value of **RUNTIME** means the annotation will be used at runtime. It will be present in the application's byte codes. The **@Target** annotation means the interceptor can be applied to a **TYPE** (class, interface or enum) and/or a method. The **@interface** annotation declared the name of the annotation.

The interceptor, `CountInterceptor`, was created next with the `increment` method. Since the method was annotated with **@AroundInvoke**, it was executed before the target method format was executed. Within the `increment` method a simple counter was incremented.

The `format` method was annotated with **@Interceptors** associating both the `PhoneNumberInterceptor` and the `CountInterceptor` with the method. When the `format` method was executed, `PhoneNumberInterceptor` was executed first followed by `CountInterceptor`.

See also

Chapter 8, *Interceptors* discusses the uses of interceptors in more depth.

Using time within an EJB

Time is a complex topic with many aspects of time being beyond the scope of this book. Within this recipe, we will examine several common problems that can occur when working with time in a Java EE application.

Getting ready

To use time in a Java application we normally use a `Date` instance in conjunction with a `Calendar` instance. The `Date` object represents a time while the `Calendar` instance maps it to a specific calendar system.

Normally we will use the `DateFormat` or a `DateFormat` derived class to convert a time into a string for display purposes. While the use of these classes appears straightforward, there are several areas where a developer can go astray.

Time is represented using an instance of the `Date` class. However, this class does not represent a date in the sense of a calendar. It is the number of milliseconds which have elapsed since the epoch, midnight January 1, 1970 GMT. The `java.util.Date` class reflects this time using the coordinated universal time (UTC). This is the current time at the Greenwich Meridian Line at the Royal Observatory in Greenwich England. GMT (Greenwich Mean Time) and UTC are essentially the same time zone. GMT is the time zone used by UTC.

The time represented by the `Date` class is not accurate enough for some scientific applications but is normally sufficient for business applications. Do not use the deprecated methods of the `Date` class. Most of these deprecated methods are concerned with getting the current day, hour, or similar measure. Instead, use `java.util.Calendar` to convert between dates and time fields.

A Date reflects a time. A Calendar represents a mapping of a Date to a particular day, month and year convention. For example, the java.util.GregorianCalendar represents a calendar system used throughout the business world. While it is not the only calendar in existence, it has found widespread usage.

How to do it...

Let's start by adding 24 hours to a Date object. Create a Date object and then, using its getTime method, add the product of 24 hours times 3600 seconds in an hour times 1000 milliseconds. The getTime method returns the time in milliseconds since the epoch.

```
Date today = new Date();
System.out.println(today);
Date tomorrow = new Date(today.getTime() + 24L * 3600L * 1000L);
System.out.println(tomorrow);
```

The results of this code sequence will be displayed similar to:

INFO: Thu Feb 03 16:28:59 CST 2011

INFO: Fri Feb 04 16:28:59 CST 2011

However, adding 24 hours is not the same as adding a calendar day. Not every day consists of 24 hours. For example, many countries use daylight saving time which means the number of hours in a day will vary depending on the time of the year. When we deal with days in this sense, then we need to use the Calendar class or a class derived from Calendar.

When we talk about the current time and date, we are usually talking about the local time. This time is dependent upon the time zone we are in, and whether daylight saving time is in effect or not.

Here we will use the java.text.DateFormat class to format Date strings. There are several ways to use this class; however the example below uses the static getDateTimeInstance method with two DateFormat.MEDIUM arguments to specify the appearance of a formatted date.

```
Calendar day = ...
DateFormat dateFormat =
  DateFormat.getDateTimeInstance(DateFormat.MEDIUM,
  DateFormat.MEDIUM);
System.out.println(dateFormat.format(day.getTime()));
```

The output will appear formatted as shown here:

INFO: Feb 3, 2011 5:02:05 PM

How it works...

The examples demonstrated differences between the `Date` class and the `Calendar` class. In the first example, the addition of 24 hours to a date worked fine. However, for days that are not 24 hours long this approach will result in incorrect values. In the `println` method, the `tomorrow` variable was displayed. Displaying a `Date` object will invoke its `toString` method that returns a string representation based on the current time zone.

The use of the `DateFormat`'s `getDateInstance` involved using two apparently very similar arguments. However, the first argument governed the formatting of the date while the second controlled the time formatting. The `DateFormat` instance returned has a `format` method. The argument of the `format` method is a `Date` object. This method formatted the time represented by the object and returned a string.

There's more...

There are two other areas we need to address:

► Inadvertent use of the default `TimeZone`
► Thread issues with the `DateFormat` class

Inadvertent Use of the Default TimeZone

The `Calendar.getInstance` uses the default local calendar. This could conceivably be set to a calendar other than `GregorianCalendar`. It also uses the local time zone. For a server-based application, this may not always be appropriate. The time in Singapore is different from the time in New York City. If we want a certain event to execute at 10:00 on every Monday for a specific client, then it is imperative to know the client's time zone.

The `TimeZone`'s `getDefault` method returns the default time zone. To get a `TimeZone` object to represent a specific time zone, use its `getTimeZone` method with a string argument representing the time zone needed. The following code sequence sets the time zone to Zurich and the date to today. The date is then formatted and displayed.

```
Calendar day = Calendar.getInstance();
TimeZone timeZone = TimeZone.getTimeZone("Europe/Zurich");
day.setTimeZone(timeZone);
day.setTime(new Date());
DateFormat dateFormat =
   DateFormat.getDateTimeInstance(DateFormat.MEDIUM,
   DateFormat.MEDIUM);
dateFormat.setTimeZone(timeZone);
System.out.println(dateFormat.format(day.getTime()));
```

The output will be similar to the following:

INFO: Feb 4, 2011 2:07:10 AM

The `getTimeZone` method accepts a string representing a time zone. Valid time zone strings can and do change over time. If an invalid string is passed, then the GMT time zone is retuned and no exceptions are thrown.

Thread issues with the DateFormat class

The methods of the `DateFormat` class are not synchronized and thus are not thread-safe. It is a good practice to use a separate instance of a `DateFormat` class per thread. The following code does not provide protection against potential synchronization problems:

```
public static final DateFormat dateFormat = new ...
```

While there is only one instance of the object, the `final` keyword means a new instance of the `DateFormat` cannot be assigned to it. However, there is nothing in the statement prohibiting the object from being modified since the `DateFormat` object is not immutable. Wrapping such an object with synchronized get and set methods can provide additional protection against unintentional modification.

How to support currency

Many applications deal with currency and it is frequently an integral component of business applications. There are many issues that complicate the representation and use of currency values such as precision and accuracy. In addition, there are differences between how currency types such as rubles and the yen are displayed. In this recipe, we will examine the data types we can use to represent currency and locale-specific issues regarding currency.

Getting ready

There are several potential data types that can be used for representing currency including:

- ▸ Floating point numbers
- ▸ Integer
- ▸ `BigDecimal`

To determine which is best we need to consider issues such as precision and accuracy. Ease of use is another concern since we will need to be able to manipulate currency values. We also need to consider the locale to insure the currency we are using is expressed in a locale-specific format.

Floating points are a poor choice for representing currency. Their major drawback is their lack of precision. To understand this limitation, consider how we represent the fraction 1/3 as a decimal number: 0.33333. We cannot precisely represent this fraction as a decimal number since it would take an infinite number of trailing 3s. The fraction 2/3 has a similar problem: 0.66666. Adding 1/3 plus 2/3 gives 1. However, adding 0.33333 plus 0.66666 gives 0.99999. Close, but it does not provide sufficient precision. While we can round the result, floating point numbers do not provide us with much control over the rounding process. Floating point numbers are not exact while currency values require exactness.

Integers could be used but it requires the developer to explicitly keep track of the decimal point. Assuming this is not too burdensome, which it probably is in operations like multiplication, we still need to display the results of our calculations. This will require us to extract the last two digits (assuming cents and dollars is our currency) and convert the result to a properly formatted string. This approach has not been widely used due to the lack of support.

The BigDecimal class is a member of the java.math package. It supports arbitrary precision decimal numbers and standard arithmetic operations. One drawback to its use is each BigDecimal object is immutable which can result in inefficiencies associated with the creation and garbage collection of objects. However, it is the preferred approach.

How to do it...

A BigDecimal number can be created using a number of overloaded constructors. One approach is to use a single double number as the argument of the constructor. Here, 1045.32 is used to create a BigDecimal object. The value is displayed without formatting and the scale method is used to determine the number of digits to the right of the decimal point.

```
BigDecimal amount;
amount = amount.add(new BigDecimal(1045.32));
System.out.println("amount Unformatted: " + amount.toString());
System.out.println("Scale of amount: " + amount.scale());
```

The console output appears as follows:

INFO: amount Unformatted: 1045.319999999999936335370875895023345947265625

INFO: Scale of amount: 42

Contrast this with creating a BigDecimal number using a string.

```
BigDecimal amount2;
amount2= new BigDecimal("1045.32");
System.out.println("amount2 Unformatted: " + amount2.toString());
System.out.println("Scale of amount: " + amount2.scale());
```

The output follows:

INFO: amount2 Unformatted: 1045.32

INFO: Scale of amount: 2

When formatting a `BigDecimal`, we can use the `java.text.NumberFormat` class. Its `getCurrencyInstance` method returns a `NumberFormat` object formatted according to a specific locale. Below, we use the `Locale.US` with the `amount2` variable:

```
NumberFormat numberFormat =
   NumberFormat.getCurrencyInstance(Locale.US);
System.out.println("amount2 formatted: " +
   numberFormat.format(amount2));
```

The output will appear as follows:

INFO: amount2 formatted: $1,045.32

Basic arithmetic operations are supported by `BigDecimal`. For example, to add two numbers we can use the `add` method.

```
BigDecimal number1 = new BigDecimal("32.54");
BigDecimal number2 = new BigDecimal("8.44");
number1 = number1.add(number2);
System.out.println(numberFormat.format(number1));
```

This results in the following console output:

INFO: $40.98

`BigDecimal` supports other operations including subtraction, multiplication, division, and exponentiation.

How it works...

The first set of code examples illustrated the use of a string to construct a `BigDecimal` object. This approach simplified the setting of its scale. The scale is determined by the number contained in the string. A number represented as a string with three digits after the decimal point would have a scale of 3. Using a string is the preferred way of converting a floating point value to a `BigDecimal`. The use of a constructor using a `float` or `double` value can sometimes be unpredictable.

The third example illustrated the use of the `NumberFormat` class to format the appearance of a number. The `getCurrencyInstance` method used a `Local` value to format the value based on a particular local.

The fourth example demonstrated how to perform arithmetic operations on `BigDecimal` objects. This is further elaborated in the next section.

There's more...

The `BigDecimal` class is a useful tool for dealing with currency. However, we need to be careful in a few areas:

▶ Understanding the implications of immutable `BigDecimal` objects

▶ Comparison of `BigDecimal` objects

▶ When to perform rounding

Understanding the implications of immutable BigDecimal objects

In the previous example, two numbers were added together and assigned to the first number.

```
BigDecimal number1 = new BigDecimal("32.54");
BigDecimal number2 = new BigDecimal("8.44");
number1 = number1.add(number2);
```

This is the correct way to add the numbers. However, do not use the following approach and expect `number1` to be modified:

```
number1.add(number2);
```

Remember, `BigDecimal` objects are immutable. This operation modifies neither `number1` nor `number2` but returns a new `BigDecimal` object containing their sum.

A common requirement is to keep a cumulative sum. The following code illustrates the essential elements of this technique:

```
BigDecimal total = BigDecimal.ZERO;
for(...) {
  total = total.add(numbers[i]);
}
```

Notice the use of `BigDecimal.ZERO`. This constant represents a zero and is used to initialize `total`. The value returned by `numbers[i]` is added with `total` and the residual value is assigned to `total`. There are two other constants available: `BigDecimal.ONE` and `BigDecimal.TEN` representing the values of 1 and 10 respectively.

Comparison of BigDecimal numbers

When comparing two `BigDecimal` numbers, we have to be careful when using the `equals` method. Normally, this is the preferred method for comparing two objects as the equality operator simply compares reference values.

The `BigDecimal`'s `equals` method bases its comparison on the values of the number and the scale used. Consider the following example. Two `BigDecimal` numbers are assigned the same number except for the number of digits to the right of the decimal point. The `equals` method returns `false`. However, the `compareTo` method works properly.

```
number1 = new BigDecimal("1.00");
number2 = new BigDecimal("1.000");
System.out.println(number1.equals(number2));
System.out.println(number1.compareTo(number2)==0);
System.out.println();
```

The output:

INFO: false

INFO: true

The `equals` method uses the number and the scale to determine equality. Since the two numbers have a different scale, they are not considered to be equal. The `compareTo` method returns a negative value if `number1` is less than `number2`, a zero if they are equal and a positive number if `number1` is greater than `number2`.

When to perform rounding

Rounding can be an important part of a computation. `BigDecimal` provides several rounding options. When rounding should be applied is dependent upon the nature of the calculation. Consider the addition of 0.134 and 0.133. If we add the numbers together and then round to two decimal places we get 0.27. However, if we round the two numbers first to 0.13 then add them together their sum is 0.26. The right approach is dependent on the problem we are trying to solve.

Rounding is supported using the `round` method. This method takes a `java.math.MathContext` object. The two argument constructor used below takes the precision as its first argument and a rounding method as its second argument. The rounding options are similar to those used with `BigDecimal` as explained shortly.

In the following example, we implement the addition problem discussed previously. The variables, `number1` and `number2`, are added together and then rounded. The numbers, `number3` and `number4` corresponding to the first two numbers, are rounded and then added. All rounding uses a precision of two digits.

```
number1 = new BigDecimal("0.0134");
number2 = new BigDecimal("0.0133");
BigDecimal number3 = number1.round(new
   MathContext(2,RoundingMode.HALF_UP));
BigDecimal number4 = number2.round(new
   MathContext(2,RoundingMode.HALF_UP));
```

```
System.out.println(number1.add(number2).round(new
    MathContext(2,RoundingMode.HALF_UP)));
System.out.println(number3.add(number4).round(new
    MathContext(2,RoundingMode.HALF_UP)));
System.out.println();
```

The output below confirms the differences in the addition using the two rounding approaches.

INFO: 0.027

INFO: 0.026

The `BigDecimal` class provides eight rounding techniques. If the rounding mode is not specified, it uses the most appropriate scale and rounding based on the operation performed. While not detailed here, the `BigDecimal.ROUND_HALF_UP` will round up if the fraction part is greater than or equal to 0.5. However, `BigDecimal.ROUND_HALF_EVEN` best minimizes errors that can accumulate over a series of calculations.

Efficient manipulation of strings

The use of strings is an important component of most applications and can contribute to poor performance if not managed correctly. This recipe examines techniques used to improve the use of strings.

Getting ready

String manipulation in Java is supported through three `java.lang` classes:

- ▶ `String` – An immutable object
- ▶ `StringBuilder` – Performs string manipulation but does not use synchronized methods
- ▶ `StringBuffer` – Performs string manipulation using synchronized methods

Each of these classes has its place. For simple strings that are not changed, the `String` class is a good choice. If strings are manipulated using operations such as concatenation, `StringBuilder` and `StringBuffer` are better choices. However, since `StringBuffer` synchronizes most of its methods to achieve thread safety, use of this class can be more expensive than using `StringBuilder`. If the string is used in a multi-threaded environment, then `StringBuffer` should be used.

A few general string guidelines:

▸ Do not use the `String` class when significant string manipulation is needed

▸ When the string length is known initialize the length of a `StringBuilder` or `StringBuffer` object using its constructor

▸ Make sure you understand how testing for string equality works

String concatenation is expensive when performed using the `String` class. This is because the `String` object is immutable. For many situations this is fine. However, if it is necessary to repeatedly change the string, then using the `String` class means new `String` objects will be created which introduces the expense of object creation and, potentially, garbage collection.

How to do it...

Consider the following `getList` method below which returns a comma-delimited string based on an array of names. The array, `names`, is initialized with four names and the `String` variable, `list`, is initialized to an empty string. Within the `for` loop, each name is concatenated to `list` with a comma appended between them. Each time the list is modified a new `String` object is created and the old one is discarded.

```java
public String getList() {
    String names[] = {"Bill", "Sue", "Mary", "Fred"};
    String list = "";
    for(int i=0; i<names.length; i++) {
      list += names[i];
      if(i < names.length-1) {
        list += ", ";
      }
    }
    return list;
}
```

A more efficient version of this method follows and uses a `StringBuilder` object instead. Notice the initialization of `list` to 100. This size is more than adequate for the data used here. Concatenation is achieved using the `append` method which adds its argument to the end of `list`. The `toString` method converts the `StringBuilder` instance to a `String` object.

```java
public String getList() {
    String names[] = {"Bill", "Sue", "Mary", "Fred"};
    StringBuilder list = new StringBuilder(100);
    for(String name : names){
      if(list.length() > 0) {
        list.append(", ");
```

```
        }
        list.append(name);
    }
    return list.toString();
}
```

Only one `StringBuilder` object and one `String` object has been created. This reduces the overhead of multiple object creation required in the first version of the method.

The initialization of the `StringBuffer` size is larger than needed. It is often possible to calculate the size beforehand which can save space but at the expense of an additional calculation.

Testing for string equality can be performed using one of several techniques. The first approach uses the equality operator.

```
if (name == "Peter") ...
```

This approach checks if the variable `name` references the string literal "Peter". Most likely this is not the case. Remember, the equality operator in this situation tests for equality of references, not if the two referenced objects are the same.

The next approach uses the `compareTo` method. While it works, it is more complicated than it needs to be. The `compareTo` operator returns a negative value if name is less than "Peter", 0 if they are equal to each other and a positive number if name follows "Peter" lexicographically.

```
if (name.compareTo("Peter") == 0) ...
```

A better approach is to use the `equals` method. Alternatively, the `equalsIgnoreCase` method can be used if the case of the strings is not important.

```
if (name.equals("Peter")) ...
```

When dealing with null strings there are two considerations which deserve attention. If we need to test for an empty string it is better to use the `length` method.

```
if (name.length() == 0) ...
```

Also, using the following statement will avoid a `NullPointerException` should `name` contain a `null` value.

```
if ("".equals(name)) ...
```

How it works...

The string list examples illustrated the efficiency gained though the use of the `StringBuilder` class. Fewer object creations were required. Several approaches were demonstrated for comparing strings. These illustrate either a more valid, convenient, or efficient technique for the comparison of two strings.

Bear in mind most compilers perform optimization on source code. Any compiler level optimization can render source level optimizations mute or at least more of a style issue. Optimizations should always begin with making sure the application is implementing the correct functionality, uses a sound architecture and the most efficient algorithms before too much effort is devoted to source level optimizations.

Index

R

S

Thank you for buying
EJB 3.1 Cookbook

About Packt Publishing

Packt, pronounced 'packed', published its first book "Mastering phpMyAdmin for Effective MySQL Management" in April 2004 and subsequently continued to specialize in publishing highly focused books on specific technologies and solutions.

Our books and publications share the experiences of your fellow IT professionals in adapting and customizing today's systems, applications, and frameworks. Our solution based books give you the knowledge and power to customize the software and technologies you're using to get the job done. Packt books are more specific and less general than the IT books you have seen in the past. Our unique business model allows us to bring you more focused information, giving you more of what you need to know, and less of what you don't.

Packt is a modern, yet unique publishing company, which focuses on producing quality, cutting-edge books for communities of developers, administrators, and newbies alike. For more information, please visit our website: www.packtpub.com.

About Packt Enterprise

In 2010, Packt launched two new brands, Packt Enterprise and Packt Open Source, in order to continue its focus on specialization. This book is part of the Packt Enterprise brand, home to books published on enterprise software – software created by major vendors, including (but not limited to) IBM, Microsoft and Oracle, often for use in other corporations. Its titles will offer information relevant to a range of users of this software, including administrators, developers, architects, and end users.

Writing for Packt

We welcome all inquiries from people who are interested in authoring. Book proposals should be sent to author@packtpub.com. If your book idea is still at an early stage and you would like to discuss it first before writing a formal book proposal, contact us; one of our commissioning editors will get in touch with you.

We're not just looking for published authors; if you have strong technical skills but no writing experience, our experienced editors can help you develop a writing career, or simply get some additional reward for your expertise.

EJB 3 Developer Guide

ISBN: 78-1-847195-60-9   Paperback: 276 pages

A Practical Guide for developers and architects to the Enterprise Java Beans Standard

1. A rapid introduction to the features of EJB 3

2. EJB 3 features explored concisely with accompanying code examples

3. Easily enhance Java applications with new, improved Enterprise Java Beans

EJB 3.0 Database Persistence with Oracle Fusion Middleware 11g

ISBN: 978-1-849681-56-8   Paperback: 448 pages

A complete guide to building EJB 3.0 database persistent applications with Oracle Fusion Middleware 11g tools

1. Integrate EJB 3.0 database persistence with Oracle Fusion Middleware tools: WebLogic Server, JDeveloper, and Enterprise Pack for Eclipse

2. Automatically create EJB 3.0 entity beans from database tables

3. Learn to wrap entity beans with session beans and create EJB 3.0 relationships

Please check **www.PacktPub.com** for information on our titles

JDBC 4.0 and Oracle JDeveloper for J2EE Development

ISBN: 978-1-847194-30-5   Paperback: 444 pages

A J2EE developer's guide to using Oracle JDeveloper's integrated database features to build data-driven applications

1. Develop your Java applications using JDBC and Oracle JDeveloper

2. Explore the new features of JDBC 4.0

3. Use JDBC and the data tools in Oracle JDeveloper

4. Configure JDBC with various application servers

Processing XML documents with Oracle JDeveloper 11g

ISBN: 978-1-847196-66-8   Paperback: 384 pages

Creating, validating, and transforming XML documents with Oracle's ID

1. Will get the reader developing applications for processing XML in JDeveloper 11g quickly and easily

2. Self-contained chapters provide thorough, comprehensive instructions on how to use JDeveloper to create, validate, parse, transform, and compare XML documents.

3. The only title to cover XML processing in Oracle JDeveloper 11g, this book includes information on the Oracle XDK 11g APIs.

Please check **www.PacktPub.com** for information on our titles

Made in the USA
Coppell, TX
15 April 2021